To Nik,

Here is your personal copy of our book along with our grateful thanks again for your faith in us and for agreeing to make such a key contribution!

We live in interesting times indeed - may your pen never sleep in your hand!

With our very best wishes

Paul & Andreas

Leverkusen, April 2020

ANDREAS KREBS / PAUL WILLIAMS

The Illusion of
INVINCIBILITY

The Rise and Fall of Organizations—
Inspired by the Incas of Peru

Forewords by Nik Gowing and Dr. Peter May

Table of Contents

Foreword by Nik Gowing

Founder and director of "Thinking the Unthinkable" and main presenter, BBC World News 1996–2014.

Business and leadership have always faced immense vulnerabilities. Enterprises begin with great energy and innovative ideas that develop through the start-up period and seed funding. Commitment and determination are vital to ensuring early success. A strong sense of self-belief and invincibility fuels a conviction that failure is not even possible.

Then comes the scaling up, and hopefully the sustaining of success. Failing to be nimble and agile, with a constant anxiety about what is being missed, has always triggered a cost. Often that price can ultimately turn out to be existential, both for brands and professional reputations.

At the start of this third decade of the twenty-first century, those pressures and that reality are sharper than ever. Business and politics are wrestling with the scale of a new disruption. It is getting deeper and wider. The timelines are shorter. Public intolerance and impatience are sharper than ever. Customers and voters alike—especially the NEXTGEN—push back against anything or anyone they don't like.

We assume the current disruptions and challenges to all are not a blip. The often-brutal realities and lessons of history should warn us to expect this challenge to what almost everyone assumes is an automatic continuation of seventy years of stability and normality since World War II. After all, it is assumed that things and fortune will always—on balance—get better.

In so many ways, we have been fortunate. Yet now, most leaders and those they serve are unable to grip the nature, scale, and implications of disruptions that are underway. Denial and disbelief tend to be the default, not a pragmatic embracing of unthinkables and unpalatables.

The way things have been is not the way they are and will soon be. Destabilisation and subversion of all we assume and have taken for granted are underway. Handling the new disruptions requires new skills and talents. But leaders, who largely qualified for the top by conforming, are neither skilled nor prepared for what needs to be a profound, earth-shaking change in their approach. Conformity that qualified them for the top disqualifies them from providing the leadership needed.

This is why this reality check assembled by Andreas Krebs and Paul Williams is so intriguing.

Their comparison of twenty-first century leadership vulnerabilities with how the Inca empire first grew at an extraordinary rate to dominate South America, then imploded ignominiously, is both sobering and inspiring. As they report, there is always a "logic to decline." But, inevitably, the leaders involved are blind to that logic. The Incas showed that. They never fully realized what threatened them until far too late.

Like so much in business, politics, and leadership, the impact of what you read here in *The Illusion of Invincibility* was catalysed by a chance set of circumstances: a corporate invitation to travel to Latin America to conduct a business workshop. The research link would not easily have come sitting in Germany. But a personal intrigue to start lifting a private veil on the realities—both remarkable and shocking—of the Inca hegemony suddenly created a wholly different range of perceptions about the travails of being a leader today.

These ever deeper insights from an altitude of up to 3,500 meters in the Andes energize all that is reported and analysed in this book.

For example, Nokia should have learned much from the Incas. The company's breath-taking journey from forestry and manufacturing rubber boots in Finland to being a world leader in mobile phones, then its crash into ignominy with little value in a corporate fire sale, matched the rise and fall of the Incas. Authoritarian leadership, overambition, conceit, and hubris marked the record of both. Even Jeff Bezos of Amazon concedes that, one day, the mega global e-retailer he created "will fail." Probably because of blindness on the part of leadership to the fragilities created by success and inflated self-belief within one of the world's largest corporations.

The overarching message from the Incas for leaders is that there must be a "stress test for your egos." So review urgently your approach to HR. Review also who you seek to work with and who you seek to work for you. And think early enough about who and what comes next, after you have left the company.

It takes cunning and intellectual gymnastics to draw cogent lessons for present day leaders from the brutality, unbridled self-confidence, and "uncontrolled egos" of a South American empire at the height of its dominance five hundred years ago. But the analogies are sobering. It works.

So take note. And consider the relevance to how you lead.

Nik Gowing, London, UK

Foreword by Prof. Dr. Peter May

Leading expert on family businesses and strategic consulting for owner-led organizations.

Business people love a success story: a story of victory, of rags to riches, of making it. We are fascinated by entrepreneurial legends, no matter whether they hail from the digital or the industrial age. The path travelled from a one-man operation to the hundred-million-turnover "hidden champion" in one or two generations or the rise of a regional player to a global multinational—these are exciting role models that invite and inspire imitation.

But how certain can we be about the factors that lead to such an ascent? In hindsight, the reasons for a successful development almost always appear obvious: timely reengineering, cost management, well-thought-out strategies, the right product, the power of innovation—all these factors are repeatedly cited as reasons for extraordinary success. And they are correct—at least at first glance.

Over the years, the collective wisdom of business administration has assembled a framework of knowledge upon which, in its eyes, proper and effective business should be conducted. With specialist areas such as cost management, accounting, marketing, and human resources, this framework provides the academic tools on which real-life business success is widely assumed to depend. Stick to the rules of bookkeeping, profit-making and numerous other systems of prescribed business wisdom and everything will remain on the right track. But if this is true, why do so many companies fail? We're all familiar with cases in which everything has been done exactly by the book, yet a business has still disappeared without trace. And such scenarios are not choosy: they can strike the mid-sized engineering company or the multibillion-dollar corporation just as readily as the small business around the corner. Failure happens despite adherence to the generally accepted rules.

It is testimony to the merits of Andreas Krebs and Paul Williams that they have written a new chapter in the narrative of entrepreneurial thinking. In *The Illusion of Invincibility*, the writers engage with two fundamental constants of human endeavor: success and failure. They have the courage to transcend the comfortable boundaries of an isolated specialist discipline and to expose overarching links and relationships, revealing valuable parallels and insights for everyone active in the business world. They place fundamental questions in a new context: Why and under what conditions do systems triumph, become resilient, and have the ability to expand their sphere of activity? What triggers turning points and what causes decline?

Conventional thought on management brings only a limited supply of answers. Though the practice of management has undergone countless refinements and improvements since the publication of Peter Drucker's magnum opus *Concept of the Corporation* in 1946, it has, at a basic level, perpetuated "the company" as a universal frame of reference. This book goes further. It draws new links in precisely the places where they appear to be of highest potential benefit and interest. It enriches our leadership knowledge with historical perspectives and with an insight into the general principles of rise and fall, an approach that is both exciting and indispensable for modern business management. Furthermore, it is certainly no accident that Krebs and Williams regularly refer, for their overarching perspective, to the fate of the Incas, as the South American empire exemplifies both sides of the story—the rise and the fall.

The rise of the Incas lasted for centuries. In today's wording, that translates to a success story with more to offer than the usual reflections on short-term management—and even the decline of the Incas (as a result of the invasion of the Spanish conquerors and the fraternal strife of two rulers) provides valuable additions to our current management know-how. In pre-Columbian times, the Incas' knowledge of management and expansion was far superior to that of other peoples of the time; highly developed agriculture, a network of transport routes and an efficient communications system were the central pillars of a state system which, thanks to an effective combination of negotiation, cooperation, and the exercise of power, was readily able to expand its sphere of activity. Placing this in the context of companies, we would speak of international expansion, increased turnover, and market share gains.

The success of the Incas endured as long as they were successful in reconciling the individual interests of the powerful with those of other stakeholders in the ever more complex system and in taming the destructive forces that worked from within. However, the growth momentum which was generated by this carefully managed balance of power did not last forever. Seemingly small changes led first to destabilization before finally ushering in the Incas' ultimate demise.

Putting aside for a moment any attempts to relate these directly to business, we can recognize a number of system laws that appear to have stood the test of centuries. One of these, it would seem, is that the seeds of failure are inherent in any enduring success, because the responsible leaders become increasingly blind to new and unknown threats. New and emerging technologies can destroy the value of established management practices in a short space of time and necessitate the development of alternative approaches. The excessive egotism and nepotism of a system's key actors push it into the danger zone and accelerate its decline. Now, all these years later, the distance of centuries creates a clarity that enables us to draw parallels between that time and the present. Today, we are also experiencing radical upheaval—the cavalry and weapons of the Spaniards were the unknown, disruptive technologies at the time of the Incas; for us it is digitization and robotization. Back then, the Spaniards' techniques of rule and war were the sources of massive uncertainty for the Incas, while for us, it is the loss of continuity and reliability in politics and the accelerating change of social values on both a micro and a macro scale. What's more, people with excessive ego still exist, as do unnecessary conflicts, nowhere more so than in business.

This book should provide an opportunity for each of us to reassess where we stand. We should review our routines, cease to simply accept established knowledge as a permanent solution, and sharpen our perception of the forces acting inside and outside the system. Only then will we be able to influence the dynamics in our favor and create what we collectively need: a conscious and well-guided transition into a new age.

Prof. Dr. Peter May, Bonn-Bad Godesberg, Germany

The Unexpected Outcome of a Trip to Peru

This book is not about the Incas, but without the Incas, it would never have been written. It's a book about the rise and fall of organizations and the key factors influencing their successes and failures. It's about good leadership, honest and perceptive self-management, inspiring visions, high-quality people selection, trustworthy values, credible corporate governance, and organizational focus for long-term survival. It's also about the mistakes, many of them self-inflicted, that often occur in each of these areas and cause organizations, large and small, to stumble and fall. This book will help you to lead your organization better; it will help you manage yourself better, as well as understand your boss and your colleagues better. Oh, and it will make you think, smile, and maybe even shudder, sometimes all at the same time. But above all, it will help prevent you from falling victim to the illusion of invincibility.

How It All Began…

I don't often go to Peru on business. In fact, it's happened just once, but that one trip was enough to light the fire under me to write this book.

When one of my clients—a Swiss company—decided to appoint a new general manager for their subsidiary in Peru, the SVP of international business operations called my office in Germany. "Paul," the client said. "Would you be Rosa's coach as she prepares to take over the new position? You'd be her sparring partner, if you will." Then came the unexpected part of the offer: while most of the coaching would take place either in Zürich or in my office near

Cologne, he suggested that I travel to Peru toward the end of the process to run a workshop for Rosa and her new leadership team.

One evening, about three weeks later, I found myself sitting around a campfire with two friends who'd both lived and worked in Latin America for a number of years. I told them about my recent phone call, and their reaction was highly enthusiastic.

"Peru!" the first said. "Wow! It's one of my favorite countries in the world. Oh, the food, the culture, the people—the Incas!"

"You've got to see *this*, you've got see *that*, you must go *here*, you must go *there*," the other exclaimed. "And, Paul," he continued, "above all, what you absolutely *must not do* is spend three days in the Lima Hilton and then come straight home again!"

"Hold your horses, guys," I said. "I don't speak a word of Spanish, and I'm not one for adventuresome holidays. And if I *did* take a trip around Peru, I would never consider doing it on my own. I'd want to do it with my wife, or with some good friends, or—"

"We'll come with you!" they interrupted.

And that was that. On a sunny November afternoon in Lima, six months later, I walked out of the hotel after the workshop and a mini-bus was waiting for me across the road. The man behind the wheel was a local—one of our guides. In the passenger seats were six tourists with familiar, smiling faces, including the two friends from the campfire. And one of them was Andreas Krebs.

We thought we'd properly researched the highly developed Inca culture of the fifteenth and sixteenth centuries. We were wrong: In the breath-taking landscape at 3,500 meters above sea level, what we gathered from our Peruvian guides made us pause to think much further. In Tipón, located about eighteen miles northeast of Cuzco, and assumed to be a former agricultural research center of the Incas, we learned more about how, in just a hundred years, the Incas created an empire stretching almost five thousand kilometers along the

Andes, from what is now Ecuador in the north to present-day Chile in the south. They efficiently organized and held together a kingdom that was home to some two hundred ethnic groups; they created surpluses through clever agricultural techniques, established food storage facilities and cared for their sick and for families who had lost their main provider, all at a time when epidemics and famine were raging in Europe. We discovered how, before integrating a tribe or nation into their empire, they would first make an offer of a "friendly takeover" and only use their considerable military force if the offer was rejected. And we learned how they consistently endeavored to integrate the conquered people into their empire and maintain peace thereafter by resettling people and developing the local infrastructure.

Originally, the trip was intended to give us a few days to relax from our day-to-day work as managers, supervisory board members, investors, and coaches. Yet we suddenly found ourselves talking about management—Inca management. How could it be that the Incas, who had neither the wheel nor a system of writing, let alone modern communication technology, had built and dominated a vast empire, while many present-day mergers fail under far more favorable conditions? How did the Incas manage to establish an accepted governing elite that lasted for many decades, while modern senior executives often have to defend themselves against allegations of egomania and arrogance? Why did so many groups and communities choose to follow the "children of the sun," while the attempts of today's business leaders to steer company conglomerates on a common course often end in failure?

Of course, the methods of a rigidly hierarchical society of the early modern period cannot simply be transferred directly to the present day. But our heated debates made one thing clear: the Incas offer us a mirror and a chance to reflect on the behaviors and methods business executives use today. What at first glance appears so distant and alien can actually hit home. The Inca elite faced challenges similar to those of today's managers: formulating clear goals, persuading others to embrace change and innovation in a tough environment, unifying different groups, and implementing plans according to rigorous standards. When we look beyond many of the current management trends and buzzwords, be it "digitization," "diversity," or "disruption," one question remains unchanged: What is essential for leaders at all levels seeking to ensure their companies or organizations can achieve sustainable success? Successful management and leadership really depend on the answers to this question—and this book provides such answers. Having served as the initial spark of inspiration, the Incas provide a backdrop throughout the book as we draw on our own business experiences and on what our interviewees—senior managers from international companies, successful family businesses, start-ups, consulting companies, public sector organizations, and NGOs—shared with us along the way (see "Our Interview Partners"). We would like to thank all of them for their trust and openness, and we have chosen to anonymize some of the more personal or controversial stories.

This book is in no way intended to be a starry-eyed romanticizing of the Incas' story. Alongside impressive expansion, their reign was also characterized by deportations, often of entire peoples and villages, child sacrifices, and the rigid regimentation of individuals, who were not free to choose their place of residence or their occupation. Furthermore, after almost a century of uninterrupted success, the Incas suffered an equally monumental downfall: in 1532, the Spanish conqueror Francisco Pizarro defeated the Incas' twelve-thousand-strong army with fewer than two hundred soldiers and captured their ruler (the "Inca") Atahualpa. Within a few years, the Inca Empire had disintegrated, although the last Inca king, by that time a puppet of the Spanish conquistadors, was not executed until 1572. For all the resourcefulness, efficiency, and consistency the Incas had shown in the domination of their empire, they seemed helpless in the face of their new adversary, which leads us to ask whether all such outstanding successes are intrinsically doomed to fail at some point—whether every great triumph carries within it the first small steps toward failure.

Here, too, the parallel with the present is immediately apparent. Every manager and executive knows the names of the "global players," the seemingly unassailable companies, that have experienced dramatic decline or, in some cases, been obliterated completely: Kodak, Nokia, AOL, Pan Am, Arthur Andersen, and many more. If we take the annual Forbes list of the world's five hundred most profitable companies as our benchmark, it quickly becomes clear that scarcely a single organization has been able to maintain its place in the gilded ranks of the world's ten most financially successful companies over a longer period of time. Perhaps it is precisely the illusion of invincibility that predestines their often rapid fall from grace. For executives and managers, this means remaining constantly vigilant, particularly in times of "guaranteed" success, searching for weaknesses and constantly working to challenge and develop both themselves and the company. Otherwise, the danger is that they may suffer the same fate as a certain German executive whose pompous attempts to create a "Global, Inc." out of the Daimler Group marked the beginning of the end of his career and cost the company and its shareholders billions of dollars.

One more thing: While we have carefully researched the information about the Incas in this book and have talked with a number of experts in Peru, the United States, and Germany, we neither intend nor are able to provide more than just an overview of this fascinating culture. There are many other books that do this job much better than we can, and we have listed some of these in the bibliography. Our view of the Incas is a selective view through the eyes of managers working within large organizations. The Incas added an unexpected layer of meaning and insight to our view of the business world, and the lessons we learned surpassed in many ways the dozens of leadership seminars and workshops—with their assorted PowerPoint presentations—that we had both witnessed over the years. Our hope is that this book succeeds in conveying at least part of the fascination of this change of perspective and that our insights, analyses, and recommendations provide sufficient information and entertainment to encourage you to read the book from start to finish. After all, there are more than enough boring management books out there!

Andreas Krebs and Paul Williams,
Langenfeld, Germany
www.inca-inc.com

"Many years of success can produce an unjustified degree of self-confidence and lead to the misguided belief: 'We can do it all.'"

DR. IRIS LÖW-FRIEDRICH, EXECUTIVE VICE PRESIDENT AND CHIEF MEDICAL OFFICER, UCB

What Goes Up Must Come Down?
A Look at the Fortune 500

Every year, *Fortune* magazine publishes the list of the top 500 companies. On this list appear the "big players," those companies with the highest revenue in the world. And yet, hardly any of these organizations manage, consistently, to maintain their ranking among the titans. Could it be that the moment of greatest triumph is also the moment of greatest vulnerability? Does every extraordinary success carry with it the seeds of its own destruction? Must everything that goes up eventually come down? If global empires can collapse and advanced civilizations like the Incas' can melt away into irrelevance in a matter of a few years, how on earth can our current business leaders and managers have any confidence that today's success can be sustained into the future? More importantly, are there any warning signs of impending doom? Of course, these are not just questions for big businesses. After all, we all know of start-ups that demonstrate meteoric growth before failing equally spectacularly, as well as more traditional family businesses that flounder, seemingly without warning, after many decades of success.

Remember Nokia?

Ask a modern-day cellphone-savvy teenager what they think about Nokia and they'll most probably give you a blank stare. Er...who? Nokia? Just a few years ago, this Finnish company ranked among the giants of the business world and dominated the global market for mobile telephones from 1998 to 2011. In 2004, Nokia made it into the top third of the Fortune 500, coming in at number 122. A small country with around five million inhabitants was the home of an undisputed leader in a key and growing global sector.

The story of Nokia reads like a Hollywood script. It is 1865, we are in the south of Finland, and an engineer called Fredrik Idestam builds a paper pulp factory on the banks of the Nokianvirta; he calls it Nokia. About thirty years later in 1898, Eduard Polón sets up the Finnish Rubber Works to manufacture rubber boots and tires. Another fifteen years go by, and Arvid Wickström establishes the Finnish Cable Works. From 1963 onward, the Cable Works manufactures wireless telephones for the army. The three businesses have already been working closely together for forty-five years when they merge to form the technology firm Nokia in 1967. The core businesses of forestry, rubber, cabling, electronics, and electric power generation are continued until deregulation of the European telecommunications market in the 1980s creates new opportunities. With the birth of the Scandinavian mobile phone company NMT (Nordic Mobile Telephone), Nokia manufactures the world's first mobile car phone in 1981 and, from 1987 onward, focuses on mobile phones and grows exponentially.[1] Other business areas like rubber, cabling, and electricity generation are hived off. The business keeps the consumer happy with technological innovations such as the "Communicator" (an early form of smartphone) and floods the market with sturdy and affordable mobile phones for the masses. In 2002, one in three mobile phones sold on the planet is a Nokia (market share of 35.8 percent), only one in six is a Motorola (15.3 percent), and fewer than one in ten is a Samsung (9.8 percent). For a long time, the highest selling mobile phone was the Nokia 1100, selling more than 250 million phones up to 2013.[2]

To the world, Nokia, with its headquarters in Espoo, Finland, appears invincible. Unfortunately, the company, too, starts to believe itself unbeatable. As Nokia reaches the pinnacle of its economic might, new competitors start to join the fray. When the first flip phones come onto the market in 2004, Nokia sticks with its tried-and-trusted designs. And when Apple launches the first smartphone with a touchscreen in 2007, CEO Olli-Pekka Kallsvuo describes the iPhone as a "niche product." In November of the same year, the front cover of *Forbes* magazine, complete with a picture of a rather self-satisfied looking Kallsvuo, asks the question: "One billion customers—Can anyone catch the cell phone king?"

Nokia's developers continue to come up with new ideas and pioneering products—for example, the first mobile phone with camera (Nokia 7650) or the Internet Tablet 770—but the organization is too slow and cumbersome to respond and is perhaps blinded by the accolades in the press. To make matters worse, a dispute breaks out among board members. Should they accelerate smartphone development or stick with making cheap handsets? Their long-serving head of the business in Germany describes the scene as "the very picture of a huge bureaucracy, populated by mobile phone functionaries with jobs for life."[3] At the beginning of the ensuing crisis, we can learn a lot about the nature of the problems by looking at how the employees of one of their larger European affiliates used dark humor to rename their meeting rooms. "Helsinki," "Berlin," and "London" became "Won't Work Here," "Will Never be Approved," and "Global Wants It."[4] ("Global" refers to the company's monolithic headquarters in Finland.)

As quickly as it had forged ahead in the previous ten years, the company now heads into decline. Nokia's market share starts to slump in 2008 and, from 2011 onward, the business operates at a loss. A cooperation agreement is put in place with Microsoft in the same year.

Its own operating system is to be ditched and Nokia mobile phones will run on MS Windows. The rest of the market looks on in amused disbelief and jokes about the two rusty old battleships heading off into the sunset together. The Nokia products are no match for the Apple iPhone or for the Android phones made by Samsung, LG and other manufacturers, and two years later, Microsoft takes over Nokia's mobile phone business. The trade magazine *connect* commented, "The Finnish mobile phone phenomenon has come to an end." Nokia positions itself today as a leading supplier of network technology. Since 1999, its share price graph looks like the outline of a mountain range, with dizzying heights around the turn of the millennium and flatlining from 2009 onward. Anyone buying a Nokia share in 2000 had to pay more than sixty dollars. By mid-2019—and for the five years before that—the share price has stagnated at around six dollars.

Those familiar with the history of the Incas will see plenty of parallels with the Nokia story. In both examples, a small nation changes the world because it is more inventive, more disciplined, and—at least, at first—more successful than the competition. Both are able to seize the moment. The growth catalyst for Nokia was deregulation of the mobile phone market, combined with know-how in wireless telecommunications. For the Incas, it was a period of unusually cold weather in the Andes and along the Pacific coast, around 1100, which allowed their superior know-how in agriculture, irrigation, and farming techniques to come to the fore. While other tribes abandoned the cold hills, and drought on the Pacific coast combined with very heavy rainfall elsewhere led to migration and conflicts, the Incas stayed true to their motto: "Bring Order to the World." They carved out thousands of terraces on steep slopes, built irrigation systems, and diverted rivers. They only planted crops that were appropriate for the prevailing climate, cultivating a variety of potato that easily lends itself to freeze-drying, for example. The Inca expansion was, to a large extent, built upon farming techniques which led to agricultural and thus economic success.

Just like the Finns, who enjoyed worldwide success with their reliable and affordable technology, the Incas exported their successful agricultural methods into neighboring lands and thereby gained more and more influence. Their Golden Age started in the reign of Pachacutec Yupanquis (1438–1471) and brought large land gains. But just like the Finns, who could hardly imagine that their run of success would ever come to an end, the Incas stuck with tried-and-trusted solutions when confronted with an opponent who played by a completely different set of rules. Just as Nokia, with its wide range of affordable products, simply could not imagine losing its market leadership to Apple, with its single, expensive product, so the Incas found it impossible to adapt to an opponent who was not to be caught out by their hitherto successful approach of offering the choice between a "friendly" takeover or being forced into submission. The Spanish conquistadors, led by Francisco Pizarro, had arrived.

Internal conflicts sealed their fate in both cases. For the Incas, it was the civil war of 1527, when Huayna Cápac divided the empire between his two sons, Atahualpa and Huáscar. Both brothers called on the tribes of their respective mothers and other allies and fought each other fiercely. By the time Francisco Pizarro reached the Inca Empire in 1532, it was already severely weakened and therefore easy prey for the invaders. Nokia's downfall was accelerated by the boardroom battle over company strategy which started in 2007 under Olli-Pekka Kallasvuo. The battle was between those pressing for a change of strategic direction, away from cheap cell phones toward smartphones, and those arguing against such a change. In both instances, powerful and seemingly invincible leaders slid away into irrelevance within a matter of a few years—on one side, the "Kings of the Andes," on the other, the masters of the mobile phone market. Is it inevitable that a continued period of success leads to a state of hubris which contains the seeds of its eventual destruction? Is the risk of failure an intrinsic part of every great triumph?

Rapid Rises, Dramatic Falls

A close look at the biggest businesses in the world, as measured by annual turnover, is a lesson in humility. In 1990, the American magazine *Fortune* published the first global Fortune 500 list, based on the previous year's sales. If you compare the top ten from this list with the top businesses in 2000 and 2017, you realize the fragility of success, no matter how outstanding the company. Only five of the original leaders are still in the top ten (highlighted below) ten years later. A further seventeen years on, just four of the 1990 leaders (also highlighted) are still there:

The Top Ten in the Fortune 500 list for 1990

Ranking	Company	Country	Turnover-1989 (US$ billion)	Sector
1.	General Motors	USA	126,974	Auto
2.	Ford	USA	96,933	Auto
3.	Exxon	USA	86,656	Oil and Gas
4.	Royal Dutch Shell	Netherlands	85,528	Oil and Gas
5.	IBM	USA	63,438	IT
6.	Toyota	Japan	60,444	Auto
7.	General Electric	USA	55,264	Ind. Holding
8.	Mobil	USA	50,976	Oil and Gas
9.	Hitachi	Japan	50,894	IT
10.	BP	UK	49,484	Oil and Gas

The Top Ten in the Fortune 500 list for 2000

Ranking	Company	Country	Turnover-1999 (US$ billion)	Sector
1.	General Motors	USA	189,058	Auto
2.	Walmart	USA	166,809	Retail
3.	ExxonMobil	USA	163,881	Oil and Gas
4.	Ford	USA	162,558	Auto
5.	DaimlerChrysler	Germany	159,986	Auto
6.	Mitsui & Co.	Japan	118,555	Ind. Holding
7.	Mitsubishi Corporation	Japan	117,766	Trading
8.	Toyota	Japan	115,671	Auto
9.	General Electric	USA	111,630	Ind. Holding
10.	Itochu	Japan	109,069	Trading

The Top Ten in the Fortune 500 list for 2018

Ranking	Company	Country	Turnover-2017 (US$ billion)	Sector
1.	Walmart	USA	500,343	Retail
2.	State Grid	China	348,903	Energy
3.	Sinopec Group	China	326,953	Energy
4.	China National Petroleum	China	326,008	Energy
5.	Royal Dutch Shell	Netherlands	311,870	Energy
6.	Toyota Motor	Japan	265,172	Motor Vehicles & Parts
7.	Volkswagen	Germany	260,028	Motor Vehicles & Parts
8.	BP	UK	244,582	Energy
9.	Exxon Mobil	USA	244,363	Energy
10.	Berkshire Hathaway	USA	242,137	Financials

The list reflects the tectonic shifts of the global economy. In 1990, the United States is leading the list with six companies, followed by Japan with two. By 2017, however, there are only three American companies and one Japanese, but three from the People's Republic of China are in second, third, and fourth place. Well-known names such as IBM (the fifth-largest company in the world in 1990; ranked 92 in 2017) or General Electric have dropped out of the top ten completely. The 1990 leader, General Motors, ranked forty-first in 2017. The oil and gas giants now dominate the list more than ever, taking six of the top ten places. Berkshire Hathaway is the first financials company to make it into the top ten.

For a long time, General Electric (GE) served as a role model for generations of business managers, ranking year after year in the top ten of the Forbes 500. How was it possible that this icon of American industry could so suddenly and comprehensively collapse? After a period of continuous decline in share price, on June 26, 2018, GE was removed from the Dow Jones Index. This was a bitter moment indeed, as GE was one of the original members of the Dow when it was launched in 1896 and had been included in the index continuously since 1907. A typical selection of those elements which guarantee decline were to be found at GE: a disintegrating corporate culture, gigantomania, blatant financial trickery, and balance sheet manipulation. In just one year, over $125 billion of the company's market capitalization was wiped out.[5]

One of the maxims of the business world is "the only thing that is certain is uncertainty," with past performance being no guarantee of future performance. Unfortunately, this almost always seems to be forgotten during prosperous times, leading to some reckless decisions. In 2000, the German car manufacturer Daimler made a brief appearance in the top ten, thanks to its merger with Chrysler. CEO Jürgen Schrempp described the merger as "a marriage made in heaven." Schrempp's ambitious plan was the creation of a "global corporation," ignoring all evidence of the problems which arise from mergers and acquisitions, and the skepticism of his own dealers. Unfortunately, the dealers were right: In 2009, the heavenly union ended in a forty-billion-dollar divorce. The DaimlerChrysler saga is a perfect example of a senior executive's unchecked egomania and a failed merger strategy. We will go into greater detail about these traps and how difficult it can be to avoid them in Chapter 8 ("Ego Beats Reality"). After all, no confident and tenacious manager who has made it to the top of the greased pole is immune from an inflated ego. So, the challenge is this: How can you stay on the right side of the fine dividing line between ambition and egomania, or between visionary drive and megalomania? How can you protect yourself from your own "Indiana Jones moment"?

Wait a minute. You're probably thinking: What's wrong with following in the heroic footsteps of the thrill-seeking movie character? Well, to be blunt, the archaeologist Indiana Jones is anything but a role model. Yes, at the end of each of his adventures he has found the prized treasures, but only after leaving behind him a trail of dust and destruction, including ruined temples and monuments. Just like the character of Dr. Jones, played by Harrison Ford, many managers tend to confuse self-interest with service for the greater good, often doing their businesses an enormous disservice as a result; since we've had some personal, front-row experience with this, in the final chapter, we'll tell you about our own Indiana Jones moments. Before that, however, in Chapter 6, we will take a closer look at the other reasons why big company mergers, like that of Daimler and Chrysler, fail so spectacularly, and explore what modern business managers might learn from the Incas and their well-crafted approach to integration.

But let's get back to the Fortune 500. The car industry provides many examples of corporate failure, and any analysis needs to address the question of corporate values. Time will tell how Volkswagen, ranked number 7 in the Fortune 500 in 2018, will fare in the light of the "Dieselgate" scandal. In the US, revenue was down tremendously soon after the irregularities were uncovered,[6] with VW having advertised its diesel cars on American television as being super clean. In one ad, an older lady holds a pure and pristine white cloth behind a car exhaust pipe with the engine running, and the cloth remains whiter than white. Those who so blatantly blur the lines of corporate values will pay—or are paying—the price (see Chapter 4). Once described by one of Europe's leading current affairs magazines, *Der Spiegel*, as "North Korea without the boot camps,"[7] the corporate leadership culture at VW is a good example of why company values have to be much more than just slogans for use at town hall meetings and offsite workshops. At VW, employees trembled with fear in front of senior management, as they could lose their jobs if they didn't meet targets and stay within budget. Consequently, they covered up and fiddled problems, and now the business is faced with much higher costs arising from fraud. Even after the manipulated software was first exposed, VW's inconsistent relationship with company values continued unabated. In the spring of 2016, while blue- and white-collar employees were in fear of losing their jobs and taking pay cuts, the top management pushed through seven-figure bonus payments for themselves, still convinced that they had done everything "right." Since then, it has become increasingly clear that management performance needs to be reevaluated, and calls are getting louder for these performance bonuses to be paid back. And rightly so! By April 2019, the diesel scandal had already cost the company twenty-nine billion euros; international investor groups were lining up with damage claims, and, most recently, another 5.4 billion euros in accruals had to be put aside by the CFO. It remains to be seen whether that will be enough.[8] Meanwhile, over seventy criminal cases against individual managers have been filed in the United States and Europe. In fact, ex-VW CEO Winterkorn and nine other VW and Audi managers no longer dare to travel to the US for fear of being arrested on the spot.

Of course, many other factors have an impact on business success, and we will take a closer look at them in the course of this book. At what point does an emotionally charged business vision start to be counterproductive (Chapter 1)? How were the Incas able to succeed over many decades in entrusting leadership to the most talented, an area where many businesses fail (Chapter 2)? What defines credible leadership (Chapter 3)? How can businesses today avoid the kinds of destructive power struggles that brought the Inca Empire to its knees? And, when faced with other people's self-interest and biases, how can managers remain level-headed and make objective decisions? A careful analysis of Inca history can provide answers to these questions. For five hundred years, the way the Incas were viewed was heavily influenced by their insatiable conquerors and Catholic missionaries. The newcomers justified their brutality by denouncing the Incas as a "primitive" culture. Bearing this in mind, it's well worth asking yourself: "Who's telling me what, and why?" (Chapter 7, "Sound Judgment.")

The Logic of Decline

Two and a half thousand years ago, Greek philosopher Heraclitus of Ephesus pointed out that "there is nothing more constant than change." In the Bible, Joseph warns the Pharaoh that seven years of famine will follow seven years of plenty (Moses 1:41). The Middle Ages produced images of the goddess Fortuna spinning the wheel of fortune—relentlessly and without any emotion. There is a clear common message. The fate of whoever happens to be at the top can quickly change. Nothing will stop Fortuna from spinning them around and down, but of course there is always a chance they will end up back at the top again.

The idea that success is fickle is probably as old as mankind. For businesses, this means that not only stunning successes are always possible, but also catastrophic collapses. And while "disruptive technology" may be a fashionable buzzword today, this idea was already the basis of Joseph Schumpeter's theory of "creative destruction" formulated more than seventy years ago. This asserted that the driving force of capitalism was innovation; new and better processes and technology continually challenge the established order, and the ground rules for production are constantly changing. From this perspective, the mechanical loom and the steam engine can be seen as agents of "disruption," only to be rendered obsolete by innovation's next throw of the dice.

Those who want to stay ahead of the game must keep changing and constantly adapt in order to remain relevant and survive. We all know examples of businesses that missed the boat and let progress pass them by. Some carried on producing typewriters even as the personal computer came to dominate. Others produced flashlights, even though every smartphone now includes a flashlight function. On top of external factors, homegrown mistakes can send a business into decline, as we saw at DaimlerChrysler, GE, and VW. As early as 2004, Gilbert Probst and Sebastian Raisch at the University of Geneva were asking themselves if there could be such a thing as a "logic of decline." They analyzed the hundred biggest corporate crises of the previous five years in the United States and Europe, looking at the fifty biggest insolvencies and fifty companies whose market capitalization had collapsed by a minimum of 40 percent in the same period.

Probst and Raisch identified four characteristics of consistent and sustainable business success:

○ Performance-driven business culture[9]
○ Strong growth
○ Willingness to embrace constant change
○ Strong ("visionary") leadership

Interestingly, 70 percent of the businesses that failed actually displayed all of these characteristics—but to excess! These organizations suffered badly from over-rapid growth, hasty change processes, excessively powerful and stubborn CEOs, and an "exaggerated performance culture."

Performance Culture

An extreme performance culture—one with high salaries and bonuses, for example—fosters rivalry, along with a mercenary attitude. Employees attracted by such a culture are quick to leave the sinking ship if the business suffers a downturn in fortune, thereby accelerating its decline.

Growth

Rapid growth frequently results from too many acquisitions in too short a time period. This not only creates obstacles for business integration, but frequently overburdens the acquirer with high debt, which in turn becomes a problem during periods of lower turnover. Good examples of this are the US conglomerates Tyco and ABB. When change is not properly managed, the result is disorientation at all levels. At ABB, following sixty takeovers and countless restructurings and changes of direction, there were moments when employees were no longer certain what the business was actually there for. The final nail in the coffin is having a top management that fails to recognize the scale of the problems because past success has made them self-satisfied, dazzled by their own brilliance, and oblivious to the dangers they are facing. The business burns out, sinks into insolvency (for example, Enron, which grew 2000 percent between 1997 and 2001), or is weighed down by mountainous debt (as seen at British Telecom, Deutsche Telekom, and France Telecom). Probst and Raisch talk about "burnout syndrome." More recent examples of this would include Porsche AG—which was assimilated into the VW group after a failed takeover attempt left it badly exposed—the ever-changing history of Infineon, and the demise of Valeant, which we analyze in Chapter 6.

Change

The collapse of successful businesses is not always determined by fate, external events, or disruptive technologies, but is frequently the result of a string of poor management decisions which, taken together—according to Probst and Raisch—form the basis of the "Logic of Decline." So far, so bad. Unfortunately, it's not the case that all a business needs to do to stay on a solid footing is to take its foot off the accelerator. The other 30 percent of businesses failed due to their inertia and weak, indecisive management. A phenomenon referred to as "Premature Aging" is when turnover stagnates, innovations are ignored, board members block reforms, and an overly benevolent business culture prevents essential personnel reductions from taking place. Examples that come to mind include Eastern Airlines, Kodak, Xerox, and Motorola.

Ideally, a business should continuously seek the right balance, looking for healthy growth and steady change, supported by proactive change management, which requires its employees to adjust and adapt without overstretching them.

Leadership

Except in periods of serious crisis, autocratic leadership is counterproductive. Successful organizations rely on mutual exchange and good governance all the way up to the top. This fosters a "defensible culture of trust" in which good performance is rewarded and poor performance is sanctioned, without turning the organization into an eat-or-be-eaten shark-infested pool.[10] All this requires a reflective and level-headed top management which acts consistently and decisively.

And yet, as convincing as these factors appear with the benefit of hindsight, introducing them into the day-to-day running of a business is highly challenging. Who can say with any degree of certainty whether we are enjoying a period of healthy growth, rather than starting to overheat? Or whether the business culture still supports an acceptable degree of competitive spirit, rather than promoting mercenary attitudes?

Moreover, there is that fundamental dilemma which the management visionary Jim Collins highlighted in his essay "How the Mighty Fall" about businesses ruined by their own success-induced complacency.[11] A business (or its leadership) must start to change course before its problems are clear for all to see. This must happen in a period when everything still appears to be running smoothly. "Amazon is not too big to fail," Jeff Bezos said recently. "In fact, I predict one day Amazon will fail. Amazon will go bankrupt. But our job is to delay it as long as possible. If you look at large companies, their lifespans tend to be thirty-plus years, not a hundred-plus years."[12]

Probst and Raisch concede that it is psychologically challenging to "change a strategy that, at least superficially, appears to be successful."[13] But it is not, apparently, impossible, as Bezos's remarks above prove, assuming he turns these observations into actions to prevent the failure he refers to. It certainly takes an enormous amount of humility, combined perhaps with a healthy fear of failure, to make such a statement when heading up one of the most successful companies ever seen on this planet. Indeed, the Amazon boss's insights would have been useful guidance for the Incas, who might then have slowed down their rapid expansion earlier, before increasing resistance had made their empire too expansive to govern.

Collins's analysis of the factors that lead to the downfall of large corporations significantly ties in with the work of his colleagues in Geneva. Based on his analysis of a combined six thousand years of company history, he highlights the key reasons for companies' decline: managers taking success for granted, greed for more power, higher revenue, greater size, and the denial of risks and threats. Once problems can no longer be ignored, frantic rescue attempts ensue, followed shortly by complete capitulation. But Collins, too, is making his observations with the benefit of hindsight. In reality, the burning question is this: How do we, the executives responsible for the day-to-day management of our businesses, recognize the early warning signals? How can we counter the logic of decline in the early stages? How do we raise our level of awareness; how do we gain deeper insights beyond the day-to-day business? The following chapters address these and other questions. At the end of each chapter, we summarize the most important takeaways under "Inca Insights." So, let's get started!

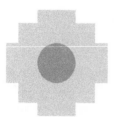

INCA INSIGHTS

- **The moment of greatest strength and success is also the moment of greatest vulnerability.**

- **Analyze your weaknesses, especially when you are starting to feel invincible!**

1 A Compelling Vision
(or the Pitfalls of Ambition?)

A company's glossy brochure or website usually includes a "vision statement" and, if you ever want to flatter a senior executive, just describe him or her as "a visionary." But, in the real world, is a vision statement *always* useful for motivation? For many decades, this certainly was the case for the Incas—up until the point when their ambition led to a dramatic downturn in fortune. Even today, the maps of their empire are still impressive, as they illustrate a period of continuous expansion achieved in just six decades and stretching around 2,500 miles down the west coast of South America. At its peak, the Inca Empire included parts of modern-day Ecuador and Peru, Bolivia, Chile and Argentina. What lay behind this rapid and almost insatiable appetite to conquer? The Inca lords found affirmation in their vision: "Bring Order to the World." Inca Pachacutec took a name which translates to "World Reformer" or "Savior of the Earth," and the empire's expansion started during his reign in 1438. The Inca "global corporation" viewed bigger as better and biggest as best, rather like today's global players in Silicon Valley—although in the end their enormous empire became practically ungovernable, so retreat was not an option. Any similarities with today's big businesses are more than just coincidence. The Incas considered every enemy of a tribe they had conquered to be a new enemy for them, which meant more military campaigns and constant further expansion. Toward the end, their ambitious vision turned into a risk which accelerated the downfall of the empire, simply because subjugated tribes could no longer be integrated quickly enough. Many of these tribes willingly joined forces with the Spanish conquistadors and ultimately helped bring down the Inca Empire.[14]

The extent of the Inca Empire in the fifteenth century

But clearly, for an extended period of time, the bold core vision of the Incas to bring order to the world held a magnetic appeal. Over many decades, it drove the actions of the elite, the export of farming and irrigation techniques, the use of resources, and the deployment of the crafting skills of the "assimilated"—always with one goal in mind: the methodical expansion of their sphere of influence and the construction of a smooth-running state apparatus. Nobody went hungry in the Inca Empire; there is no archaeological evidence of any malnourishment, something that cannot be claimed about Europe in the fifteenth century. That said, hardly anyone enjoyed any personal liberty in the Inca Empire. Whole villages were resettled, tradesmen packed off to major population centers, and forced labor employed. The reason why the Inca vision of an ordered world was both appealing and compelling across a wide geographical area also has to do with the fact that it was perfectly suited to the times. Starting in the eleventh century, climate change—drought inland and devastating rainfall on the coast—led to famine and continual conflict. Following a period of chaos, the Inca proposition to bring order to the world was obviously so attractive that many of the indigenous peoples were happy to accept a "friendly takeover" offer, putting up little or no resistance.

Many large businesses are launched with a modern vision, which guides and inspires strategic decision-making and everyday actions. This sort of vision can inspire, cajole, and motivate. Some well-known examples include Bill Gates's ambitious target to get "a PC on every desk, in every house" and Google's claim "to provide access to the world's information in one click."[15] Both these visions define the beginning of a new era which both Microsoft and Google have decisively influenced and continue to do so.

Likewise, Jeff Bezos's vision to make Amazon "the most customer-friendly business in the world" and Steve Jobs's typically succinct definition—"a vision is how you will make the world a better place"—not to forget his equally modest claim to be making a dent in the universe.[16] In this sort of company, the Inca proposition to bring order to the world does not seem too far out of place. Anyway, Jobs took it on himself, both personally and for his business, to be radical ("think different") and to risk being highly focused rather than just producing "me too" products.[17] It is no surprise, then, that visions are sometimes hailed as the ideal route to business success. As the demise of the Inca Empire shows, however, this is dangerous thinking. And, anyway, how many of these visions were in fact only formulated after the event? So, when do you need a vision, what should it look like, and what are the associated risks for an organization?

"We Don't Need a Vision—Just Reliable Delivery!"

Sooner or later, anybody who works for a large organization will be confronted with workshops dealing with "visions," "missions," or "statements of intent." However, these concepts quickly become fuzzy and blurred, and then strange things start to happen. In our opinion, a proper vision is the setting of an ambitious but nevertheless realistic goal, which serves to inspire both existing and future employees and other stakeholders. Okay, Steve Jobs's "dent in the universe" may not have been realistic, but it was memorable, and the majority of people will have known what he meant.

Don't Fiddle While Rome Burns!

During an international meeting of a large life sciences company, Andreas Krebs experienced firsthand how not to go about launching a vision.

Here's some background: Some countries were experiencing severe problems with their supply of a key product because certain raw materials were not being delivered on time, and there was a high risk of a major loss of sales. Board members, along with the most important leaders from different countries, were engaged in a heated discussion on the issue when the CEO announced that they had a tight schedule and needed to move on to the next agenda item: A

Vision for Technical Operations ("technical operations" being the business area responsible for production and supply). Despite raised eyebrows, the colleague from TO started with a promotional film, heavily laced with sugary slogans about wanting to be the best, then continued with a detailed PowerPoint presentation on the new TO vision. She had just managed to get to slide number three when the leader from France, unable to hold back any longer, blurted out, "Hey guys, we don't need to be the best. A regular supply would be fine!" There was laughter all around, and some sympathy for the lady from TO charged with the thankless task of presenting a vision at the worst possible moment. And, while the whole situation may not have been quite as dramatic as Rome burning, she certainly went home that evening with a different set of priorities than she'd had when she arrived.

A business working out a vision in the midst of a crisis is a bit like a captain gathering his crew during a Force Twelve storm to extoll the attractions of a destination which they may never reach. And yet, such madness is not that uncommon. Why? "Get the vision right and the rest will take care of itself" would be the wrong conclusion to draw, even if successful businesses often have an inspiring vision of their future and their value in the world. Visions are not simply the result of a distillation process which can be hurriedly cobbled together. Knut Bleicher, economist and former head of St. Gallen Business School in Switzerland, says: "Visions cannot be created on a whiteboard— they must be allowed to develop naturally, as part of a never-ending process."[18]

Was Bezos really driven from the very outset to become the world leader in customer focus, as the Amazon website claims?[19] When Bill Gates dropped out of Harvard, was he really dreaming of putting a PC on everybody's desk? Or did these visions only emerge after their first successes? How much marketing, how much image-building, how much retrospective connecting-the-dots is hidden behind these legends? We simply don't know and can only speculate. What we do know is that, for visions to really inspire and motivate, they must provoke a positive emotional response from all involved and be plausible. They have to be "lived" every day by all levels of the company. They have to be intuitive, be consistent, and reflect the firm's DNA; otherwise, they will just provoke cynicism and ridicule. Ideally, a vision should communicate the essence and core purpose of a business by encapsulating it in an ambitious and emotionally charged long-term objective. Employees will only buy into a vision if it both inspires them beyond their daily routine and resonates with their normal activities and day-to-day experience. Even the Incas, with their vision of "good order," could not just rely on divine guidance, but needed to highlight their successes to win credibility for their vision with neighboring tribes.

Contrary to many assertions, you cannot simply derive objectives, strategies, and values from a vision. It is a bit like a revolving spiral in which norms, values, rules, routine practice, specific business objectives, and an overarching vision all intertwine. By using the slogan "The Best or Nothing," Mercedes-Benz fuses an appreciation of quality with a pride in its business. Even today, not without reason, Daimler employees in the Schwabia area of southwestern Germany are proud to say that they are part of the "Daimler family." The fact that Mercedes-Benz can continue the vision of the company's founders and incorporate it into advertising campaigns points to a well-anchored long-term objective with which workers can easily identify.[20] The words "The Best or Nothing" are carved into the ceiling of Herr Daimler's former garden pavilion, which can be seen in the Gottlieb Daimler Museum in Stuttgart.[21] Such visions, deeply rooted in the DNA of a business, serve to boost morale, give a sense of purpose, and help to see everyone through difficult times. But what if you don't have a legendary slogan coined by a business founder to refer to when you are searching for a vision? In the next section, we share an anecdote from the world of business.

Inspiring visions are grounded in the reality of daily business practice.

On Eagles Flying through Circus Tents

If visions are to engage people emotionally, they should not be imposed from the top along the lines of "Vision X will come into force on January 1, 20XX!" Psychologically and practically, that simply won't work. Instead, many organizations go back to the basic educational principle of actively involving those who are going to be most affected. Fundamentally, for an organization looking to build a solid basis for a vision, it is good practice to involve as many employees as possible in the process. In many companies, this leads to a veritable flood of meetings and workshops at all levels and, unfortunately, the outcome is often the dreaded lowest common denominator: It does no real harm to anyone but, as a consequence, doesn't get anyone particularly excited either. So far, so ineffectual. But we're afraid it gets worse...

The Wonderful World of Workshops

A large company adopted the following vision: being ranked in the top ten in its sector within fifteen years. In addition to standard workshops on long-term goals and strategy, "vision workshops" were organized at different levels (department, region, country) to allow each unit to redefine itself in the context of this Vision 2025. One of the originators of the vision, a consultant in the team running the workshops, was particularly keen on using an "ice breaker" exercise involving metaphors, and there was a special moment at the beginning of each workshop when every participant was asked to write down how they would describe themselves. No limits on people's imagination were set, creativity was encouraged, and comparisons were explicitly invited with the world at large, be they animal, vegetable, or mineral. Everyone had to write down on a card how they saw themselves in their particular area of the business, and the following results were the most popular: ringmaster, court jester, mermaid, fortune teller, queen bee (surrounded by useless drones), condor, large eagle, little eagle, supertanker, speedboat, bull in a china shop, Pied Piper of Hamelin, four-star general, private (who only *takes* orders), interior minister, foreign minister, magician, etc.

Alarm bells should have started ringing once the drones and bulls in china shops cropped up. But, as you may have experienced yourself, when this type of exercise gathers momentum, there is often a very fine dividing line between the inspired and the absurd, and no one really wants to be the killjoy.

The next step was to cluster the terms on the cards, using colored stickers to form a ranking until a common consensus was reached which everyone could take on board. Some wonderful images emerged: "Fly, little eagle, fly!" "The noble eagle soars majestically through the circus tent," "A supertanker travelling as fast as a speedboat," or our favorite, "The court jester rides bareback on the mighty condor."

Hundreds of "Vision Workshops" started like this and, to the delight of the consultants, were rolled out across the whole of the organization, both nationally and worldwide. While we can look back on all this now with a wry smile, at the time it was taken very seriously by those involved. Well, most of them.

It is just as risky to derive visions from a condensed bundle of brainstorming contributions as it is to outsource everything to an external consulting firm. For a vision to work well, it has to reflect corporate culture and form the basis of a long-term objective, which will motivate, serve as a guide in day-to-day business, and encourage the "wow" factor. If an organization wants to be "the most customer-friendly business in the world," every decision taken at all levels of the business must be measured against this vision. This applies equally to how staff react to customer complaints through to management making strategic decisions. A good vision enhances a project to an extent where people say, "Hey, I want to be part of that!" and motivates by giving purpose to the work of each and every individual involved. It should be clear and concise, so that all employees can understand it, which conveniently rules out long-winded marketing blurb. Purely numerical statements involving market share or financial targets are also taboo and can, indeed, be quite dangerous—but more about that in a few moments, under "Why Striving for Increased Market Share Is Not a Vision."

First of all, how many of the following would capture your heart and convince you to give everything?

- *"We aspire to be the leading client-centric global universal bank. We serve shareholders best by putting our clients first and by building a global network of balanced business underpinned by strong capital and liquidity."* (Deutsche Bank)
- *"We are 'The Chemical Company' successfully operating in all major markets."* (BASF)

- *"Our vision: world-leading brands and technology."* (Henkel)
- *"GM's vision is to be the world leader in transportation products and related services. We will earn our customers' enthusiasm through continuous improvement driven by the integrity, teamwork, and innovation of GM people."* (General Motors)
- *"To operate the best omni-channel specialty retail business in America, helping both our customers and booksellers reach their aspirations, while being a credit to the communities we serve."* (Barnes & Noble)[22]

The longer the slogan, the more it arouses skepticism. To become "the most customer-friendly business in the world" may well inspire. But "…the leading client-centric global universal bank, serving the best interests of its shareholders"? Likewise, references to performance objectives or market share targets fail to inspire. Which business *doesn't* want to "succeed in all its main markets" or deliver "top performance"? This type of wording ignores completely that powerful visions feed on strong emotions. Admittedly, this is easier for non-profit organizations to achieve than businesses. It is, however, not impossible.

- *"UNICEF's vision: A world where the rights of every child are realized."*
- *"Amnesty International's vision: A world in which every person enjoys all the human rights enshrined in the Universal Declaration of Human Rights and other international human rights standards."*
- *"Syngenta: Using Innovation to Feed the World."*
- *"Google's vision: to provide access to the world's information in one click."*
- *"To become the world's most loved, most flown and most profitable airline."* (Southwest Airlines)[23]

Simon Sinek, the successful TED speaker, author, and management consultant, links this with the "Start with why" effect.[24] Almost everyone knows *what* a business does, and some people know *how* it does it, but it is rarely clear *why* it does what it does. Most visions get stuck at the level of *"what* we do," as shown above. That's the reason they are so long and boring. "Why" visions inspire, are meaningful, and provide a real vision: A fair chance for every child, improving everyday life, making information available at all times to everyone, feeding the world. This "why" is also the key difference of mission statements, which are often confused with visions. Just as a reminder: A mission statement describes *what* a company wants to do now and *how* it will do it, whereas a vision statement outlines *why* a company exists and *where* it wants to be in the future. Management visionary Jim Collins uses the catchphrase "Big, Hairy, Audacious Goals" (BHAG) instead of visions, meaning a picture of a very large, bold, extremely challenging ("hairy") distant objective, an inspiring "Mount Everest" which the business wants to conquer in the next ten to thirty years.[25] Good BHAGs—pronounced "bee-hags"—are not just marketing talk; they drive things forward forcefully and effectively. The bar is thus set pretty high, and so it's not surprising that, despite the surfeit of visions, a really cracking, inspiring vision is rare.

Why Striving for Increased Market Share Is Not a Vision

So, you'd like to be "number one" in your industry? Well, what might seem like an exciting and motivating target is something you might want to think about a little more carefully before proceeding. Is that really a sensible objective? Watch out if your top management starts to toy with the idea of such a so-called vision. Maybe VW wouldn't be involved in constant legal battles if former CEO Martin Winterkorn hadn't announced his objective to topple Toyota from its title of largest automobile manufacturer in the world.[26] A good vision guides workforce behavior positively, whereas overambition can take it in the opposite direction. Would there be an exhaust emissions scandal caused by "cheating software" if VW hadn't wanted to expand its markets in the US in order to reach its ambitious targets? Would Deutsche Bank have been hijacked by investment bankers with their "boom or bust" mentality if, like many other banks toward the end of the nineties, it had not wanted to join the ranks of global players, cost what it may? Would the Inca Empire have been able to put up sterner resistance against the Spanish if it had started earlier to shift from rapid expansion to internal consolidation? The focus on a goal such as "being number one" gives employees the impression that anything goes, as long as the activity is helping to achieve this target. In the cases of VW, Enron, Arthur Andersen, and others, it created a values-free zone, in which behavior was no longer subject to accepted company values or even those of wider society.

We look at this issue more closely in Chapter 4, "Fair Play or Shifting Values." The following example illustrates some of the other dangers of seeking to be Number One.

"Vision 2020" or How to Provoke Poor Investments

It is the turn of the millennium and we are at a Eurostoxx 50 company, an engineering business in the process of launching its "Vision 2020" which foresees a large-scale transformation, creating thousands of jobs and generating billions in turnover. Within the next twenty years, one of its key business units should, once again, rank in the top five in the world. In the previous ten years, the business has dropped out of the top five, falling to sixteenth place, so the vision seems to make sense and be strategically sound. It is communicated worldwide across the organization by means of a large number of meetings and workshops, and ambitious targets are set. So, why did the whole initiative eventually fail, considering how much was invested in the new business approach and how many employees embraced and adopted it enthusiastically? Here are four reasons, all of which are applicable to other businesses.

1. It did not have the full backing of the Board

The goal of getting back into the "Top Five" was only ever going to be achievable through the company acquiring at least one of its biggest competitors. However, the board was not prepared to support such ambitious M&A activity, and this in turn led to frustration among the senior management of the operational business unit, which made many attempts to start negotiations with takeover candidates. All these initiatives were blocked by the board at some stage in the evaluation process, and countless man-hours at middle management level were wasted. The skepticism with which the chairman of the board rejected the vision of the business unit was tangible and, although the vision had been formally approved at board level, the chairman openly scorned his business unit colleagues in meetings and at company events.

2. The overall objective was too ambitious

In many cases, employees and managers were driven by the extremely ambitious targets to take what was actually inappropriate action, albeit consistent with the vision, as they assumed that any activity which increased growth and market share was justified. This led, among other things, to some absurd situations in which non-core M&A activities in emerging markets were approved with enthusiasm. So, for example, a local business in the Philippines was taken over with no global or even regional integration strategy in place, and a similar amount of money was spent in Colombia on the acquisition of a stake in a newly established distribution company. Our interview partner, at the time a junior manager, was directly involved and had to deal with the critical discussions with other business divisions and corporate functions which followed. They strongly doubted the wisdom of these activities, which, with the benefit of hindsight, seems well founded. Similar things took place in other markets.

3. Discussions about the vision were too focused on soft factors

Vision workshops focused too much on values, teamwork, and how people interacted with each other. These are, of course, extremely important aspects, but in this case the more measurable, harder factors such as profitability and practical delivery were not considered enough. A lot of employees misunderstood this apparently very "soft" approach and treated it as an open invitation to do their own thing (see Point 2 above).

4. Responsibility for communicating the vision to the grassroots was delegated

Junior managers were appointed "vision coaches" and given the job of conveying the vision to individual departments and divisions. This had the negative effect of diluting responsibility so that many middle managers no longer felt accountable for embracing the vision and all the changes that came with it, which detracted from the acceptance of the whole project.

From the example above, by implication, we can derive some rules of thumb on how to deal with business visions:

1. Avoid expressing visions in concrete numbers. A numerical target risks misconduct (technical, legal, moral) because employees, under the yoke of a fixed number, no longer do what is best or right, but instead do whatever is needed to achieve the target.

2. Do not propagate messages or mottoes which senior executives have not fully bought into.

3. When you are formulating a vision, critically examine its implications as a guide to day-to-day actions and objectively discuss the consequences. What does it mean to feel bound by this vision?

4. Make sure that the vision is really accepted in the business and not just perceived as an optional nice-to-have. This includes everybody: senior managers, department heads, team leaders, and rank-and-file employees.

5. Don't stubbornly stick to the original path, but be open to criticism and adjust the vision if errors or undesirable behaviors emerge (unlike the Incas, who were incapable of changing course once the original direction, permeated with religious significance, was set).

6. Consider what impact your vision may have on your various stakeholders.

One of our interview partners shows us why these rules are important. Gerd Stürz, Head of Life Sciences (Germany, Austria, Switzerland) at EY, told us about his negative experience with solely concentrating on growth targets. Commenting on an international consulting firm for which "top line growth" became its official objective, he said:

Suddenly, the principal focus was no longer on quality but on growth. Later, this was seen to have been the final nail in the organization's coffin, when it lost all credibility in the face of the scandal-laced insolvency of one of its clients. This was due to the external perception that their misguided business strategy, focusing solely on growth, was an important contributory factor to the client's downfall.

Anything Is Better than Bullshit Bingo

If this vision thing is so difficult, then why bother? Our experience suggests that visions are important and answer the question posed by employees and other stakeholders: "What's in it for me?" It encourages them to identify more closely with the business. You can earn money anywhere, so why would you want to work for this company? In an era when, for many people, work is about more than just putting bread on the table, a compelling vision can act as an invitation to be part of an exciting project. Identifying with something that feels important is one of the keys for motivation. Then again, identity is highly emotional. It's no coincidence that every year the Gallup Institute, in its well-known "Engagement Index," measures the level of "emotional attachment" workers have to their employers.[27] When people feel that they're an important part of something bigger, they get involved in a different way than those who see themselves as small cogs in a big machine. The same message is conveyed by the tale of three stonemasons working on the Cologne Cathedral. When asked what they are doing, one replies, sullenly, "I'm chiseling away at a stone." Another says, "I am working to feed my family," while the third explains, with a sparkle in his eye, "I'm building a cathedral!"

As well as identity, a vision creates solidarity—a connection between employees which can, in some instances, reach across continents. Sometimes this works its way into company jargon, such as when workers at Google refer to themselves, globally, as "Googlers." The bigger a business, the more useful it is to have something visionary which binds it together. Ideally, it promotes a sense of community, even though face-to-face interaction seldom or never occurs. Another theme in one of our interviews was the need in large organizations to have a sense of community in order to enjoy mutual success.

Dr. Christoph Straub, CEO of BARMER, one of Europe's largest Health Funds, told us about his work as the CEO of a group of hospitals:

I was taken on to integrate a portfolio of several independent clinics and merge them into a single hospital care provider. It should have been possible. After all, others manage it. Nevertheless, we failed because we never worked on the shared identity of the business. It is very difficult to create an identity if the only principle which applies in the business is "Every man for himself" and if the organizational structure is designed, from the top down, so that people have to fight each other. The image we portrayed to the outside world of the clinics being a strong unit was not reflected internally, neither in terms of business culture nor organizational structure. When faced with financial problems, we weren't able to find any innovative ideas on how to improve the situation. We could have solved these issues, but finding a common solution was not part of the DNA of the business.

This report, based on direct experience, is interesting for two reasons. First, because the reference to a shared identity highlights the importance of a unifying vision. And secondly, because Christoph Straub also makes it clear that words alone cannot achieve anything if the actions of management and the business culture are more inclined to divide than to unite. A vision which is more like a behavioral letter of intent serves as an official invitation to the employees. Whether it is accepted depends on whether the employees perceive the invitation as credible, given their daily business reality. "Are you serious?" "Is that consistent with our values?" (see Chapter 4) and "Is that realistic?" Both the macro level (vision) and micro level (daily interactions) have to work and complement each other.

This also means that, as long as a business is still working on a vision that is not ready to be published, much can still be gained by chipping away at the micro level to secure engagement and cooperation from the workforce. What can help are the core questions which the Gallup Institute uses to measure the emotional attachment and loyalty of employees to a business. How many of the following questions would your colleagues or subordinates say "yes" to? The more questions that are answered in the affirmative, the higher the motivation and engagement of those concerned. A closer look at the twelve criteria used by Gallup reveals a combination of appreciative management style, efficient organization, opportunities for self-development, and a fair and positive working environment. That's hardly rocket science, is it?

The Twelve Elements of Great Managing —The Gallup Questions[28]

1. Do you know what is expected of you at work?

2. Do you have the materials and equipment to do your work right?

3. At work, do you have the opportunity to do what you do best every day?

4. In the last seven days, have you received recognition or praise for doing good work?

5. Does your supervisor, or someone at work, seem to care about you as a person?

6. Is there someone at work who encourages your development?

7. At work, do your opinions seem to count?

8. Does the mission/purpose of your company make you feel your job is important?

9. Are your associates (fellow employees) committed to doing quality work?

10. Do you have a best friend at work?

11. In the last six months, has someone at work talked with you about your progress?

12. In the last year, have you had opportunities to learn and grow?

Before a business uses empty statements, interchangeable platitudes, or just the blindingly obvious to create a vision—in short, before it indulges in bullshit bingo—it would be better to forgo all forms of so-called visionary statements. And that applies to start-ups too. However gripping the success stories of Jeff Bezos, Mark Zuckerberg, Larry Page, and Sergey Brin may be, not one of them was a first mover, not one of them started out as a gifted visionary with a great new idea. Writing in the magazine *Brand eins,* Thomas Range is blunt: "Amazon's founder Jeff Bezos didn't invent online retail. Ebay's founders didn't invent the online auction. Google's founders Larry Page and Sergey Brin didn't invent the search engine. Mark Zuckerberg did not invent social media with Facebook. And the founders of AirBnB didn't invent private online room rental."[29] What is common to these and other successful entrepreneurs is a sense for what the market is looking for and systematic and disciplined development and implementation of their business model. If you have been a customer of the one-time online bookseller Amazon for more than ten years, then you will have witnessed firsthand the company's constantly expanding range of products and digital services.

Conclusion: It takes lots of small steps to set up a business and hold it steady on the long road to success. The best moment to accelerate this process with an appealing vision, for customers and the workforce alike, is probably not in the first tentative phase, but when the business is already well underway and the signs are multiplying that "there's something in this." Indeed, that something then becomes the script for an inspiring yet realistic vision. And only then does a vision become an engine of progress and a motivator of people, rather than just a naïve, potentially embarrassing, and, worst of all, distracting delusion of grandeur.

A Stress Test for Your Vision

Who is actually responsible for the "vision" of a business? For the Incas, it was clear. The Inca himself, anointed by the Sun God, determined the path, and it is not that much different in modern organizations. A vision statement can only be effective if the leadership team is fully on board and everyone in the business buys into it. Furthermore, it is top management that must have the courage to adopt Collins's "Big Hairy Audacious Goal" idea and then appoint and work with a competent team on creating a sustainable vision. Not only large businesses benefit from well-documented and ambitious long-term goals, but also small companies and family businesses, non-profit organizations, clubs, departments, teams, and every single one of us, as we work out what we want to achieve in our lives. Regular reflection on the question "Where are we actually going?" generally leads to greater success and satisfaction, provided that the vision properly embodies the concept of a motivating and meaningful way forward described in this chapter. Let's find out.

Your Vision Test

1. Now is a good moment for a (new) vision. (Unfavorable times are, for example, during a serious crisis or a start-up period.) ☐

2. The vision can be captured in one sentence. It does not need any further explanation and is crystal clear to everyone inside and outside the business. ☐

3. The vision is distinct and unique; it could not be applicable to any other organization. ☐

4. The vision is emotionally compelling. It goes beyond purely economic targets or milestones. ☐

5. The vision fully reflects the culture and values of the organization. ☐

6. The vision unleashes the desired behavioral responses. ☐

7. The vision is relevant and meaningful for everyone. ☐

8. The vision answers the question: Why does the world need this business/ organization? ☐

9. The vision reinforces a positive image of the organization (external perception). ☐

10. The vision is both ambitious and credible (a realistic long-term objective). ☐

INCA INSIGHTS

- **Set yourself big targets.**

- **Appeal to the hearts and minds of everyone in your organization.**

- **Keep a close and constant eye on whether your vision is still taking you where you really want to go, and nowhere else.**

"You can't train someone to be smart. That's something they just have to bring with them!"

—DR. TIMM VOLMER, CEO SMARTSTEP CONSULTING

---

2 Talent before Seniority

(or the Creeping Danger of Mediocrity?)

The success of a business depends on the skills of its people. So, be honest: How many of your team colleagues would you re-employ? How many of them are just "OK" and how many do you put up with because you think you have no choice? After all, an incompetent employee can harm their employer and a dishonest one can ruin them. Considering the risk, it is remarkable how carefree some businesses are when hiring new people. The Incas would probably have been astonished by these questions. Their elite leaders were subjected to rigorous training in special schools called *Yachaywasi* and Machu Picchu is believed to have housed one of these "Inca Business Schools," where sons of both the Inca nobility and tribal chiefs from the conquered territories were educated.[30] Seventeenth-century chroniclers describe the curriculum in detail: history, religion, and poetry, as well as arithmetic, bookkeeping, statistics, statecraft, law, medical procedures, and of course warcraft, weaponry, and hand-to-hand combat. All in all, it was a course of study reminiscent of a cross between modern military academies and elite universities. In addition, the curriculum included topics such as discipline, self-control, and pain endurance. The training ended with a month-long test under the supervision of the ruling Inca and, if you passed, you were eligible for jobs in administration and in the military.

The sons of the Inca princes, too, had to excel in the elite school and earn their place in the Inca nobility, just like the potential successor to the throne, who had to pass some particularly strict tests. "On the basis of these merits, he earned...the right to govern, and this was much more important than the fact that he just happened to be his father's first-born," writes Garcilaso de la Vega in 1609[31]. Yes, the new ruler was selected from among the Inca's sons, but this was often a wide circle of candidates, and by law, succession was determined by who was the most able for the position. Furthermore, in determining his succession, the Inca was assisted by a council made up of twenty relatives, all of which sounds well thought through. Automatic succession and poorly prepared personnel decisions are rarely blessed with good fortune, and a decision to rely on your "second choice" frequently comes back to haunt you. But don't we still fall into these traps far too often?

Once again, the Incas are capable of really shaking us out of the conviction that ours is the most advanced era, and sometimes the twenty-first century is astonishingly archaic. Laws of inheritance under which a farm automatically passes to the eldest son still hold sway in parts of Europe. Siblings, especially daughters, are "subsidiary heirs," which is a polite way of saying they have no rights of inheritance. It is much the same in many family-run businesses. A poll conducted by the I.F.M., the Research Institute for Family-Owned Businesses, in Bonn, Germany, revealed that more than two-thirds of the owners of medium-sized businesses with over 250 employees would like management succession to stay in the family. Above all, sons are preferred (57.6 percent), little different from centuries ago, and there is no mention here of tough selection procedures or demanding probationary periods in which the candidates have to prove themselves worthy of the position.[32] In this respect, the Incas were astonishingly farsighted.

What Happens When the Prince Automatically Becomes King?

Otto von Bismarck once mockingly observed, "The first generation creates the wealth, the second manages it, the third studies art history, and the fourth generation squanders it all." Even if one of Germany's most famous political leaders and *Reichskanzler* was talking about the economy of the nineteenth century, it is undeniable: even today, countless owner-managed businesses find it difficult to arrange for a qualified successor. Indeed, it has been shown that almost three-quarters of all such companies—which, after all, play a major role in Europe, with up to 70 percent of GDP in some countries—have "absolutely no" or "currently no" succession planning in place. Clearly, they live in a world with no traffic accidents, illnesses, or other similar strokes of fate. The illusion of invincibility is powerful, even among otherwise considered and prudent business people.[33]

While a high value is placed on innovation in technology, software, and marketing, when it comes to another key success factor—leadership—hope is often the guiding principle. Just like hundreds of years ago, mothers and fathers want to believe that their legacy is in the safe hands of their sons and daughters. From a human point of view, that is understandable, however risky it may be from a business perspective. Rarely are the potential consequences of such an approach so openly exposed as in the following example.

"The Best Man Needs Help"

Such was the headline the German newspaper *taz* placed above the picture of Konstantin Neven DuMont in October 2010. He was the heir to the fourth-largest newspaper publisher in Germany and, at the time, a board member at the media group M. DuMont Schauberg.[34]

The business had been under family control since the beginning of the nineteenth century and, as far as the current patriarch Alfred Neven DuMont was concerned, that was the way it was going to stay, so he brought his son Konstantin Neven DuMont into his circle of top managers. Insiders at the firm were somewhat skeptical about the abilities of his successor, but the new arrival was nevertheless happy to give the journalists a more than confident statement: "I have the qualifications and have already proven that I can do the job at least as well as all those people from the financial sector or the managing directors from other publishing houses."[35]

A dispute over business strategy between father and son—not least about how to tackle the challenges of digitization—broke out and was further aggravated by an interview Konstantin Neven DuMont gave to the *Bild* newspaper. *Bild* was the biggest competitor of the family's tabloid newspaper, *Express*, and the interview had not been discussed with the other members of senior management, who could hardly have been happy about it. There were consequences as *Bild*, quite naturally, took full advantage of the situation.

In November 2010, Alfred Neven DuMont relieved his son of all duties in the business. At the end of 2012, Konstantin Neven DuMont transferred his shares back to his parents and, between 2013 and 2017, he was bought out of the business.

The family learned from its mistakes. The family representatives, Christian DuMont Schütte and Isabella Neven DuMont, now exercise control at supervisory board level, while an external manager runs the operational businesses.

If you find yourself shaking your head in a combination of amusement and disbelief, you might want to think about that just for a moment. Let's face it: Even in "normal" families, arguments erupt and emotions can often run high on straightforward day-to-day issues. So how much more difficult must it be to find agreement between parents, siblings, cousins, and more distant relatives on matters of business strategy, division of responsibilities, and the distribution of considerable wealth? The heiress to a large family dynasty described the challenge very aptly as follows: "We have to somehow combine this highly subjective environment with the real-life numbers and facts to come up with sensible enterprise decisions."[36]

Anyone who can maintain composure as they navigate this emotional minefield commands our respect. It is one of the most deep-rooted of human instincts for parents to view their children through rose-tinted glasses. Equally human is the all-too-critical attitude of many patriarchs, whose fear of the loss of power and status prevents a timely handover to a younger successor, or the belief of many founders in their own invincibility, which can completely suffocate the next generation. And all of this is taking place in an increasingly fast-moving and global era which is crying out, louder than ever before, for smart leadership.

"In the twenty-first century it will be far less about simply handing down material assets and far more about passing on the entrepreneurial mentality and aptitude to the next generation," says Peter May, one of Europe's leading experts on family businesses.[37]

The Incas also lived in an era of change, constantly faced with new challenges. And they would have been equally familiar with power battles, jealousy, envy, and family feuds, all of which makes their disciplined approach to leadership development even more admirable—an approach which limited personal preference through compulsory training followed by testing and assessment in front of a central board. Indeed, it is noteworthy and indicative that their eventual downfall was accelerated, at least in part, by a departure from this disciplined approach, leading to a less than clear succession policy and a subsequent weakening of the Inca Empire (see Chapter 5, "Tackling the Real Opponent"). But it is not only family businesses that make mistakes when recruiting their senior managers. Christine Wolff, an experienced business manager and non-executive member of a number of boards, considers "wrong personnel decisions" to be the most serious mistakes she has made in her career to date and identifies the most common pitfalls.

From Christine Wolff, multiple board member:

There are four typical mistakes made in the area of personnel management, all of which I have made myself:

1. Hanging on to average or bad managers for too long
2. Promoting the wrong people, either because you are under time pressure or because you are not focusing on their actual qualifications
3. Giving the job to the person who screams loudest, just to reduce the pressure at that moment
4. Promoting or transferring someone to another department to get them out of the way

And what have I learned from this? If possible, try to avoid time pressure, because under stress everyone makes mistakes. You should be well-structured in your approach, take time to look closely at the qualifications of each candidate, and it is never too soon to start actively developing talented people, something that is often overlooked.

We wonder if you have ever made one (or more) of these mistakes. We certainly have. One thing is certain: If the real cost (in dollars and cents) of poor personnel decisions were included in budgets in the same way as investment in technology or marketing, then recruitment and selection methods would look very different. Let's do the mental arithmetic for a moment and add together annual salary, bonus, and employer's Social Security contributions, costs for advertising the position, headhunter and search fees, and the salaries and time of internal people involved in the selection process, not to mention the time required to ensure a professional onboarding for the new recruit once they've agreed to start. Even for relatively junior positions, you will quickly be up to a six-figure sum and can triple that in the case of making a poor appointment, not only because the whole process has to start again from scratch, but also because the wrong person in the wrong place can have serious financial impact due to, among other things, lost orders, lost revenue, compliance issues, and resignations from frustrated colleagues. The latter effect refers to the situation when the inappropriate new recruit has people reporting to them, as it is well-known that people *join* companies but *leave* incompetent bosses. We have no doubt that, if there were more widespread and robust financial scrutiny of HR processes such as these, the temptation to make off-the-cuff decisions or follow the path of least resistance in matters of recruitment or career development would virtually disappear.

A successful business that wants to stay that way is well advised to take great care in the way it goes about recruitment and selection. However, the reality is often very different. In his talks, Andreas Krebs particularly enjoys the moment when he invites his listeners to take part in a short exercise. "Think of your ten most important key people. Imagine you could recruit them again from scratch. Who would you keep?" Immediately, you can see on the faces of the assembled managers the mental screening process, as they think through the names in their departments. "Her? Yes, immediately! And him? Not in a million years!" Within just a couple of minutes, at least in their heads, most departments have shrunk dramatically. On one occasion, a clearly frustrated manager answered the question by loudly shouting out "None of them!" Most would retain no more than half of their colleagues, and the remainder would not be rehired. So, what does this actually mean? Are we working with people, in our team, in whom we don't really have any confidence? And we are not talking about serious weaknesses which could justify sacking people, but just the everyday frustration of team members delivering average, ordinary, unexciting work. But whose fault is this ultimately? The employees themselves? Or perhaps those who recruit carelessly and surround themselves with the mediocre, only to then complain about their lack of inspiration and good ideas?

And, just in case you are thinking, "Well, I had no choice" because you inherited your team, ask yourself this: What's your plan to shift these colleagues from a "perhaps keep" to a "solid yes"? And then from a "solid yes" to an "absolutely must retain"?

Dilettantism, Disinterest, and Delegation

This apparently simple exercise ("Which of my colleagues would I hire again?") is an acid test for any leader. Anyone who would prefer to see most of their team move on should ask themselves why they were hired in the first place or why they have allowed them to carry on working without doing something about it. How did it come to this? Where were mistakes made? Managers who have been in their companies or roles or business sectors for a long time frequently swear by their intuition, their "gut feeling," when it comes to candidate assessment. Now, we don't want to dismiss or devalue the importance of life experience or the insight into human nature gained through many years in the workplace. The question is whether you can consistently rely on this intuition in the heat of the moment, whether this intuition is equally relevant for different business functions and age groups, or whether our intuitive insight and gut feeling really are as good as we would like to believe. One of our interviewees, a highly experienced leader and human resources expert, gave us food for thought.

From Dr. Alexander von Preen, CEO of Intersport eG:

I don't think that this sense [a reliable first impression of candidates] stays with you forever. The longer you are in a position of authority (let's say ten years), the more time this intuition has to decay and wither. You start making poor decisions. Your antennae get rusty and stuck in time. Society changes a lot, different age groups tick differently, life conditions change, education changes, values change, etc. I see this over and over again, also among top managers. Your instinct for people can deteriorate over time and you have to be aware of this.

Wise words, indeed. And let's be very frank: Can you ever really "know" another person? If the answer is yes, then it certainly is a process that normally takes a number of years. And a colleague who excels in his current job can just as easily fail in the next. We all know the classic example of the good performer who's been moved into the wrong job for the wrong reasons—the best salesman who is rewarded with a promotion to a management position and fails abysmally. The change is detrimental to the company and very tough for the individual, yet it happens over and over again.

From Christine Wolff, multiple board member:

I come from the engineering sector, mainly working with engineers, scientists, etc., technically top-notch people. And I have made the basic error of not being careful enough about moving very good technicians into management roles. It's a mistake to assume that a good technician is also automatically a good manager. Some are, but some aren't and don't even want to be—and it's a mistake that can potentially do damage to the business.

In my case, it was different. I am an average scientist, but I have better leadership skills. Hardly a week had gone by in my job and I had pulled together my first team and worked with groups to achieve good results. It wouldn't have helped the company much if I'd carried on working on the technical side. Others can do that better.

This is a straight-to-the-point and very succinct example of putting the principle of "talent before seniority" into practice. Unfortunately, the idea is frequently turned on its head when proven specialists are rewarded with management positions. Company loyalty and good performance over an extended period of time in a specific position is rewarded, rather than considering what a person can do best and whether this is what is actually needed in the future role. Anyone who closely monitors when and where colleagues blossom and flourish, and where they do not, is somewhat better placed to avoid such mistakes. In order to fill leadership positions with the right people (those with the best chance of success, see below), it would be helpful to move away from the idea that career progression is solely defined by how many people report to you or the size of the budget you control. Do we really value specialist skills enough? The Incas used to elevate proven craftsmen to the central court. How do we show that we value colleagues who are "only" experts, but whose expertise is critical to the company's success? Anybody who understands the basics of motivation knows it's not principally a question of money, but rather has to do with recognition, appreciation and being seen to have the right status in the organization.

Returning to the topic of assessing colleagues, it has long been known that human perception and judgment are highly unreliable and subjective. But how many of us fall into the trap of believing that these frailties only apply to everyone else? Perhaps it's worthwhile to take another look at the seven common causes of poor judgment:

1. Our perception is highly selective. We cannot process all the information our senses pick up. That's the reason the police are generally skeptical about eyewitnesses, as five bystanders at the scene of a crime have probably seen five different-colored cars. Black, blue, or maybe gray? And how often do you actually see your team members in action? Do you really know what they do well or what they are not so good at? And who do you focus your attention on during team meetings?

2. Perceptions and judgments are guided by our expectations; we see what we want to see, and this can lead to self-fulfilling prophecies. US psychologists Robert Rosenthal and Lenore F. Jacobson conducted a famous experiment in the mid-1960s. They led some primary school teachers to believe that, with the help of scientific testing, they had identified the 20 percent of pupils who were just about to begin a development spurt. In reality, the children had been chosen at random, but at the end of the school year this group had, in fact, outperformed their classmates, presumably because they had had more attention and affirmation from the teachers.[38] So, does that mean, for example, that so-called "high potentials" are our beacon of hope because they really are better? Or is it because we expect them to be better?

3. We allow ourselves to be blinded by one characteristic or attribute which outshines all others—the "halo effect"—for example, above-average height suggesting assertiveness, good looks suggesting intelligence, or self-assurance suggesting a higher readiness to work hard and be committed. Did you know that height and income are correlated? Or that most CEOs of Fortune 500 companies and most US presidents (about 90 percent) are taller than average?[39] So much for intrinsic values.

4. We prefer people who are like ourselves; it's the "similar-to-me effect." Someone with a similar background, maybe even somebody who went to the same business school: well, she *must* be good! Psychologists say that sympathy is essentially perceived similarity. Who could disagree with giving a promotion to a pleasant colleague? Sociologist and elite researcher Michael Hartmann goes further. Talking about how top jobs in the economy and society at large are filled, he states that social background and appearance are more important than skills and performance.[40] Furthermore, in an increasingly global work

environment, self-awareness of the phenomenon of ethnic bias is becoming ever more important.

5. We always look for confirmation of first impressions, and first impressions are made subconsciously and in a flash. Since our perceptions are selective (see point 1 above), it is extremely easy to then confirm our expectations. Look how long it took to see Bernard Madoff, one of the biggest investment fraudsters of all time, in the right light. Although there had been plenty of indications for years, nobody wanted to believe that the former chairman of NASDAQ and member of the NASD Board of Governors could have been capable of such dishonesty. Due to his extremely confident and convincing manner and his numerous donations to charities and cultural institutions (including many board positions in theaters, foundations, and schools), many philanthropic organizations entrusted him with their money; only after it became more and more clear that he had embezzled over sixty billion dollars and had ruined about 4,800 investors did the full extent of his duplicity become visible. He was sentenced on June 29, 2009, to 150 years of imprisonment.

6. All sorts of things can influence how we assess people—general beliefs, prior experience, kitchen-sink psychology—and sometimes this works out well enough, but not always. In fact, we often draw conclusions which are, to put it bluntly, devoid of any logic whatsoever: "If someone demonstrates he really wants the job during the interview phase, then he's bound to make a big effort later on as well," or "Someone coming from a family of entrepreneurs is much more likely to be driven and ambitious than someone whose father was a civil servant," and there are plenty more examples like these.

7. We generalize our own view of the world and project it onto others. So, somebody who has enthusiastically taken on leadership responsibility can quickly fall into the trap of believing that this must also be the dream of every other colleague or candidate. Or someone who enjoys being praised in public cannot imagine that another colleague might find such an experience unpleasant and embarrassing.

All in all, we tend to overestimate our objectivity when assessing others, something psychologists call "the illusion of sound judgment."[41] With this in mind, it seems pretty rash to be taking an important hiring decision almost off the cuff, following a sixty- to ninety-minute discussion. And yet the job interview remains the most popular way of making hiring decisions. After all, who really wants to spend long and intensive days at an assessment center? Admittedly, it is possible to learn a lot about a person in the course of a well-prepared and properly structured conversation, even more so if the questions are well thought through and derived from a clear description of the position. But how often is this really the case? Or is it more often than not something like this: Your assistant knocks gently on the door and reminds you that your meeting with Mr. or Ms. X is in a few minutes. You grab the file, take a quick glance at the candidate's resume, and rush off to meet them. Everything else is down to "intuition," how you feel on the day and, with any luck, your colleague from the Human Resources department who is sitting in on the meeting. Paul Williams spent a number of years as a senior manager in HR and knows this problem all too well. He has drawn up the following list of "rules," based on his experience running hundreds of interviews alongside senior line managers. Paul is happy to leave it up to the reader to decide how seriously to take the list:

Rules of Thumb for Job Interviews

The amount of time a recruiting manager spends talking (about) himself during an interview is directly proportional to his level of seniority in the organization.

The capacity of a manager to listen carefully to a candidate during an interview is inversely proportional to his level of seniority in the organization.

The more senior a manager is, the greater the probability that he will answer the question that he has just asked *himself*, rather than waiting for the candidate to speak.

The more a manager speaks (about) himself during the interview, the better his impression will be of the candidate.

While we've discussed the issues concerning human perception and intuition, and addressed the dangers of poor preparation, there is another, equally serious and problematic issue with recruitment which we have not yet mentioned at all, namely the self-interest of the department head which, shocker, is not always driven solely by the best interests of the business. "As hire As, Bs hire Cs" is a well-known phenomenon; a poor boss is seldom interested in bringing unnecessary competition into their area of responsibility and usually prefers mediocrity, which they can more easily control. And if by chance a top performer lands in their department, then they are unlikely to hang around for very long. Nevertheless, a lot of organizations actually do seem to manage to just muddle along. It has been shown often enough that a performance-driven company culture is one of the cornerstones of sustainable business success (see Probst and Raisch, *The Logic of Business Failure*, 2004).[42] The question is not whether we "manage to muddle along," but rather "How much better could it be if we actually had the right people in the key positions?" Unfortunately (or perhaps fortunately), it can take quite some time, particularly in large companies, for the full impact of poor personnel decisions to be reflected in the bottom line. And, equally, managers are often slow to correct mistakes. Let's not underestimate the loss of potential business brought about by having the wrong person in an important position for too long.

So, what might be an alternative to the traditional job interview? Well, for one thing, it is certainly not following the popular trend of outsourcing the whole process to external consultants, even if being able to blame them when things don't work out is an attractive proposition. There is no doubt that the standard array of techniques such as personality type and interaction style tests, assessment centers, and structured interviews have their place. But these can only work well if all those involved, both internal staff and external consultants, have agreed on a detailed brief for the position to be filled and have the full support of senior managers within the business. When it comes to recruitment and development from within the company, especially for key positions and the selection of next-generation leaders, it is advisable to refer to internal assessments, 360-degree feedback tools, and experiences gained from personal interactions over many years, in favor of management audits run by external consultants. And it's downright negligent when top management steers clear of important personnel decisions, thinking these are better left to the HR department and the relevant line managers. An experienced CEO we've worked with for many years once said, "The most important decision we make as a company is who we hire and then systematically develop." We thoroughly agree!

Are You a Consumer or a Producer of Talent?

A large American corporation introduced a special remuneration system for its board members. Twenty percent of variable income was linked to the "talent" balance of each director. Was their division able to supply talent for the top two hundred senior management positions, or did they have to recruit externally for crucial vacancies or even draw on talent from other divisions? The key question was "Are you a net producer or a net consumer of talent?"

This process proved to be very effective, not only in terms of remuneration, but also because it helped to establish consistent talent development as a core

One of our interviewees elegantly describes how a top manager can nurture talent and benefit from the process along the way. His following statement is reminiscent of the placement method the Inca lords used. They'd deploy to the various regions graduates of their elite *Yachaywasi* Academy who'd been selected as students from either their own or the region's upper class.

From Dr. Alexander von Preen, CEO of Intersport eG:

For me, the development of junior staff is a very exciting and crucial part of my job. I have implemented a scheme in which I recruit five young people every year as assistants and project managers. They report directly to me and they learn about my management skills, my competencies, and my specific, personal expectations. I let them into my inner circle, I invite them as guests to private events and treat them as part of the family. I soon give them a lot of responsibility and involve them in business matters which are otherwise confidential, e.g. strategic planning. After eighteen months, I place these people into the wider organization and they are my key pillars of contact into the company, my most trusted colleagues across the whole network.

Talented people are all around us and not just in our own specific areas of responsibility. What matters is being genuinely interested in people and having the willingness to give some of them a chance, just like in this example:

From Elevator Operator to Senior Salesman

In emerging economies, there are many people who can look back on unusual careers. One such example is the elevator operator who used to greet Andreas Krebs every day on his way up to the tenth floor of his office building in Guatemala City: this guy was smart, helpful, and friendly, probably in his early twenties. At the time, the business was looking for people to join the supermarket promotions team, and Andreas gave a tip-off to the responsible sales manager. He spoke with the lift operator, and then the challenges and his new life began. The man earned about eighty dollars per month working in the elevator, lower than the minimum wage, which is not unusual in developing countries. He needed a scooter for the new job, so his whole family rallied round and found the money. Instead of fifty dollars, he now earned $280, the absolute minimum for such a job in the Guatemalan branch of a Eurostoxx company.

But he didn't let this go to his head—quite the contrary. Next came evening school and lots more training, and he duly rose from promoter to salesman, from salesman to senior salesman, and then further. It's what you might call a mini fairy tale, but the charm of it is that it's true and that it contains two simple but important messages: Firstly, if you work hard, are ambitious, and really want to be successful, then all you need is one chance. And secondly, it pays off for leaders to keep an eye out for those who have earned just such a chance.

Rule Number 1: No Compromises!

If we were to give just one piece of advice when it comes to choosing new employees, then it would be this: Don't compromise! No "Well, it might work out," no "That's the best currently available," no "We need to do this quickly." When you consider how much negative impact and collateral damage can be caused by hiring the wrong person for a key position, then such laxity in personnel decisions is, at the very least, extremely short-sighted. Rolf Hoffmann, one of our interview partners, put it very succinctly: "Nothing is more expensive than wrong hires!" Did you know, for example, that when managers are transferred to a new department, they actually take with them, albeit it unwittingly, the average sick days recorded in their old department into their new one? This emerged in a study at a large European corporation in which managers with high absenteeism due to ill-health were put in charge of departments with low levels of sick leave. After one year, the levels of sick leave in the new department had risen to the same levels as in their previous areas of responsibility, and the study showed that this phenomenon also works in the other direction.[43]

One of the biggest obstacles in filling positions successfully is dealing with so-called "blockers": specialists or managers who have reached their performance peak, but who are blocking important operational or strategic positions in the organization. They are mostly in the second half of their careers but still too far away from normal retirement, and a redundancy package is considered too expensive. But how expensive is it to keep someone in a key position when they are only moderately effective? How much additional value could be created for the business with the right person in the job? In the absence of other alternatives, a redundancy offer is almost always worth it, allowing the position to be freed up for better candidates with a more promising leadership and development prognosis. Are you wincing slightly at the use of the rather unflattering word "blocker"? True, it is not a particularly attractive term, but it's not uncommon in the HR world. And the situation can be made more difficult because these people are often solid performers, and it doesn't seem fair to move them. Nevertheless, they can still create value for the business in less prominent positions while making way for people better suited to the task in hand.

Management visionary Jim Collins has been following the strategies of particularly successful companies for years and has come up with the snappy formula "First who, then what—get the right people on the bus." You just need the right team to deliver sustainable commercial success. Statements like this come across as somewhat banal, but if it is so simple, why do we find it so difficult to put into practice? Why do so many managers say they would not rehire half of their department? In the process of filling job vacancies, Collins talks about managers being rigorous and acting in a consistent way.

In describing "How to be Rigorous," he recommends the following:

- Practical Discipline #1: When in doubt, don't hire—keep looking.
- Practical Discipline #2: When you know you need to make a people change, act.
- Practical Discipline #3: Put your best people on your biggest opportunities, not your biggest problems.[44]

How often do managers procrastinate when faced with tricky personnel decisions because they are afraid of conflict? How often are capable people worn down in crisis-riven departments, though they could do so much better elsewhere? During the DaimlerChrysler debacle, critical voices were quick to point out that Daimler's own management was in danger of being depleted by sending too many people to the US.

It Really Is All About People

Colin Powell, former US General and Secretary of State, summed up his most important leadership principles in his book *My American Journey*. In it, he reminds us of some rudimentary truths:

"Organization doesn't really accomplish anything. Plans don't accomplish anything, either. Theories of management don't much matter. Endeavors succeed or fail because of the people involved. Only by attracting the best people will you accomplish great things."[45]

No compromise also means getting away from the idea that you can "develop" workers at will and mold them according to your own thinking, as if you were retooling a machine. Of course people can learn, of course they can develop further, but within limits. An introverted technician will not, in all probability, make a convincing salesman or an empathetic manager. First, people must want to change; secondly, the conditions must be right to allow for the corresponding learning and development to take place; and thirdly, they must have certain core skills and personality traits which match those required for the new career direction. The sticking point is often step number one.

Factor F—Beware of Taking Shortcuts in the Selection Process

For several years, Paul Williams was responsible for the international trainee recruitment program at a EUROSTOXX company. A large number of graduates needed to be assessed on their suitability for a leadership career, so every year the focus fell on four to six international business schools and the resumes of candidates were pre-screened on criteria such as overseas studies, foreign languages, and interesting extracurricular activities. The number of candidates was whittled down further in thirty-minute "speed interviews" to decide who would then be invited to an assessment center. The key question was, which criteria should be used in the interviews? Thirty minutes was insufficient time for an in-depth behavioral event interview, so it had to be something short and sweet.

"We came up with the 'Factor F,' the F being short for 'fascination.' The thinking was that those who, in the future, were to lead other people must be able to connect with them, enthuse them, and capture their imagination. Factor F was defined as follows: can this person—in a very short time—awaken my interest in them and really captivate me? How passionate are they when they are talking about topic X? Am I drawn in or is it just a dry monologue?"

Many talented trainees who then went on to be very successful were identified using this technique, but some mistakes were made, too. For example, in one resume, "Parrots" was listed under hobbies. It transpired that the candidate had taken over the care of two macaws, large parrots from South America, and these are highly intelligent and sociable creatures, which can live up to sixty years. Paul Williams, biologist and animal lover, was so intrigued that about twenty minutes of the interview revolved around these birds, and it was captivating to listen to, full of enthusiasm and, well, fascinating. And yet, how much did this have to do with leadership skills and the suitability for a career in management? The candidate made it to the assessment center and into the firm, but it quickly became clear that he was not going to be successful and he duly left the company.

There was, of course, a lesson to be learned by Paul personally, but also one regarding the selection methodology. Leadership is more than just telling a fascinating story, and it will not have been the first or indeed the last career launched on the strength of a strong presentation. Good communication skills and a well-developed "Factor F" *can* be an indicator of success later on but, to come up with a sound decision regarding a positive prognosis in a leadership career, you need to have far more breadth and depth in your selection process than was demonstrated here.

Faced with the complex challenge of making a measured assessment of a colleague or candidate, there is a huge temptation to seek refuge in focusing on seemingly meaningful but irrelevant criteria. The fact is that neither studying at X nor living abroad in Y is a guarantee of success, as the following study shows:

What Makes a Successful CEO?

In May 2017, the *Harvard Business Review* published an article about an amazing project. Over a ten-year period, the "CEO Genome Project" collected data on more than seventeen thousand top business leaders (so-called "C-Suite" executives). Among these were two thousand CEOs. The data was enhanced by four- to five-hour-long interviews as well as by related conversations, such as interviews with colleagues, superiors, stakeholders, etc. The study covered career background, work performance, and, above all else, patterns of behavior.

The main target of the research was to find out why these people were appointed in the first place and what had helped them to be successful over a long period. Those questioned came from all sectors and from businesses of all sizes—from small firms to Fortune 100 companies. Although the research focused on Americans, it was felt that the findings could apply to similar countries and cultures. The most important conclusions were:

– Although charismatic and self-confident candidates are often preferred for top positions, it is the more introverted and analytical candidates who, ultimately, are more successful.

- Forty-five percent of all CEOs had made at least one serious mistake in their career which cost them their job and cost their firm a lot of money. Seven percent of this group signed up straightaway as CEO at another firm.

- There is no correlation between educational background and qualifications and proven success. Only 7 percent of the "high-performing" CEOs went to one of the top universities, and 8 percent had no tertiary qualifications at all.

- Four decisive characteristics of successful leaders emerged, and out of the thirty core competencies listed, more than 50 percent of the candidates evidenced at least two of the following characteristics:

  • Deciding with speed and conviction

  • Engaging for impact

  • Adapting proactively

  • Delivering reliably[46]

Even if these core competencies sound somewhat generalized, they provide a clear focus with respect to current and future leadership challenges:

- Deciding with speed and conviction: It is better to make decisions than not to decide. In the VUCA world (volatility, uncertainty, complexity, and ambiguity), there is only limited time for analysis and consideration; quick and effective action is becoming ever more important.

- Engaging for impact: Sound stakeholder management and networking with your most important business partners provides an information advantage and thereby greater certainty when it comes to decision-making. This, too, is an important key to success (see Chapter 7, "Judgment").

- Adapting proactively: The most successful executives spend more than half their time on long-term goals, challenges, and risks (see Chapter 5, "Fight the Real Enemy" and above all the section on risk management). Successful managers consider crisis management part of their job, thus preparing them much better for reversals and setbacks.

- Delivering reliably: Again, this is not surprising. Long-lasting and demonstrable success strengthens leaders and promotes greater success. To quote the study: "Boards and investors love a steady hand."

Even if you are not always looking for your next CEO, it is well worthwhile asking "Behavioral Event Questions" from the Genome Project, which focus on the most relevant characteristics as far as success is concerned, and using these to evaluate a potential manager. This type of questioning reveals how the candidate has up to now solved a particular problem or mastered a similar situation, and this can say a great deal about how they would deal with a similar situation in the future. For example, you can ask specific questions about contextual or situational evidence as to when and where a candidate has shown a particular behavior. A candidate will prompt such questioning if they make claims about their personal strengths and characteristics, such as "I am a good team player" or "I am assertive and get things done." The following questions are helpful for an interviewer in this context:

○ Where have you shown that you get things done? What were the circumstances?
○ What was the task?
○ What exactly did *you* do?
○ What was the result or outcome?

A useful acronym for this approach is "STAR" (Situation-Task-Action-Result).

Further information can be derived from additional situational questions which assess the behavioral options and link achieved outcomes with personal characteristics. These are effective in almost every interview, not just for positions with leadership responsibility. For example, you can ask about:

○ Tasks for which the candidate's personal strengths were ideally suited and those for which they felt less suited or even found rather unpleasant
○ What the candidate valued in former bosses, and what not

- The biggest challenge that a candidate had overcome in their career to date, and how they managed it
- An example of the most recent or most influential learning experience the candidates had, where they had seen positive impact on their personal development, and how
- A major success and how it came about
- Suggestions and ideas for solving a tricky situation in the new job

By doing this, you are anchoring the conversation in the daily routine of the business. To round things off, we would like to augment this with a methodology that goes further in anchoring the assessment in the specific environment in question and thus leads to better decision-making, especially in internal appointments. At the same time, it gives us an opportunity to distance ourselves from the rather overused concept of "potential."

Prognosis, Not Potential

Twenty years ago, McKinsey declared the outbreak of the "war for talent." Since then, there has been much talk about the "high-potentials" which a business must attract in order to stay successful. Given the fact that, in the meantime, organizations are in a battle for the best people at every level—not just for management—the question arises as to whether "potential," as a concept, is not leading us down a blind alley. We have personally experienced how a whole pool of "potentials" suddenly were no longer seen as such, simply because there was a change of top management at the company in question. Bizarre as it seems at first glance, there can be many reasons for this. The list of people with "potential" was perhaps unconvincing, for example, because it was drawn up by a weak management. Or the "top potentials" were viewed by the new decision-makers as threats, only to then go on to great careers outside the company. Our skepticism is confirmed by an experienced HR professional and former Olympic trainer in fencing.

From Johannes Thoennessen, psychologist and consultant:

I find the concept of "potential" very vague. I can only measure potential if I know precisely what someone is supposed to have potential for. For instance, I can say whether a sportsman has the potential, at some point in the future, to run a hundred meters in ten seconds or whether he will never break fifteen seconds. By contrast, the challenges and demands required in leading people are so varied that I can almost completely rule out being able to measure potential in this context. The whole concept of leadership is just too complicated. And no one has yet been able to really answer the question "What makes a successful manager or leader?" All sorts of people, with totally varying skills, can be extremely successful leaders. That alone shows that it is impossible to define a generalized concept of potential.

Another major problem with the concept of potential is that someone either has "potential" or they don't. On this understanding, whether a person is successful or not rests exclusively with that person, so that other systemic factors, such as a change of decision-makers with a different understanding of leadership, are ignored and at the same time "an extremely high potential for demotivation" is created, as underlined by Johannes Thoennessen. If less than 10 percent of an organization are considered to be "high potentials," then the best part of 90 percent are going to be frustrated. Rather ironically, the 1998 McKinsey report, which set off the high-potential hype, completely fails to identify which characteristics make some employees more successful than others.[47] The more you look into it, the more "potential" is exposed as a rather meaningless label. Even more confusing then are the batteries of tests and analyses that ostensibly measure potential, but often without any reference to the context or the precise circumstances of the business in question.

It would be fairer, more relevant, and above all more in tune with real life, to ask whether candidate X, faced with conditions Y (company culture, leadership insight, business sector, colleagues, customer or market requirements), has what it takes to be successful and then to ask whether earlier successes can back this up. Such a prognosis is not focused exclusively on personality traits but also looks at the situation as a whole—a truly systemic approach. At the same time, this "prognosis" already takes into account different viewpoints and possible mistakes. After all, a well-researched weather or share price forecast comes with a high probability of being accurate, but it can, in the end, fail to materialize. And so it is with "prognosis," which is thus more subtle, more nuanced, and ultimately less dogmatic than "potential."

We are still left with the question of how we can gain reliable insight into the prognoses of employees. One practical tool, DECIDE®, helps predict the probability of success based on past performance.[48] At the heart of this tool is the principle, "The best predictor of future behavior is past behavior." Ahead of a possible promotion, restructuring, or new appointment, between five and eight assessors, all of whom have worked with the candidate in a broad range of situations, are asked to provide a structured assessment. They are given various scenarios dealing with typical challenges faced by the candidate's target position daily. For example, leading a demanding team, presenting to an important client, or negotiating with a major supplier. The assessors decide which of these tasks they personally would entrust to the candidate and which they would not. Next, they give the reasons for this decision, resulting in a differentiated picture of the candidate's strengths and weaknesses. For lovers of statistics, the final summary also shows how many of the assessors answered yes or no for each category. In this way, DECIDE® combines the advantages of the 360-degree feedback approach with those of an assessment center. The process cleverly makes use of people's ability to look ahead and picture how somebody would behave in challenging or even critical situations. It relies on intuition and holistic perception, while at the same time minimizing errors of individual judgment by asking a range of assessors and, very importantly, focusing everyone's attention on real-life work situations.

Our experience suggests that this approach is more reliable than the widely used competency models. These assign lists of competencies to individual positions, but the lists are frequently either too short, and therefore don't tell us very much, or too complicated, because it is nigh impossible to formulate and validate all-encompassing competency lists for every key position in the company. The concept of structured peer-group questioning also works well when testing external candidates for their suitability for a position. Here is Johannes Thoennessen once again.

When you bring together decision-makers and give them the opportunity to get to know a candidate better and find out what he's done in the past, then they automatically draw comparisons with their inner perceptions about successful managers in their areas of responsibility and can conclude, "He behaves like colleague X and so that could work well for us too." Of course, you cannot model this with mathematical precision, but you can be reasonably certain of getting a good forecast. It's often a problem when only one person is asked, as he can only offer his one viewpoint. If, on the other hand, you pull together the insight of several people then the forecast will be much more reliable.

To cite Colin Powell once more, it's people, not organizations, who get things done, and those of us who take this to heart will never again fall into the trap of taking personnel decisions lightly. Indeed, it would be laudable if the modern business world could, in this respect, emulate the Incas, who valued the skills of the different peoples in their empire and encouraged and promoted their talented stonemasons, dexterous potters, and *quipu* experts. The Incas paid close attention to which people had which skills, and they subjected their next generation of leaders to rigorous testing. Can we really claim to consistently do the same today?

Here's an extract from our interview with Dr. Doris Day, dermatologist and entrepreneur, on the reality behind developing oneself and helping others to develop—assuming they are prepared to listen.

Being Patient with the Impatient

"Early on in my career, I had many jobs to keep things going while building up my own office practice. I moonlighted as a prison doctor, had a full-time position at a hospital, and worked at a university student health care center, and this has all made me a stronger, better business owner. I've sat in every chair, done every job in my office, I have answered the phones, stocked the rooms, counted inventory and taken out the garbage. I still do the payroll and check outgoing payments and orders. I basically understand every function of every staff member and how important entry-level work is and, unfortunately, this is often not emphasized enough. A lot of people just want to start at the top with an office full of patients and everything arranged for them, but there is value in working your way up.

This observation has had an impact on me as a leader and developer of my business, and I have great respect for people who've taken the time to work their way up and build a practice for themselves. On the other hand, I have to try to remain patient with people who are impatient, because when I see someone who just jumps in and wants to put themselves in your shoes and they don't get all the steps it took to walk in those shoes, it can be a little bit disappointing. And because we're in an age of immediate gratification and also since social media has been edited or curated rather than being authentic and true, there's the danger of a misperception that you can just hop into those shoes.

I am happy to help anybody who wants help. I am still learning so much, both about my craft and about my business practices, and I know to never get comfortable or complacent but am happy to share anything I know with anyone who wants to learn from my experience, my mistakes, and my success. Some are happy to take advantage of my offer. However, most simply want the answer and the end result but they don't want to listen to what it takes to get there. It's absolutely okay to be impatient and demanding on others and I'm sure I was the same at times, but finding the right balance for everyone involved is the challenge."

Michael von Truchsess, a long-standing colleague and board member, provided us with a most interesting example of rigor concerning people selection and development from his company. He told us how, every year, during his annual performance management discussions, he found that one particular question proved especially useful: "Who in the organization has helped you in reaching your goals over the last twelve months?" He and his senior colleagues had to list five names, irrespective of their position, function, hierarchy, or location. Every year, jaws dropped on reading the evaluation. Many well-known names from the top ranks of the organization and many "potentials" never featured on the lists, whereas other apparently less visible and less prominent colleagues were clearly very important and supportive and were having far more impact on company performance. As he then added rather drily, serious conversations needed to be had with colleagues whose names hadn't featured on the list for two or three years in a row, accompanied by the simple question: "What are we paying these people for?"

Jack Welch, ex-GE leadership legend, had an interesting and unusual way of assessing people, as mentioned by another of our interview partners.

From Gerd Stürz, Head of Life Sciences (Germany, Austria, Switzerland) at EY:

Jack Welch had this matrix. On the x-axis, he divided people into those who had values and those with no values, and on the y-axis into those with ambition and those with no ambition. So, he had four boxes, and everyone he met—whether professionally or personally—

was assigned to one of these boxes. I got to know this system from a very successful manager early on in my career and started using it myself. It is incredibly helpful:

Those people with both ambition and values, they are the stars. Not only should you get to know them, but you must work with them and develop and promote them.

Then you have those with no ambition and no values. They don't normally do any damage, but they don't achieve anything either.

The third group are those with values but no apparent ambition. They are interesting because they can be developed, but you need to invest time in finding out if that's possible.

And finally, there are those with ambition and no values. You must identify these people quickly and keep them as far away as possible— away from your business, from your family, from your partner, from wherever. These people are really dangerous.

A Stress Test for Key Aspects of Your Human Resources Policy

The prerequisite for good people selection and development is that you give it the attention and time it deserves and invest the necessary care and financial resources. Is this the case in your organization? And are your people really viewed and treated as your most precious asset?

Stress Test

Are people really the heart of your company? Let's find out. Yes or No?

1. The top management of your business is closely involved with the selection and recruitment of managers.

---

2. In a few short words, you can describe why your business is more attractive for ambitious candidates than your largest competitor. ☐

3. Your business vision is not an embarrassing paper tiger, indistinguishable from ten other so-called visions, but an attractive and distinctive statement about your company. ☐

4. Your HR department is not an overflow for employees who "need to be parked somewhere," but a highly respected and professional team which is fully acquainted with the core activities of your business. ☐

5. You have a proven and well-structured selection procedure to fill vacancies. ☐

6. You have no place for practices such as passing on problem people to other departments, best buddy promotion, or the selection of people simply because they may be easy to manage. ☐

7. Poor personnel decisions are not tolerated long-term, but promptly corrected. ☐

8. You have a performance culture based on fairness, which combines respectful appreciation with transparent and ambitious targets. ☐

9. When it comes to promotions, what matters is who is best qualified for the job, not who has been there the longest. ☐

10. To have worked at your organization is seen as positive, upgrades any resume, and is not considered to be a black mark. ☐

INCA INSIGHTS

- As far as personnel decisions are concerned: no nepotism, no favors, no compromises!

- Choose people who have proven themselves in a relevant setting and have a positive prognosis for future success.

- Be as careful with hiring someone as with choosing your spouse: If in doubt, say no!

"When General Foster came over and spoke with you, you had the feeling that, at that moment, you were at the center of his universe. He knew who you were and what you were doing, even though hundreds of officers reported to him."

—DR. DAVID EBSWORTH, EXPERIENCED CEO, CHAIRMAN, AND BOARD MEMBER

---

3 Achieving Results through Others

(or the Case of the Leader-Sham?)

Not every business can be rescued by good leaders, but poor leadership can take any company under if given the chance. So how can a leader get the best out of his team and drive the organization forward? The Inca elite was highly successful in managing this over several decades, and it no doubt helped that they were the Sun God's chosen people. We don't know exactly what their management style was, but it is a fair guess to say that it was probably closest to what we would call "very directive" today. What we do know is that the administration and infrastructure of the empire were superbly well organized, whether road-building or irrigation, planting techniques or food storage, toll collection or military campaigns. A sophisticated division of powers between the headquarters in Cuzco and branch offices in various provinces ensured that executive decisions were quickly and efficiently implemented. And in so doing, the Incas were not, in any way, pussyfooting. Whole villages were resettled and communities torn apart. You were told where to live and what work to do. They exercised absolute power, not unlike the Divine Right of Kings in Europe in the Middle Ages, only with a better feel for organization, but nevertheless a system that nobody would want to see return.

With this system, however, the Incas did guarantee that the common folk survived and thrived. They made sure that nobody went hungry and provided shelter, clothing, tools to work with, and health care. They also supported the families of fallen soldiers and others in need. Many researchers and experts view this as "an early example of the modern socialist state."[49] You could also describe it by saying that the Incas were highly demanding, but at the same time offered something in return. Nowadays we would call this give-and-take reciprocity. When you look at it more closely, the Inca leadership drew its legitimacy not only from the Sun God, but also from providing structure and prosperity across the empire. And this is directly transferable to leadership in the modern age. How exactly do you provide value to your colleagues and your company? How does your team benefit from having you as their boss?

Leadership Style versus Leadership Instruments

It is important to distinguish between leadership style and leadership tools or instruments. As mentioned above, the leadership style of the Incas is generally recognized as having been highly autocratic, directive, without compromise, and with the authority centered very strongly on the Inca himself. We are certainly a long way away from recommending such an approach which, after all, ultimately contributed to the downfall of the empire.

In contrast, the range of leadership instruments developed and utilized by the Incas, such as offering a clear vision to the existing population and to those peoples potentially to be acquired, the merit-oriented selection of successors for the Inca, the clear definition of values and sanctioning when these values were not adhered to, and the highly developed communication systems around the empire are, we believe, legitimate sources of inspiration for our times.

Frederick II of Prussia, also known as Frederick the Great, called himself the "first servant of the State." At the time, this was revolutionary: a leader who defined himself by the added value he brought to his realm. Aside from his understanding of authoritarian governance, this leadership concept is still relevant today. The effectiveness of a leader is judged, first and foremost, by the results they achieve with and through their colleagues. Can they hold things steady during a crisis? Can they maintain a successful course when times are good? Do they anticipate the next set of challenges? In a world full of well-educated individualists, they will only succeed by convincing the people they lead. This can happen in a variety of ways, but there are a number of fundamental and interdependent aspects that are key, and that is what this chapter is all about.

On Rock and Roll Women and Jars of Honey

We have gotten used to the Gallup Institute coming up with the same numbers every year about employee engagement and motivation. Give or take a few percentage points, the study always tells the same story. About a sixth of the workforce is highly motivated, another sixth has as good as resigned, doing very little or even harming the business, and two-thirds work strictly according to the book. In practice, this means that most employees do just enough to fulfil their employment contracts and then focus on getting home as punctually as possible.[50] What goes through your head when you look at your department with these numbers in mind? Or is your company the exception that proves the rule? And, anyway, how do you go about measuring this? How can you be certain that you really are surrounded by high-performing, active, and, more importantly, proactive colleagues?

Here's one idea, easy to implement and undoubtedly indicative: Ask yourself the simple question—When was the last time a member of your team really positively surprised you? When did you last have a genuine "Wow" moment at work? What we mean by this is that wonderful feeling you get when you look at a piece of work or a job done and think "Yes! That's *exactly* how I imagined it! Spot on. Just perfect!" And it gets better, as the colleague in question goes on to say, "And for this part I thought about a different approach, and here I added something new, and I thought the closing sequence would benefit from being developed a bit further, so I did this." And the whole thing is now far better than what you had originally had in mind. Wouldn't it be nice to have this marvelous feeling more often?

Unfortunately, daily reality would appear to be somewhat different. During his leadership talks, Andreas Krebs often asks people about their last "Wow" moment. One New Jersey audience, with a mixture of people from business and politics, was typical. Only a few claimed to have such an experience about once a week, for about half it was "now and then," and for the remaining third it was "never!"

Why is this the case? Ever since the publication of Reinhard K. Sprenger's bestseller *The Motivation Myth*, there has been little to add to our knowledge about motivation and its drivers. Generations of future leaders, including us, have sat through leadership seminars and stared at the slide showing Maslow's "pyramid of needs" (dating back to 1943!), with appreciation and self-fulfillment at the top and basic physiological needs and security at the bottom. And we know that the motivation triggered by a higher salary is notoriously short-lived. Fifteen years later, Frederick Herzberg confirmed this in a different way, describing factors which simply ensure that people are "not discontented," such as acceptable working conditions, a reasonable salary, and a secure job, and adopted the term "hygiene factors" for these. The other side of his model describes the factors which really inspire people to "go the extra mile," the motivating factors, such as opportunities for self-development, the chance to experience success, and the receipt of appropriate recognition.[51] Three decades later (and now in its twentieth edition), Sprenger pointedly showed that the art of motivation lies, above all else, in not demotivating people, and that some of the most widely used so-called motivation tools, such as bonuses and other financial incentives, are viewed by the average recipient at best as a hard-earned part of the standard package or, at worst, as rightful damages for all the pain endured.[52] But if this is all so well known, why does so little change in practice?

The answer is simple. We are know-how giants but mere dwarves when it comes to implementation. We know what we ought to do, but we don't do it. If the motivation experts are correct, the level of motivation in a team is directly linked to the personality of the manager and how he or she views their people. Motivation cannot be induced using goal agreement processes or long-term incentive programs, or be delegated to the boss's secretary, known for her affable good humor and unique ability to translate the boss's obscure messaging into understandable English. Anyone who wants engaged and enthusiastic employees has to allow them to experience successes, take a genuine interest in what they do, and reward them with real, personalized recognition. That's it! Easily said, but unfortunately, not quite so easily done. And by the way, this doesn't just apply to "the others;" it applies to just about every one of us and we include, without hesitation, ourselves here too.

"Keep Up The Good Work!" Disinterest Thinly Disguised as Praise

During his tenure as Head of Asia, Andreas Krebs had a boss who wasn't really all that concerned about the special challenges involved and the equally special solutions sometimes needed to manage in these countries. This person was more a connoisseur of the southern European culture, with no particular interest in the so-called "emerging markets." On top of that, the numbers were good in the Asian region and everything seemed to be running smoothly, so his "leadership" was limited to signing where he was asked to sign, approving where he was asked to approve, but always accompanied by a mandatory "Well done! Keep up the good work!"—a verbal pat on the head. And yet, despite the free hand Andreas had been given, there was a bitter aftertaste: the feeling that his boss just wasn't that bothered about what he was doing. At this point, some might argue that leaders have to be able to motivate themselves. That may well be, and, indeed, the business was running well in Asia, but the approach still left Andreas with the feeling of lost opportunity and "what might have been" had his boss made more of an effort to engage with the specific challenges, successes, and failures in the region. As an experienced sparring partner with a different perspective, he could surely have expanded the company's thinking about the region or, through genuine recognition, encouraged even greater efforts.

There is a very thin line between laissez-faire and plain disinterest. And real empowerment looks completely different, based on appreciative discussion and exchange, creating new, well-thought-through growth opportunities for people and products, and not just nodding things through with an indifferent, "Sure, just get on with it…"

P.S. In many respects, the successor to this boss was the exact opposite: meticulous, distrustful, hyper hands-on, a classical micromanager. Not surprisingly, very quickly people were yearning for the return of the disinterested predecessor…or, even better, someone who could combine both approaches and know when to apply them!

If leaders really are expected to be self-motivated, why does one of our interview partners still speak so enthusiastically, many years after the event, when he recalls how his boss dropped by to congratulate him on a great success and to thank him personally? Why does a long-serving CEO like David Ebsworth, quoted at the beginning of this chapter, still remember, decades later, how during his time in the military, a general was able to make him feel valued and respected with just a few well-chosen words? Nobody really believes that a bonus or salary increase paid twenty years ago and accompanied by a few dry, standard phrases in an internal mail would have the same long-term impact. People crave recognition, and the human psyche does not automatically change just because you have climbed a few rungs up the career ladder. Sometimes it is good to remember that and to think about your own need for recognition and attention when deciding how to do the same for others. Appreciation is something which is expressed on an equal footing, is credible, and is concrete—not, like so much well-intended praise, generalized and handed down from on high. It is worth considering that what sounds like a good slogan may not always have the desired effect. "If I can dream it, you can do it" was a particular favorite of one of our ex-bosses. It sounded smart and amusing at first, and was undoubtedly intended to motivate, but on closer inspection ran the risk of causing more perspiration than inspiration.

That brings us back to how we view other people. Sprenger is convinced that every human being is motivated and fundamentally willing to work hard. There is nothing new about this. Back in 1960, in his book *The Human Side of Enterprise*, Douglas McGregor contrasted "Theory X" with "Theory Y" of mankind. Theory X asserts that humans are naturally unmotivated and shy away from responsibility, requiring close management and constant monitoring. Theory Y is exactly the opposite, where people are essentially ready to work hard and want to develop themselves and to assume responsibility. Whichever theory you subscribe to, it is highly likely that your choice will, sooner or later, be empirically confirmed. If you tightly control your team, supervise them closely and pounce on every mistake they make, then most of the team will quickly start to find workarounds, hiding mistakes from you and only doing the bare minimum. After all, if you don't actually do very much, then you can't get too much wrong. And furthermore, if your favored approach is for your people to "simply do what you say," then you can be sure they will do exactly that. The result of this leadership strategy? Well, exactly what you expected—you knew it all along! You cannot trust the individuals in your team and quite obviously have to permanently push them to get any kind of output. Or you could try the opposite approach. Make it clear to your team that you trust them, give them the freedom to organize things the way it suits them best, give them responsibility, actively support and encourage them. Most people will feel motivated by such an environment and you will feel confirmed in your decision to choose this approach.

By this time, you may well be asking yourself what on earth rock and roll women and jars of honey have to do with all of this. Well, we think the story below illustrates that most people possess a natural motivation for demonstrating passion and excellence in some aspect of their life, the only problem being that it is not always the pile of problems lying on their desk at work that fires up this desire to perform.

Thomas's Honey Shop and the Shy Controller

One of Andreas Krebs's favorite stories is about his Head of Marketing in Asia who, based in Germany, just did not want to do any business travel between April and October. This was unusual, as normally people are quite keen on doing trips to Asia, but Thomas always came up with an excuse not to go, even though a large number of meetings and conferences took place during this part of the year. And by the way, there are two very interesting leadership questions addressed here.

Andreas takes up the story:

> One day, after I'd been running the department for about a year and a half, a colleague sat down in front of me and had two jars of honey with her in a little bag. I asked her about them and she answered, "Oh, they're from Thomas's honey shop!" I was slightly taken aback, which she must have noticed, and she continued, "Didn't you know? All of us buy our honey from our in-house beekeeper and amateur honey producer." She left the room and, a few minutes later, I went across the hall into Thomas L.'s office and asked him if he wouldn't mind showing me his honey shop. He walked toward a large gray aluminum filing cupboard of the sort that were standard issue at the time, at which point I noticed for the first time that he had two of these. (Everyone else, including me, had only one!) He opened the door and revealed the contents. The cupboard was filled from top to bottom with honey. There was clover honey, lavender honey, orchard honey, all beautifully organized by blossom type, creamy or liquid, light or dark, and there were little price labels on each jar and informational leaflets about the work of amateur apiarists and beekeeping.

Thomas L. was, understandably, rather unsure about how to react, so to relieve the awkwardness, I asked him to tell me about his hobby as a manager and caretaker of four honeybee colonies. As he started to talk about his bees, I saw how his whole body language changed, how his eyes sparkled with the passion, enthusiasm, and identification he felt for his hobby; I saw straight away what was going on. And the second leadership question? Well, of course, strictly speaking, you are not allowed to run a honey shop in the company, even if it is just a hobby and no matter how endearing it sounds. Then again, did I want to be the one to close down the little "business"? You are probably, and quite rightly, thinking, "Where would it all end if everyone did something like that?" and I may not have been acting by the letter of the law, but I tried to be pragmatic and sensitive. If you want to jump on the fast track to becoming the bad guy, then go ahead and close down the cute little store where everyone buys their honey!

In the end, we did a deal. Thomas L. had to find a solution which allowed him to go on business trips all year round and I would take no further action regarding his honey shop. So, he found a fellow beekeeper in his club who, when necessary, could look after the bee colonies when Thomas had to travel and, as a positive side effect of this approach, I cemented my friendship with Paul Williams, who was my HR Business Partner at the time, by not mentioning a single word to him about the whole story until a couple of years later. He is grateful to me for that to this day!

In a similar vein, a competent if somewhat reticent colleague in financial controlling put in her holiday request for the middle of the budget phase, which was very unusual to say the least. When I asked her about this, she explained that she was going on tour with her band. I found out that this lady, a good but very quiet member of the team, was the accordion player in a well-known local Irish rock band. On stage, she was a real rock lady, in the office the shy number two in controlling, who arrived at eight o'clock in the morning, did her job well enough and left at quarter to five in the afternoon to catch her bus.

So, there we have it: the core of the whole topic of motivation. Every single employee can be inspired, and every member of your team has a passion for something. Capturing and channeling some of this emotion and engagement for the good of the company is the key. The best way to start going about this is to give people the feeling that their contribution really matters, and by being genuinely interested in them. Those who feel recognized and valued are the people most likely to give you something back in return. And this genuine interest might well include showing appreciation for amateur beekeepers and rock singers, just so long as they do their job well. So, if you offer your employees inspiring goals and the chance to show what they can do and be part of demonstrable successes, you will never have to worry about having to motivate people. Most of us love to be successful and, even more, to be part of something bigger. That is what drives the fascination of companies like Google, Porsche, or Adidas.[53] Part of your job as a manager is to communicate clearly the story that you and your team are writing together. What is it about your company or business that inspires you? We hope and assume that you are well able to answer this question, as a demotivated leader will always struggle to sustain the motivation of his employees.

It is fairly easy to check whether you are on the right track when it comes to showing appreciation and interest. Imagine it's 7:45 p.m. and you need to call a close colleague or a member of your team at home for an important reason. Could you hold a conversation over the telephone with their partner for two or three minutes? Do you even know whether your colleague actually lives with someone, whether they have children, and, if so, whether they are still at school or perhaps at university? Does your colleague have any hobbies? Are there any other issues which are currently on their mind? Of course, some of you will say, "Do I want to know that? Do I really need to know that?" Of course not. We're only talking about your single most valuable resource! Many companies, perhaps your own as well, have statements in their visions or missions on the lines of "People are at the heart of our company" or similar. So how does that translate into practical behavior?

From Dr. Timm Volmer, CEO, Smartstep Consulting:

> *It was a really important moment for me. I had just finished a major project when the CEO came into the meeting to say a personal thank you, bringing with him a bottle of champagne. Looking back at why that made such a deep impression on me, it was the sudden realization that I was actually working for human beings. And that moment of realization has stayed with me and I always enjoy my work most when there is a human dimension.*

It was just a small gesture, yet it made a long-lasting impression on one of Europe's top health economists that he still remembers to this day. An example of "low cost, high touch" at its finest!

Human gestures can't substitute for monetary awards, but they do tend to be considerably more memorable for the recipient. If you want to be a good manager of people, it helps a lot if you actually *like* people. This is not us becoming over-emotional, even if such statements give the impression of being too touchy-feely. Liking people is not incompatible with the strategic demands of leadership, such as setting clear guidelines, delegating responsibility, checking on results, and acting decisively if someone breaks the rules. And, if the situation demands it, firing people. None of this alters the fact that "leadership," at its core, is based upon a personal relationship. The well-known leadership expert, Oswald Neuberger, stresses that leadership requires two people: one who leads and one who consents to be led.[54]

Aside from the military, being led is largely voluntary nowadays. Only if team members are really convinced about following you (which assumes mutual trust, respect, and, ideally, empathy) will they bring all their know-how, skills, and creativity to bear. We only need look at what has happened at some well-respected banks to see the consequences when employees work for bonuses and not for people. Or Volkswagen, where fear rather than respect and trust appear to reign. And the consequences of a culture of autocratic decision-making could be witnessed at Samsung, where the new smartphone Galaxy Note 7 was the subject of a full recall due to batteries igniting without warning. In traditional Confucian style, the firm's patriarch, Lee Kun-hee has ruled Samsung with an iron fist for decades, where "even small mistakes are punished by getting rid of the managers responsible."[55] If you were an employee in this sort of environment, would you warn about possible problems with the new flagship product? At the end of the day, treating every single employee in an organization with respect is a question of basic human dignity.

A Question of Trust. Who Packs the Parachute?

There is a very effective exercise you can do to find out how much trust you have in your team members and peers and, at least as interesting, how much trust they have in you. We use this during presentations and ask each person to imagine they are at a skydiving training school, but are not yet able to pack their own parachutes. The other participants on the course can include your team members, peers, your boss, your spouse or partner, whoever you choose, and they have all learned to pack their parachutes. The exercise begins harmlessly enough with the question "Who would you take a packed parachute from?" From your boss? From which of your colleagues? From which of your team members? From your life partner? So far, the audience is still enjoying the exercise and is fully on board. It starts to go quiet when the question is turned around. Who would take your parachute? Would your colleagues and coworkers rush to choose one of the parachutes you had packed? Or would yours be the last one to be chosen, like the class nerd in team selection during the sports lesson back at school?

You can carry out this exercise during a workshop as well, in two different variations. The less threatening version is to ask everyone to write down whose parachute they would take, and at the end everyone is given their results confidentially. The tougher approach is to do it openly, where everyone can see how many people would choose the respective parachutes, revealing who enjoys the highest level of trust and who, if anyone, has no one's trust. We should point out that this is a potentially very challenging exercise for any team or group of colleagues and should be handled with care. So, what do you think? How many would rush across and take your parachute?

As illustrated above, trust has to be earned, you can't demand or force somebody to trust you. Furthermore, one of the most fascinating and most challenging aspects for many managers is the fact that you have to place your trust in others before they can be expected to trust you. In other words, you have to pay in first before you can take out. One of the most effective ways to pay into the trust account is to make yourself openly vulnerable in some way, placing your trust in others to help you out and look after you. That's a difficult thought for most of us, and even more so for many managers, brought up on the personal understanding and the organizational expectation that they are in control of the situation, whatever it happens to be. One of our interview partners conveyed how he gained the trust of his team with a story that gave us goosebumps the first time we heard it. We decided to call it "Running for My Life."

From Rolf Hoffmann, Executive and General Manager in various countries from 1994 to 2016:

The company I was working for moved me to South Africa in 1995 to head up the business. Nelson Mandela had just come to power, the Springboks, as their national rugby team are called, had just won the Rugby World Cup, and it was, to put it mildly, a very interesting period in South Africa's history.

I inherited an all-white management team and, pretty typical for the time, there was a huge distance, in all senses of the word, between the white office staff and their black colleagues. The black employees all worked in production and none of them had ever set foot in the administrative building. Meanwhile, to try and support the transition to a truly non-apartheid society, the government had just started introducing quotas designed to ensure that black people would be employed in other positions across organizations and not just in jobs on the shop floor. When we discussed this topic at one of my first board meetings, my management team told me that they were not happy about the quotas, but I made it clear that I would be acting on the directive. However, that was easier said than done, as I knew I didn't have the trust of the black employees and I realized I had to find other ways to break through these decades of discrimination and suspicion if I was going to get anything done in the company.

I had noticed that some of the production people would meet, twice a week, at five o'clock in front of the manufacturing facility and go running. So, I approached the foreman one day and an interesting dialogue followed:

"I notice that you guys go out running regularly and wondered if I could come along?" I said.

He looked at me like I had three heads. "But we run through the townships and it wouldn't be safe," he replied.

I looked straight at him and said, "Well I guess I'd have to count on you guys to protect me then."

He hesitated, then said, rather reluctantly: "Let me check with the boys and I'll let you know." He came back to me a few days later and told me that my idea had caused a good deal of surprise and some raised eyebrows in the team, but okay, I could come along.

So, a week later, there we were, this Teutonic steam engine, trundling along with all these African impalas and gazelles. And sure enough, they kept me in the middle of the group and we ran through some of the really dicey neighborhoods of Johannesburg without incident, month in, month out, for as long as I was there. Of course, we did other things to move the company forward in a time of massive change *in the country, but this was really how I broke the ice and gained the trust of the black members of the team, because I literally put my life in their hands. If they had left me alone in the township, there is no way I would have made it out of there in one piece.*

Personal Responsibility: The Last Table

In theory, most managers look for employees who think independently and take personal responsibility for their actions. The reality is different. We neutralize personal responsibility with detailed decision-making and approval procedures, rules and regulations. Large businesses, in particular, grow into enormous bureaucracies in which people behave as though they were in a game of Mikado: He who twitches first loses the "game" and ends up doing the work. The traditional family business, with an old-school patriarchal boss, is also seldom a paragon of democracy. And in start-ups, you can often see how, in a rapidly growing organization, it is still a closely-knit group of founders that calls the shots and later arrivals are reduced to subsidiary roles in an outer circle. Then again, the following also applies: It takes two to complete the degradation of personal responsibility, one to impose constraints and one who consents to be constrained. It can also be quite a convenient method to downplay individual initiative by deferring to "the powers that be."

"There Is Nothing We Can Do!"

We ran a workshop over several days for an internationally operating business. The company's organizational model was extremely complicated, on the lines of "double matrix, triple helix." The majority of people in this particular team felt trapped in at least one matrix and had three or more bosses to whom they reported, or colleagues with whom they had to very closely confer and constantly align. As a result, responsibility was spread extremely thinly across the organization, with everyone bearing some responsibility and therefore, at the end of the day, no one really carrying the can: ideal conditions for B and C players and a nightmare for high performers.

The workshop participants were a team of top managers who were responsible for looking after and developing a key product. Very quickly it became clear that most of the participants were extremely frustrated because they "could do nothing"; they saw themselves as victims of the complexity in the firm's structure. We then dared to do something which, apparently, no one inside the company had done for quite some time. We suggested taking a close look at the firm's leadership principles, and lo and behold, there it was in black and white, exactly what the participants were looking for: wonderful statements like "Debugs the organization and organizes networks effectively while living the values." The team had simply not demanded that they be implemented or, even worse, many were not familiar with the leadership principles at all. And so the core topic of the workshop became taking this declaration of intent seriously and using it to work out how to break free from the self-inflicted matrix misery.

We come across this type of self-limitation quite frequently when working with companies. The solution is there, but everyone has gotten so used to looking at the bars across the windows that they can no longer see that the cell door is actually wide open.

Once employees have been weaned off personal responsibility—and with it, individual initiative—then it is not easy to restore it. Publicly admonishing or punishing those who have made mistakes is guaranteed to kill off any chance of individual responsibility. Apparently, there are leaders who believe that you must occasionally "throw someone to the lions" in order to get everybody else back in line. We can only hope that these people stick to lion training, since handling complex issues with a browbeaten team can be a complete lottery. Be that as it may, a new management entering a business cannot simply flick a switch and reset a deeply ingrained business culture, as Dr. Christoph Straub described to us.

From Dr. Christoph Straub, Managing Director at BARMER:

One of my biggest mistakes was to try a new product launch at short notice following years of retrenchment. It was all about providing finance for additional services, within reason, so that we, as a health insurance provider, could offer more service for the same price, and therefore become a more attractive proposition to both present and future clients. It didn't work. There were voices within the organization who warned, "This business has been programmed to operate with black-and-white decision-making for twenty years—at operational and at management level. Taking personal responsibility for operational decisions, using judgment in difficult cases, allowing people to make mistakes, and then correcting them accordingly? We are just not able to do that." And they were right. Our results that year were poor, the major cause being the introduction of this extra service. We simply switched from "No" to "Yes" and ended up having to reverse most of the changes. Creating a culture of personal responsibility involves much more than simply sending managers on training courses covering "Taking Responsibility," "Responsible Decision-Making," or "Getting Your Team Behind You."

It is clearly far more preferable never to reach the point where your employees feel a necessity to shy away from acting on their own initiative. Personal responsibility grows out of self-confidence, is rooted in personal freedom and nurtured with encouragement. Anyone who assumes responsibility runs the risk of making mistakes, but people who show initiative must be allowed to make mistakes. Those who are willing to take responsibility for their actions are sticking their heads above the parapet, they are taking a position, not hiding behind others "who want it done this way." They deserve respect and need to be trusted. And with that, we come back full circle to motivation. Personal responsibility, including the opportunity for personal development and enjoying success on the one hand, and motivation on the other, are for many, if not for everyone, two sides of the same coin. This has been shown to be the case in many studies. Who enjoys just carrying out jobs and doing as they are told? It's no surprise that many employees end up preferring to find their self-fulfillment in their spare time.

So, if personal responsibility is built on trust, then it requires trust from the managers, expressed as, "I have confidence in you." This, of course, brings with it the risk of occasional disappointment, but that is also part of the trust equation. And where there is no risk, then there is no need for trust. The ideal situation is when a culture of the "last table" emerges. This metaphor grew out of an unforgettable experience Andreas Krebs had as a new board member of a US corporation.

"The Last Table" or We Are the Company!

Where does responsibility begin and where does it end? How often in our career has every one of us said, "The firm must…" or "Someone ought to…"? Irrespective of where we are in the hierarchy, phrases like these are part of daily language, not only in companies, but also, of course, in public administration, NGOs, government, in organizations everywhere. For me (Andreas Krebs), this approach came to an unexpected and abrupt end. At my first board meeting in corporate America, I was directed to my new place at the table, where my predecessor used to sit, and I sat back and observed proceedings. I was made to feel very welcome but kept a low profile for my maiden meeting.

At the second meeting, there were a list of international topics which were my area of responsibility. I was invited by the CEO, Bernard Poussot, to offer my point of view and I started to contribute. I began most of my statements with "The company should…" or "The company must…" but, after a short while, Bernard interrupted me and asked, "Andreas, what do you mean by 'the company'?" and made a point of turning to look behind him. "There is no one else here! What you see here, these ten people sitting around the table, this is 'the company.' This is the last table! And even more important: You are the company now!" Everyone roared with laughter and Bernard said, "Yes, that's happened to all of us. But this is where the buck stops and from now on you, too, are 'the company' and I'm quite sure you know what that means!"

And indeed, I did understand. And, from then on, never again forgot the difference between responsibility, which can be delegated, and accountability,

> which cannot. I was grateful for the lesson, which had been respectfully, but unforgettably, given to me. In hindsight, I wish this had happened earlier in my career. How often in our daily life do we act as though we are sitting at "the last table"?

Of course, not all of us have a seat at the last table, but we often have more freedom than we think. Anybody at their workplace trying to implement what they think is the best and the most sensible course of action for their business or organization is able to assume responsibility for these actions. The supermarket check-out assistant who chats with a colleague in the presence of customers and raves about the great offers at the discount store next door where "the shopping experience is far better" has failed to grasp this just as much as the top manager who fails to take a clear stance on critical business issues and act accordingly. How strong an example do you set to your employees when it comes to sitting at the last table? This starts by being straightforward and bidding farewell to endless discussions and the serial postponement of dealing with problems. It continues by getting into the habit at every team meeting of asking the questions: "Is the solution here in the room? Who will take charge? Can we make a decision right away and if so, what is that decision?"

At which point, we would like to propose a way of introducing the concept of personal responsibility into your organization's culture.

Beyond Delegation: Pull Leadership

Sometimes you need a gentle shove to leave your comfort zone, to enjoy personal development and a greater willingness to take on responsibility. Andreas Krebs found this out in an unusual, never-to-be-forgotten way! He was head of the business in Germany when a new US HQ board member was appointed. His new boss was responsible for Europe and other parts of the globe, whereby the major national markets, including Germany, reported directly to him.

He started his first personal conversation with Andreas along the following lines: "You are doing a great job. You are on the right track. You're a real success." More appreciative words followed. Andreas started to relax and thought, "So far, so good." Then his new boss said, "Please use the next three months to get yourself into a position where you can be available to devote 30 to 40 percent of your work time to my level. You will be working with me and a small strategy team to create added value at the EMEA regional level.[56] You will be involved in international projects; on some of them you will lead, on others you will be acting as a strategy team member. At the same time, we'll be working on setting a new direction for the whole group (twenty-five billion dollars in revenue, about fifty thousand employees). You'll be helping me to do my job even better."

That signaled the end of Andreas's moment of relaxation. So how exactly was that supposed to work? But the new boss wasn't quite finished. "What I don't want you to do is to add this to your current workload. If you haven't got the right people in Germany ($1 billion turnover) who are capable of taking on some of your responsibilities, then you need to find better people. And you shouldn't just delegate, but build up and develop people, in this case top-notch local managers who can create added value for you and make you even better!"

Andreas was impressed. This guy was doing precisely the opposite of what normally happened! Usually, we direct our leadership and management focus "downward," correcting and adjusting; here, there was no correction involved, but instead the opportunity was being offered to add value at higher levels in the organization. The board member was opening up opportunities for Andreas over and above the country level, which needed to be grabbed. This approach had a remarkable pull effect. The performance of the business was dramatically improved, not just at one level, but with a cascading effect right down into the organization. Andreas's best people took on some of his country responsibilities, and so their own roles and responsibilities were significantly enhanced. They had to "upgrade" themselves, which was something most of them were very happy and able to do, and their resumes received a boost as well. Everyone adopted a more strategic approach to work, and the work in general became more exciting and interesting.

The senior manager brought about a radical change in the local business culture and, at the time, it was called "Achieving results through others." In this book, we call it Beyond Delegation and Pull Leadership because, importantly, this has very little to do with classical delegation and monitoring of results. This is much more about handing over complete tasks and areas of responsibility, setting ambitious targets, demonstrating a high level of trust, and allowing others to grow and be part of a bigger success story. This form of leadership elevates the concept of "more personal responsibility" to the status of a fundamental principle. And as the challenges we face become more fast-moving, complex, and demanding, businesses will need to rely more on people being able to cope with higher levels of empowerment in the form of self-regulating freedom and *responsible autonomy*. Otherwise they will be faced with being stranded like rudderless ships in a stormy sea.

The pull effect of Beyond Delegation has significant impact on the development of staff as well as on the operational side of the business, generally bringing the very best out of people. In this way, the potential in an organization can be truly unleashed and lift itself up to a completely new level. It must be said, though, that this approach requires consistent and, at times, the tougher side of leadership— for example, making the decision to replace good people, who have essentially done nothing wrong, with even better people, if it becomes apparent that the incumbent team are overstretched by the new approach. Pull Leadership must be well thought through and implemented to avoid creating new problems in the organization. The core principles described here are not necessarily new, but it is rare for them to be applied in practice with the rigor that Beyond Delegation requires.

Fundamentally, Pull Leadership draws people into new areas of activity and performance. Sometimes this happens quite literally and brings a new job title with it, sometimes the initial impact is more on attitude and at a conceptual level, as it sinks in to the individual that there are new tasks to be fulfilled with a significant increase in personal responsibility within their existing position. Sometimes, both happen at the same time. Either way, as the manager of these people, it is vital to monitor and support them carefully as they face what may be both technical and personal challenges. There are two straightforward and well-known models that can be of great help to you as a leader when accompanying team members during this process:

1. The Learning Zones Model

You are probably familiar with the difference between comfort zone, learning zone, and panic zone. In our comfort zone, we feel secure, we can carry out the tasks assigned to us well, and we have most of what we are doing under control. In the learning zone, we are less secure, as we have new challenges to overcome, but, if these challenges are sensibly dosed, it can feel exciting and motivating. Finally, in the panic zone, we feel helplessly overstretched and are at risk of either paralysis, running around like a headless chicken, or, if this status becomes the norm, we may develop physical or mental overload and potentially serious health issues. This means that constructive, positive personal development takes place in the learning zone. Only someone who is willing and, to some extent, brave enough to step into this zone will be able to take on new tasks, learn to master them and, in so doing, be an active part of the new culture. If they are not prepared to do this, then they may very quickly become a problem.

There is a simple test you can use to find out if, when faced with Pull Leadership, you are more likely to be part of the solution or part of the problem. Think back over the past few months for a moment. If you were not regularly in a work situation where you felt just a little bit nervous or even anxious, then you probably have not left your comfort zone for a while. And by the way, never leaving your comfort zone has the unfortunate side effect that this zone starts to shrink after a while; staying still is actually going backward. Successful Pull Leadership is all about coaxing and encouraging colleagues out of their comfort zone. And the good part about it is that it can become a habit for all concerned, just as much as you can get used to relentlessly plodding along the same comfortable path. Your job as a leader is to constantly assess whether you are getting the balance right for each person in your area of responsibility. The new tasks and challenges should not be such that individuals, or even whole business sections, find themselves constantly in the panic zone and subject to unacceptably high stress levels. This would be counterproductive and, in some cases, may lead to burnout or other signs of chronic physical and/or psychological overstretch.

2. The Situational Leadership Model

A second helpful concept which can accompany this process is the well-known "Situational Leadership Model" from Hersey and Blanchard. Depending on the "maturity" of an employee, it gives very clear guidelines on how to vary leadership style toward this person over time and, depending on the precise task, indicates whether a "directing" or "supporting" approach is more appropriate. "Maturity" in this context is taken to be a combination of a team member's technical skills and engagement (self-confidence and motivation).[57] There is hardly a leadership workshop which does not refer to this model. Moreover, it draws attention to the fact that trust and encouragement are both very important leadership tools, which are particularly effective when dealing with the most "mature" employees (technically competent people with a high capacity for self-motivation).

When implementing Pull Leadership, you are relying much more on trust than before, as people's job scope and responsibilities are expanded, while at the same time loosening the reins of delegation further. Looked at in this way, it could be argued that Pull Leadership adds a new, fifth style to the four leadership styles identified by Hersey and Blanchard—directing, coaching, supporting, and delegating—which we would propose calling "confronting with new opportunities." As such, it is especially important that an employee is aware that they are not being left to cope on their own and that any justified concerns or fears arising from the new challenges will be listened to and taken seriously. In working with this process, a leader must know their people very well and encourage a regular exchange of views in both team meetings and individual conversations. Introducing Pull Leadership is demanding for all concerned and, particularly in the early transition phase, the leader will need to keep a close eye on key people and look after them well. The long-term benefits for both the performance of the organization and all those involved are well worth the effort.

But be warned, Pull Leadership also clearly exposes where and when people are not able to keep up, either in terms of mindset, because they lack the right attitude and willingness to try something new, or for technical or intellectual reasons. When things go wrong, leaders are called upon to face the consequences and to act quickly. Some colleagues will be very quick to grasp the advantages of Pull Leadership, and the really good ones will implement it and positively surprise you with their ability to adapt and grow. If all goes well, everyone benefits. Beyond Delegation advances individual employees, upgrades their skills with a view to further career advancement, and the whole organization benefits.

Even the Inca Emperor couldn't control everything that was happening in the outer reaches of his huge empire and had to trust that his leadership strategy was working. This meant granting privileges to local chieftains and allowing them to continue being responsible for their regions. At the same time, provincial princes were obliged to deliver good results, supported by an efficient system of administration. Alliances through marriage and educating the sons of the chieftains in the Inca's "Elite Academy" (interpreted by some researchers as hostage-taking in disguise) made up the rest of the picture. From today's perspective, this looks like a well-thought-through system which was extremely effective over long distances. Naturally, we cannot copy the Inca approach exactly, but you must admire their basic approach and clearly-thought-through leadership model. Either way, then or now, the development of such a model, or at least the living of it, is a matter for top management.

Complete Leadership: More Than a Question of Style

Typically, a range of leadership styles are outlined during management seminars and, when the cooperative leadership style is mentioned, everyone nods in agreement. So far, so ineffectual, really. Rather than carrying out a theoretical exposition dealing with questions of style, it would be much better to examine the individual personality traits which have a much bigger impact on leadership behavior—at least in times of stress and high pressure—than any academic theories. It was no different for the Incas. During the bloody civil war, which ultimately led to the downfall of the empire, all their leadership virtues were quickly forgotten to make way for pure ambition. By themselves, leadership models are of little use if the right people are not available to bring them to life. The way a leader behaves is a product of personality, environment, and practical experience (nature and nurture). Whether a leadership style turns out in practice to be credible and effective has more to do with the individual than anything else. How does this apply to the best-known approaches to leadership?

Charismatic Leadership: This is leadership based on the profound and extraordinary impact one personality can have on other people. Names like Martin Luther King, Florence Nightingale, Gandhi, Eva Perón, Winston Churchill, Nelson Mandela, or the young woman behind the Fridays for Future movement, Greta Thunberg, spring to mind. Of course, charisma alone is not enough. All these people had something they wanted to say and do and were prepared to take risks to achieve it. And perhaps most important of all, they took concrete steps to turn their vision into reality. Then again, charisma can be a double-edged sword, as shown by the example of Bernard Madoff in Chapter 2. A more positive example can be found in the memoirs of a former percussionist of the Vienna Philharmonic—and thanks to one of our interviewees for telling us the following story.

Timpanists are usually only required sporadically during a concert, so they tend to read a book or listen to the music when they're not playing. Once, during a rehearsal with a guest conductor, the overall orchestral sound suddenly changed completely and everything seemed to come together perfectly. What had happened? The timpanist looked up and saw that the conducting legend Wilhelm Furtwängler had come into the concert hall, as he was interested in hearing what was going on. In an instant, everything changed: The orchestra became a whole, a single unit, and the music itself was at once gripping and uplifting. "Furtwängler just needs to walk into the room and we all start playing at our very best!" said the timpanist. Furtwängler simply had the power of personality. "And we enjoyed playing for him because he was fair, treated people with respect, and had so much charisma."

Values-Based Leadership: This is almost the opposite of charismatic leadership. These people do not lead from the front, but stand behind the organization and lead from there. Up front are the visions, values, and goals of the business. These are so attractive and provide such strong guidance that the employees can easily identify and align themselves with them. A good example is the success story of Southwest Airlines.[58] Herb Kelleher founded Southwest in 1971, amid the crisis then engulfing the American airline industry, and was able to build one of America's most successful airlines. Since 1972, he has recorded forty-five consecutive years of profitability.[59]

Here are a couple of extracts from his philosophy:

- "A company is stronger if it is bound by love rather than by fear."
- "If the employees come first, then they're happy…. A motivated employee treats the customer well. The customer is happy so they keep coming back, which pleases the shareholders. It's not one of the enduring mysteries of all time; it is just the way it works."

We often quote these statements in leadership talks, and what makes them even more attractive is that they are easy to illustrate with real examples. For example, how would you like to see a member of your team leave your office after a difficult conversation? With a clenched fist in his pocket, muttering something very unflattering about your parentage? This happens all too often in organizations everywhere. Or would you prefer them to think, "Okay, that was not particularly pleasant, but it was fair; he listened to me and much of what he said was right. Dammit, I'll show him that I can get the job done!" Is that the direction in which you lead the conversation? And by the way, we don't pretend for one moment that such a discussion is easy. It requires good preparation to achieve the double objective of making your point clear but keeping the employee sufficiently motivated to want to try harder and not just throw in the towel.

Participative Leadership: From our point of view, this is the leadership style most likely to provide sustainable operational success in complex and fast-moving times, because it actively engages with the skills and ideas of the employees and lends itself to being combined with Beyond Delegation and Pull Leadership. This demands a reflective leader, someone who does not succumb to the illusion of their own invincibility, but who understands that their success relies largely on the creativity and support of the team. For this, you need managers who thrive on daily interaction with their direct reports, as well as other stakeholders at all levels of the organization. Are you accessible and easily approached? Or do you preach the proverbial "open door" policy, only to have it guarded by a whole entourage of assistants, secretaries, and assorted other barriers, human or otherwise? Do you actually make contact and talk with the "small people"? Do you, for example, arrange regular meetings with colleagues from all corners and levels of the organization, where they can ask you anything they want and can expect a clear answer? And does anyone actually turn up? Like the parachute exercise, this is also a good test of how much trust people have in who you are and what you say and do. Or maybe you restrict yourself to "fireside chats" with so-called high-potentials, preferably in the presence of senior members of the HR department and other colleagues from the board? We are tempted to say, forget it! It might achieve something, but the majority of these events are window dressing and, at the end of the day, nobody gains very much out of them. It is far better to hold direct conversations with employees, unfiltered and undiluted by support staff, enabling you to stay close to your people and to the market.

I Heard It from Jack!

Jack Welch, legendary CEO of General Electric (GE), is often quoted and rightly so, as he was undoubtedly responsible for identifying and implementing some important leadership concepts and ideas. Welch spent about a third of his time in the GE Academy, in workshops for those on the first rung of management (group leader, factory shift manager, small department head), right up to the top echelons of management. He was always present for one to two hours, gave a short speech and/or answered questions from his employees, and all without prior knowledge—everything unfiltered, direct, and clear. How could the CEO of such a large company have justified spending so much time at in-house seminars? For Jack Welch, the answer was simple. That was where he had the greatest leverage in getting his messages across. In this way, he gained direct access to all levels of the organization without having to go over the heads of the hierarchy in between and without risking having his message diluted by those same heads. People went back to their departments, their countries, to their corners of the organization, and said, "I heard it from Jack!"

Directive Leadership: You are probably wondering why we are even mentioning this here, the authoritarian style of leadership where managers essentially give orders and expect them to be carried out without question. However, it remains very much part of global business practice. True, in the Western world, it is mainly to be seen in the military, the police, and patriarch-led companies. For our colleagues in the Middle East and Asia, it is still highly prevalent and is unlikely to change in a hurry, so managers more used to a North American or European culture need to remain flexible. In politics too, this leadership style is currently making an unexpected comeback. We're sure the reader will have no difficulty in bringing to mind prominent examples of a new, authoritarian, egocentric, and surprisingly popular political class from around the world.

When Straight Talking Unleashes Unexpected Enthusiasm!

We were at a training course on "High Performance Behavior" with a group of international country heads in London when the participants were confronted with a classic scenario: "The business is not faring well, the company is under severe pressure, the market and competitive environment is very challenging. You are the new management team, and in one hour you must present and justify your proposed turnaround measures."

After two days of training, it was clear to everyone that only an interdisciplinary team effort could meet this objective—a coordinated plan, intensively debated, participative leadership to bring everyone on board, combined with the development of common goals which everyone has bought into, etc.

For one of the four working groups, this all seemed a bit too simple and mainstream, so just for fun, they went for a slightly different approach. They were the last group to report and, in contrast to the previous three teams, presented something along the following lines:

- "Times are tough, and tough times call for tough measures. We are going to outline them here and they will be implemented immediately."

- "With a Force Nine storm blowing in the market, there is clearly no time for long-winded discussions, round tables, and workshops."

- "If you don't like it, speak up now."

- "Any questions? No? Good, then this is what our new direction will look like and after this meeting, we'll get started straightaway. And we expect top performance, no excuses, from everyone!"

This was presented by Detlef Britzke, all six foot six inches of him, with incredible conviction. Stunned silence. The trainer team looked questioningly at each other. Unbelievable. This group had obviously not grasped a single thing that had been taught over the previous two days. The Asians, on the other hand, who had just helped develop a "soft" consensus solution in another group (as a concession to the Europeans perhaps?) reacted quite differently. After a short pause, they could no longer hold back and gave free rein to their enthusiasm:

- The lady from Singapore: "Yes, this is absolutely the right thing to do!"

- The Filipino: "That's exactly how we would have done it in Manila!"

- The Indian: "It's the only way to go!"

- The Chinese colleague: "Good sense at last!"

Which of these variants is "leader-sham," then? Perhaps, when it comes to cooperation in a global organization, we clearly have to accept that there are different ways to reach the same goal. A confident leader must decide to what extent they will (or must) accommodate such differing expectations about what appropriate leadership actually looks like in different settings.

Transformational Leadership: Our final offering in this summary of leadership styles was first outlined by the American, Bernard Bass, in 1985. It also relies heavily on a leader's charisma, and transformational leadership is all about talking to and connecting with your employees on an emotional level and capturing their imagination with an overarching vision. In addition, it encourages them to question existing procedures and promote innovation ("intellectual stimulation") and takes into account the individual needs and strengths of people. From this fertile platform—at least that is the hope—the employees' potential is free to blossom and they are better able to tackle new challenges. The business can respond with greater flexibility and innovation,[60] and it will come as no surprise that transformational leadership rapidly became the go-to management style with the advent of the so-called VUCA world, where new risks arise in a setting characterized by "Volatility, Uncertainty, Complexity, and Ambiguity." Ultimately, transformational leadership is, by definition, all about flexibility and change. Having said that, it has the problem of overlooking all the legitimate doubts about whether charisma is a valuable core competency when discussing good leadership. Enron boss Jeff Skilling and investment fraudster Bernard Madoff were also unquestionably charismatic. On top of that, it turns out that translating the theory of transformational leadership into daily practice is not quite as straightforward as was originally hoped.[61]

Before subjecting a business to transformational change, it would be a good idea if managers—especially in large corporations—simply developed a better eye for those employees who are actually able and willing to drive forward innovation, provided they are given extra space to operate. It sounds less sexy but is probably more effective.

As far as we're concerned, if there is such a thing as an ideal or complete leadership style, then it is embodied by those who begin with themselves, so have a clear understanding of their own strengths and weaknesses, know how to counterbalance these weaknesses with "complementary" colleagues around them, and have the ability to adjust their style depending on the overall context, situation, personality, and skill set of the person they are addressing. And then, last but not least, they remember that their view of the world remains as subjective as the next person's. Well, we never said it was easy! There will always be those who want to be set clear targets and for whom an emotional and interactive style is a turn-off, just like there are those who flourish and prosper if given extra space, no rules, and the chance to bring their dog to work. So, irrespective of style, here is a list of personality traits which are desirable for successful leadership, without claiming that the list is in any way exhaustive:

- Ambition and drive to meet a target and turn a vision into reality
- Courage and optimism to get through crises and keep employees on board
- Integrity and openness to create and sustain trust
- Self-reflection and the ability to observe and control your own ego (and not, for example, surround yourself with fawning "yes men")
- Resilience to stress and independence (the ability to withstand headwinds and take unpopular decisions)
- Stamina and determination

Leadership is exciting and, at the same time, very demanding. If everyone likes you, that is probably a sign of mediocrity. A leader puts themselves in the spotlight, forgoes the protection of the pack, and must be able to maintain a degree of distance from the rest of the team. Of course, complete leadership is not always easy, especially when you are new in a position and do not have an answer ready for every problem. We have heard many senior executives say quite openly, "I don't know the answer either." You may think that makes you look more human. The truth is, you can lose a large amount of respect and increase uncertainty with such a statement, with people concluding: "Well, if he doesn't know it, then who the hell does?" It is better to formulate a phase of uncertainty more confidently. "We don't have a solution today, but we will work on it (together) and keep you posted on progress." And of course, if you say this, then it is your responsibility to ensure that it actually happens. New bosses or colleagues who "have a lot to learn" are particularly tiresome. On day one, they are making it clear that they don't have a clue. That may be so; nevertheless, it is unhelpful and, in the context of successful business leadership, disastrous. You can appear honest and humble and open to input without looking helpless, and without going to the other extreme of overestimating yourself and acting as if you know everything.

1:10 or 1:10,000? Leadership ≠ Leadership

It is pointless asking whether someone "can lead." This just perpetuates the myth of the born leader who can handle any situation. It makes more sense to ask whether someone is suitable for a particular leadership function or a particular management level. After all, there are an enormous number of different leadership roles in every organization, and even experienced managers have to find their feet in a new role. What matters is to correctly assess and understand the set of skills required in the new position and to what extent these differ from the previous position. Furthermore, understanding the "power and authority of office" that comes with the new role and then exercising this in a measured and responsible fashion is of utmost importance. The strategic demands will change, as will the daily tasks, external perception, and framework. Even with fifteen or twenty years' experience in leadership positions, this adjustment does not come automatically. We noticed that our interview partners, almost all of them very experienced executives, were particularly sensitive to this topic. The big consultancy firms, for example, with their "up or out" or "grow or go" career progression, are particularly rigorous in questioning whether a colleague will be able to master the next but one career move.

From Gerd Stürz, Head of Life Sciences (Germany, Austria, Switzerland) at EY:

> *There is nobody here who is still a junior consultant after ten years, or still a manager after twenty years. Here, you either advance in your career or you go. We do not have to fire anyone. Many go into industry and do a good job there. From the outset, we accompany this process. With every promotion, we ask ourselves whether this colleague will also be able to handle the next level up. So, if someone is to be promoted from consultant to senior consultant, we also ask the question, can they go on to become a manager? And if we think that they can't do it, then we say to them straightaway, "Look, there are a few things here you need to be aware of; otherwise, we are going to have a problem in a couple of years' time." That sounds harsh, but I think it is very fair.*

We have experienced this ourselves. Not everyone can manage a department where the span of control goes beyond 1:10. In contrast, some can lead very well through people, thus leading through other leaders. Then there are those who lead large organizations without losing the ability to handle one-on-one situations with employees at all levels, from upper management to the blue-collar employee on the shop floor. The really great leaders can do all of the above: lead tens of thousands and at the same time give an individual the feeling that, for a few moments, she is all that matters to them, just like General Foster in the quote at the beginning of this chapter. Being able to switch from big to small and back to big again—that is truly a key part of complete leadership!

The "Leadership Pipeline" model of Charan, Drotter, and Noel (2011) focuses on the idea that leadership comes in a large variety of guises and that, if you wish to progress, you cannot afford to stop learning. The authors, themselves experienced top managers, formulated their theory based on countless examples in the corporate world. They assert that every level of leadership calls for the setting of new priorities, new skills, and adjusted values, taken to be the yardstick for judging success in the next position. Charan and his colleagues describe seven levels of management for multinational corporations, and five levels for traditional family businesses, with the managing director at the top.

Level 7   Enterprise manager
Level 6   Group manager
Level 5   Business manager (managing director)
Level 4   Functional manager
Level 3   Manager of managers
Level 2   Manager of others
Level 1   Manager of self

What is important are the transitions between levels, referred to by Charan et al. as "leadership passages," and every such transition requires a new round of investment in the personal development of the chosen person. Astonishingly and regrettably, in most organizations this does not happen, although such a process would clearly increase the chances of such moves succeeding and, as a result, unleash further potential in the organization.

Farsighted businesses make sure that those with a positive leadership prognosis are systematically trained, from team leader right up to the top of the organization, creating a rich and well-filled people pipeline to guarantee the long-term success of the business. Broadly speaking, as you progress along the pipeline, functional responsibility decreases as strategic, and later representative, tasks increase. So, leadership cannot, in our opinion, be regarded merely as a single concept. It is more appropriate to talk about it as a collection, over time, of diverse and multifactorial leadership challenges.

A Stress Test for Leadership

Anyone who wants to operate successfully at the highest level needs to be well networked in business and political circles, sensitive to the interests of various stakeholders, global in outlook, strategically smart, a good communicator, and resilient in times of crisis. A pinch of well-managed charisma can help, and more important than anything else is a solid dose of honest self-management, personal integrity, and empathy.

Leadership or Leader-Sham? Let's find out!

1. Your company has a leadership program that identifies suitable people and provides targeted, individual support. ☐

2. Those who are suited to leadership rise to the top, not those who have the right contacts. ☐

3. Management misconduct (e.g. bullying, harassment) is actively addressed and punished. ☐

4. Bullies and people with unstable personalities are not given leadership responsibilities in your organization. ☐

5. No departments stand out as having significantly higher levels of sickness or more frequent cases of employee burnout than others. ☐

6. The company encourages a culture of personal responsibility and employee development. ☐

7. Senior management has not lost contact with the "small people" in the company. ☐

---

8. All levels of the organization have confidence in top management. ☐

9. People are the heart of the company and statements in a similar spirit are not simply a PR exercise, but are also reflected in daily practice. ☐

10. Management ensures there are clear targets and good working conditions for people at all levels in the company. ☐

11. Creativity, initiative, and commitment are rewarded. ☐

12. Difficult decisions concerning cutbacks and measures such as downsizing are dealt with as fairly as possible. ☐

13. There are no unofficial practices such as "Divide and conquer," "Knowledge is power," or "You are either for me or against me." ☐

INCA INSIGHTS

- **Act responsibly, in the spirit of the "Last Table."**

- **Create an upward pull by handing over meaningful tasks to your best people.**

- **Think about your personality and your actions: Do you do everything possible to make your employees more successful? Would you actually enjoy having yourself as a boss?**

> "Credibility in leadership processes ensues when managers act consistently. People's behavior can be changed by setting clear boundaries, which also means that where there are rewards, there must be penalties as well."
>
> —DR. ALEXANDER VON PREEN, CEO INTERSPORT EG

---

4 Fair Play
(or Just Pretending?)

We tend to feel morally superior to earlier civilizations. But how robust are our values, really? Hardly a week goes by without a new scandal from the business world and other areas of life coming to light. The Inca Empire is an excellent illustration of the important role strong values can play in a society. The words *Ama sua, ama llulla, ama quella* can be seen inscribed on the walls of houses in Cuzco, and to this day, in the mountains of Peru, farmers still use this as a greeting. The saying is an old Inca phrase which has survived down the centuries. Roughly translated, it means, "The People of the Sun do not steal, do not lie, and are not lazy." From these principles, we can assume that the Andean state had strict rules. Indeed, laziness was punishable by death, as was the destruction of bridges or the killing of seabirds. There were no taxes to pay, but instead an ingenious system of "compulsory contributions" was put in place: the crop harvest was shared equally among the Inca, the priest, and the village community. Everybody had to serve the empire.

The Americas specialist René Oth describes Inca society as "puritan," even though foreign rulers were showered with precious welcome gifts and important victories or completed projects were celebrated with great festivities. Karoline Noack, an expert in ancient American history, calls this "ritualized generosity."[62] Those who stuck to the rules benefited from the empire's perfect system of logistics, from the highly developed farming methods and the tradesmen's skills, which guaranteed a supply of the basics in life for all, and there was a culture of give and take, even when it came to religion. Assimilated tribes had to bow down before the Sun God, but at the same time their gods and religious rituals were integrated into the Inca culture.[63] What we are left with is the image of a highly regulated society, organized down to the last detail and built on strong values. Presumably, the question of whether something was right or wrong in Inca society was rarely asked, as this overarching set of values held the widespread empire together. Tragically, the civil war between rival Inca half-brothers undermined these values, weakened this unwritten agreement, and accelerated the decline of the empire.

It was not enough for the Inca rulers just to integrate their subjects into a highly efficient administrative and economic system. Their vision to "bring order to the world" was based on a code of values propagating a system of mutual cooperation, therefore creating a fair society. Even to this day, common norms and values build a bond which holds a society together and creates a code of conduct for each individual to follow. It can be said that a decline in values irrevocably leads to a state of increased disorder and chaos.

The business world actually „discovered" the topic of values decades ago, and you may well be sick to death of hearing about it. Google the word "corporate values" and you'll get about twenty-nine million hits. However, do the same with "corporate profits" and you'll be lucky to get 2.6 million. This demonstrates that the term "corporate values" has become firmly established in our vocabulary.[64] So, on the one hand, we see an enormous amount of activity from companies regarding their values and, at the same time, we hear of one new scandal after the next. What is going on here? Can it be that companies are doing an awful lot of window dressing, with sometimes very little substance behind it? And if this is to change, what exactly needs to happen?

Sweet Talk, Empty Promises?

The world of official "values" statements is apparently in good shape. PWC surveyed around 1,400 CEOs across eighty countries under the banner "Redefining Success in a Changing World." Their findings concluded that "76 percent of CEOs around the world agree: In (the) future, success cannot only be measured in terms of profits generated...but must also involve creating societal values."[65]

Decision-makers seem to be sensitized to the topic of "values," possibly as a result of the financial crisis and various corporate scandals on both sides of the Atlantic. In Germany, the Values-based Leadership Commission specializes in monitoring this issue and regularly asks around seven hundred business leaders across all levels of management which values they consider most important. Primarily, it asks them to rank six core values in order of importance: Trust, Responsibility, Integrity, Respect, Sustainability, and Courage. Since 2010, the first three of these have always come out on top, while Courage consistently brings up the rear. In 2018, only 3 percent of managers put it at the top of the list, which comes as something of a surprise. After all, when it comes to conflict situations, how are you able to stand up for the values you and your company believe in and represent if you lack personal courage?[66]

More doubts creep in when reviewing a survey of management and employees in the bigger family-owned businesses, carried out by the consultancy firm Rochus Mummert. Whereas all the executives surveyed were unanimous in their claim that their companies had defined their values, which their workforce was familiar with, only 50 percent of their rank-and-file employees agreed. The results among middle management weren't much better; they only polled 53 percent. But it gets worse. A mere 17 percent of those surveyed thought that their bosses actually "lived" these values.[67]

One of the biggest corporate scandals of recent decades demonstrates why we chose the title "Just Pretending" for this chapter. The bribery affair involving Siemens is a classic example of how a large corporation, blinded by its own success, can delude itself into believing that it can continually flout the law without being sanctioned. All it felt it needed to do was keep up the pretense of good corporate governance, including having a code of ethics and an anti-corruption officer. However, the Siemens scandal severely damaged its top managers' reputations and led to fines amounting to more than three billion dollars and numerous court actions, some of which are still unresolved today.[68]

Siemens—"The Firm"

I can no longer bear this fake outrage that top management comes out with. One of the most influential news magazines in German-speaking countries, *Der Spiegel*, was quoting the Siemens CFO in the Telephone Landline Division at the height of the bribery scandal back in April 2008.[69] He wasn't the only one to speak out, other employees did too. And not only were public prosecutors in Germany on the case, but also those in the United States, Switzerland, Italy, and Greece. Slowly but surely, the biggest case of corruption in German post-war history was unraveled, as it became increasingly clear that bribery was an integral part of the business strategy of one of Europe's leading technology companies.

Using an ingenious network of offshore bank accounts and mailbox companies, the whole operation was organized with breathtaking efficiency, including a form for approving "Commission for Customer Orders," which required two signatures. To be safe, the signatures were to be placed on removable Post-it notes, with a printed reminder on the form: "Stick yellow note here"!

So how could things be allowed to get that far? The following is an explanation, but by no means an exoneration.

Unbelievable as it may seem from today's perspective, until 1999, according to German law, bribery outside Germany's borders was not a criminal offense. In fact, the "sweeteners" were officially tax-deductible! Being a global corporation, Siemens exploited this to the fullest, as they probably believed it was the only way of closing deals in the Middle East, South America, and Sub-Saharan Africa. And despite significant changes to the bribery law in 1999, Siemens carried on in the same old way. The culture appeared to be so entrenched that anyone who had grown up in the system—and many senior managers had been in the company for the whole of their careers—felt they lived in a world with its own set of rules. One top manager is reported to have said, "Governments may come and go, but there'll always be a Siemens!"

What was missing at Siemens was a completely unambiguous statement from the very top along the lines of "this will no longer be accepted"—a zero-tolerance approach, just like the Incas had for what they perceived as serious misdemeanors. Instead, it was business as usual conducted behind a carefully constructed façade of ethical correctness. If values are to be more than just fair-weather slogans or image-building tools, then there must be clear consequences for actions and behaviors that infringe on them.

Statements like this are always in danger of coming across as somewhat self-righteous. Isn't this hype about values exaggerated anyway? Some may say, with justification, that you can't make an omelet without breaking a few eggs. And setting ambitious business goals and then supporting them with phrases like "Just do it. And I don't care how you get it done!" can only reinforce this impression. But where does it all end if ethical and legal constraints are ignored? Decades ago, management visionaries like Jim Collins identified a link between strong core values, in the form of a "core ideology," and outstandingly successful businesses. Studies like those of Rochus Mummert have also established a link between a values-driven culture and good business performance.[70] It is well worth looking at the Credo of Johnson & Johnson, which is short, to the point, very specific, and unchanged since 1943! Interestingly, J & J defines this credo as more than just a moral compass, but a general recipe for business success. And one of the most important points to note is that it starts with patients and customers, then goes on to employees and teams, then to communities and society and finally to the shareholders. There are plenty of companies that go the other way around.

And because it is so impressive, durable, and still relevant after almost eighty years, you can find it in full right here:

Johnson & Johnson—Our Credo

We believe our first responsibility is to the patients, doctors and nurses, to mothers and fathers and all others who use our products and services. In meeting their needs everything we do must be of high quality. We must constantly strive to provide value, reduce our costs and maintain reasonable prices. Customers' orders must be serviced promptly and accurately. Our business partners must have an opportunity to make a fair profit.

We are responsible to our employees who work with us throughout the world. We must provide an inclusive work environment where each person must be considered as an individual. We must respect their diversity and dignity and recognize their merit. They must have a sense of security, fulfillment and purpose in their jobs. Compensation must be fair and adequate and working conditions clean, orderly and safe. We must support the health and well-being of our employees and help them fulfill their family and other personal responsibilities. Employees must feel free to make suggestions and complaints. There must be equal opportunity for employment, development and advancement for those qualified. We must provide highly capable leaders and their actions must be just and ethical.

We are responsible to the communities in which we live and work and to the world community as well. We must help people be healthier by supporting better access and care in more places around the world. We must be good citizens—support good works and charities, better health and education, and bear our fair share of taxes. We must maintain in good order the property we are privileged to use, protecting the environment and natural resources.

Our final responsibility is to our stockholders. Business must make a sound profit. We must experiment with new ideas. Research must be carried on, innovative programs developed, investments made for the future and mistakes paid for. New equipment must be purchased, new facilities provided and new products launched. Reserves must be created to provide for adverse times. When we operate according to these principles, the stockholders should realize a fair return.

You may be skeptical about overstating the significance of any single factor in business success. But it must be conceded that where values such as personal responsibility, integrity, or mutual respect are not found and, equally importantly, not lived by management, then moral standards run wild. We would welcome seeing more companies sharing the insights of the Protestant theologian Wolfgang Huber, and his coauthors Peter Barrenstein, management consultant, and Friedhelm Wachs, negotiation specialist, from the foreword to their highly readable book *Protestant. Successful. Business.* For example, "We are absolutely convinced that no business can survive over time if it is purely motivated by the self-interest of those involved. Businesses which are only driven by short-term profit targets will sooner or later suffer downturns. And no business in the world can prevail in the longer term if it unleashes or even cultivates all the worst characteristics of mankind. Everything disintegrates because basic mutual trust, which is so essential for the functioning of day-to-day business processes, is undermined."[71]

Why should employees play by the rules if top management doesn't do likewise? This decaying of standards damages the business at various levels. We are not just talking about financial damage brought about by fiddling the books, but also about reputational loss, damaged business relationships and, not to be underestimated, the costs of legions of expensive lawyers and any resultant fines and penalties. Referring back to our earlier metaphor, you end up cracking more and more eggs. Eventually this can pose existential risks, as can be seen in the following examples of recent business scandals.

In the long run, it is quite clear that breaches of compliance do not pay. Just look at the current crises at GE, Deutsche Bank, and VW Group, and the cartel-like structure of the car industry. Once American lawyers get involved, it starts to get really expensive. Maybe one of the reasons why the United States is a global power is its system of steep fines and tough rulings on fraud and bribery. In a world of global connectivity and high-speed communications, there is no room for non-compliance. What can begin as a local issue in a far-flung corner of the globe can flash, five minutes later, across the breaking news ticker of the *New York Times*. Given this scenario, the importance and positive impact of a clearly defined values system becomes all the more obvious. Values help you make decisions when faced with a dilemma, and shared values help a large group of individuals to find orientation and commit to a common goal. Which brings us elegantly back to the Incas.

The Price of Ignoring Values—A Selection of Scandals[72]

Company	What happened	Penalties
WorldCom	Inflated assets by as much as eleven billion dollars, leading to thirty thousand lost jobs and $180 billion in losses for investors.	CFO was fired, controller resigned, and the company filed for bankruptcy. CEO Ebbers sentenced to twenty-five years for fraud, conspiracy, and filing false documents with regulators. **Special note:** Following the WorldCom scandal, the US Congress passed the Sarbanes-Oxley Act, introducing the most sweeping set of new business regulations since the 1930s.
Enron	Kept huge debts off the balance sheet. Shareholders lost seventy-five billion dollars, thousands of employees and investors lost their retirement funds, and many employees lost their jobs. Arthur Andersen was found guilty of fudging Enron's accounts.	CEO Skilling got twenty-four years in prison. The company filed for bankruptcy. **Special note:** *Fortune* named Enron "America's Most Innovative Company" for six years in a row prior to the scandal.
Tyco	CEO and CFO embezzled $150 million and inflated company income by $500 million.	CEO Kozlowski and CFO Swartz were given long prison sentences. A class-action lawsuit forced Tyco to pay $2.92 billion to investors.
Lehman Brothers	Hid over fifty billion dollars in loans disguised as sales.	Forced into the largest bankruptcy in US history. SEC didn't prosecute due to lack of evidence. **Special note:** In 2007, one year before the outbreak of the financial crisis, Lehman Brothers was ranked the number one "Most Admired Securities Firm" by Fortune magazine.
Bernie Madoff	Tricked investors out of $64.8 billion through the largest Ponzi scheme ever.	150 years in prison for Madoff plus $170 billion restitution. Prison sentences also for other corporate officers.

Undercover Investigation, Bottom-up!

How do you embed values in a business and communicate them throughout the whole organization? Obviously, just posting a Code of Conduct on the company intranet, never to be seen again, is not enough. There is nothing wrong with a written statement of values, and, if it is the result of a cooperative effort by a cross-section of employees, all the better. It is vital that it is clearly communicated by senior executives, and it is also helpful if the information is handed out to every new recruit. Furthermore, it can be made the subject of team meetings and give orientation when values conflicts emerge in day-to-day working situations. However, most important of all is that actions and not words are allowed to communicate and demonstrate what the values really mean in terms of behavior, both inside the organization and in interactions with external stakeholders. At Siemens, it apparently never occurred to anyone to question the long-established practice of bribery, even though the boss, Heinrich von Pierer, in his book *Profit and Morals*, published in 2003, wrote that honesty is one of the core values essential for Siemens's success. As he commented shrewdly and, under the circumstances, somewhat cynically: "In the long run you cannot cover up deception, fraud, and corruption."[73]

Employees have a very fine feeling for whether company principles are to be taken seriously or are simply there for show. It all starts with the way you interact with other people in the organization, something that one of our interviewees, Catherine von Fürstenberg-Dussmann, tested out in a spectacular fashion:

Values in Daily Life—or Complete Leaders Show No Arrogance

The Dussmann Group has 63,500 employees in eighteen countries and generates revenue in excess of two billion euros.[74] Its core business is in services such as catering, security, building services, and commercial cleaning. Following the early death of the company founder, Peter Dussmann, his widow Catherine von Fürstenberg-Dussmann took the reins of the company. A trained actress, she had been a full-time housewife and mother for twenty-eight years. But before she formally took charge of the company in 2008, she took the chance to take a look behind the scenes of her own business and worked undercover for several weeks, disguised as a cleaning lady and kitchen helper. During a conversation with us, she explained that she wanted to get to know how the business really functioned, how people treated each other, knowing full well how difficult this would be once she had taken up her new position.

Two particularly memorable experiences revealed to her the prevailing attitude to values of some members of top management. After a long night of cleaning, and still disguised as a cleaning lady, she encountered the then-CEO and CFO in the corridor on the seventh floor of the head office. The two men came swaggering toward her in a straight line, forcing her to move to one side and make way for them to avoid a head-on collision. She greeted them, but neither of them reacted. She was completely ignored and as far as these two "gentlemen" were concerned, she simply didn't exist. It was the same story when she was cleaning the floor of the underground garage for a major client. She recalls constantly having to dodge left and right to avoid being run over by all these oh-so-important executives speeding past her in their Porsches and Mercedes. Not one of them greeted her, not one of them acknowledged her presence. Once again, she simply didn't exist. Incidentally, she chose to part company with the CEO and CFO, having confirmed her suspicions concerning their lack of human integrity.[75]

Small gestures can make a big impact. An exaggerated claim? We don't think so! Highfalutin statements on values, respect, and integrity are meaningless if they are not reflected every single day in the way people interact with each other. People are keenly aware of such contradictions, but sadly a lot of managers completely underestimate the symbolic power of their actions. And the further up the ladder they climb, the greater the impact of their every move. And here is a warning: Some well-meaning gestures can backfire completely. For example, if you think it's enough to turn up once a year, on December 23, to sing a couple of carols with the late shift and to say a few moving words about how people are the most important asset in the company, then you might want to think again. What you see as tears of emotion could well just be tears of disappointment, anger, and frustration. In the immortal words of Dr. Samuel Johnson, "The road to hell is paved with good intentions."

A poorly timed decision by management can be equally destructive—for example, deciding to outsource company canteen services "to reduce costs" at the same time as renewing the company car fleet. You can talk all you want about the benefits of long-term automobile leasing contracts; the damage is done. And of course, it also works the other way around, with one seemingly small gesture able to create positive impact and bring about a real change in business culture.

From Christine Wolff, multiple board member:

> *I worked at the HQ in London and I had an enormous, typical English office: huge desk, heavy furniture, leather sofa, receptionist. And then, there was the aptly named "work floor": tiny cubicles, some without any natural daylight, eighty people squeezed in between mountains of paper. I thought, I don't believe this. So, I had my office walls taken down at once and said, "You can find space here for sixteen of these people." With that, across the whole European organization, all the standard discussions about "I need the biggest office" were silenced.*

We hardly need mention here that it is not about how big your office is, but about the ability to engage with people, at every level, on equal terms. And on top of that, to make sure that your own actions are guided by the values that have been adopted for the business. This can also mean speaking out, even when it feels uncomfortable and you are not directly responsible for whatever has happened. Paul Williams remembers as if it were yesterday the very unpleasant feeling when, as a young HR manager, he learned that anyone who knowingly tolerates alcoholism in the workplace (or anywhere else for that matter) is himself classified as a "passive alcoholic." Equally, anyone turning a blind eye on corruption, abuse of power, criminal activity, or any other action of this nature is not only endangering the company's economic well-being, but completely compromising their own integrity as well.

It Might Be Legal, but Is It Legitimate?

You can have a big impact as a manager simply through the power of setting an example, and this applies to every level of the corporate hierarchy. The Incas were aware of this too. Future leaders had to pass extremely tough tests before they could assume responsibilities. Punishments became harsher the higher they climbed the social ranks. The same rules applied to everyone, whether to the common people or the chieftains. This helped the ruling classes to find acceptance among the population.

For some time now, appropriate conduct in an organization has been dealt with under the banner of "compliance." Having said that, rather surprisingly, discussions about values and discussions about compliance were, for many years, seemingly independent of each other: on the one side, statesmanlike presentations from top management about responsibility and integrity, on the other, high-level meetings to ensure that the necessary internal procedures and legal preconditions were in place to avoid incurring court cases and subsequent liabilities. At some corporations, compliance declarations are still treated as PYA ("Protect Your Ass") processes and are routinely signed by managers in order to protect the board.[76] However, slowly but surely, there appears to be a change of attitude creeping through the business world as to whether a purely legalistic approach to compliance is the right way forward.

There is no well-known large corporation which does not have a compliance management system in place, and the managers of more and more mid-sized companies are increasingly concerned about the plethora of statutory regulations which are now part and parcel of doing international business. Of course, compliance systems did nothing to prevent the misdemeanors at Parmalat, Arthur Andersen, Sociéte Générale, Barclays, Barings Bank, and Facebook. Moreover, internal bureaucracy and written declarations are nothing more than ineffectual paper tigers so long as the key decision-makers in a business do not communicate with absolute clarity the message, "We are serious about this!" A CEO who sets ambitious sales and financial targets without tolerating any internal dissent may well be acting in line with formal compliance rules. But if he or she doesn't explicitly ask, "Is this legally acceptable?" then the underlying message is "I don't care *how* you get it done!" This results in a culture of duplicity, with compliance providing a thin veil of virtue to distract onlookers, while behind the scenes, questionable practice continues unabated. And if someone should see behind the veneer, then the explanation is usually along the lines of "bad behavior of a few rotten apples in department X or Y." Fair play, this is not.

In its 2013 Code of Values, which was supposed to herald a change in corporate culture, Deutsche Bank writes, "We will do what is right, not just what is allowed."[77] They had better get a move on. An article in an important European police journal looked closely at the activities of Deutsche Bank and drew comparisons to methods used in organized crime, stating also that "players in the financial services sector (had) worked out a strategic plan for a global orgy of enrichment."[78] In October 2016, the European current affairs magazine *Der Spiegel* implied that recent CEOs of the company were akin to financial godfather figures, and so it should come as no surprise that, according to a study by the Bertelsmann Foundation, less than a third of the population trusts businesses quoted on the stock exchange to be "good for society." The figure rises to 66 percent for SMEs (small and medium-sized enterprises) and 70 percent for family-owned businesses.[79]

Such reports are a bitter pill to swallow, especially for the competent, engaged, and honest employees at all levels who make up the vast majority, even in the companies mentioned. And there is another question that large corporations need to consider: What is the long-term impact on social cohesion and social harmony if, despite all the talk about corporate social responsibility, many people consider these businesses to be nothing more than profit-driven tricksters? For example, where will it lead if companies claiming to be doing what is "right," and not just what is "legally allowed" are also the very same companies that then "optimize" corporate taxes to such a degree that the costs for maintaining basic public infrastructure have to be borne solely by society in general, with only minimal contributions coming from these large and often highly profitable companies? Or when tax optimization becomes the sole driver for decisions, such as the closure of departments or even whole business units, even if there is no obvious broader commercial rationale? Or if small suppliers are driven close to insolvency simply because large corporations take months to settle their bills? We would like to see managers ask themselves far more often, "Is what we are planning to do not just legal, but also legitimate?" Would your plans survive the classic camera test? Would you be able to explain them in simple terms in a live interview for the local evening news?

Many of these questions cannot be answered in isolation or by individual businesses. Instead, they need to be answered at a political and societal level. And what can you do? Well, you can start by making clear that compliance is much more than just a bureaucratic "Cover Your Ass" strategy. If compliance is to be taken seriously, it needs credible ambassadors. Values and compliance need to be seen as two sides of the same coin, and that is the challenge for every senior leader in organizations.

Here are some other facts from a recent study by EY which, unfortunately, don't give strong grounds for optimism:

- In only half of all businesses contacted did employees receive a letter from the management about the company Code of Conduct. In most cases, this information was just posted on the firm's own intranet.
- Less than 50 percent of the businesses take compliance into consideration when it comes to salary reviews.
- Compliance-related criteria such as "integrity" and "leading by example" are only considered by 36 percent of businesses when it comes to promotions.
- "Clawback clauses" had only been agreed with 18 percent of managers, from whom salary and bonus payments can thus be reclaimed where compliance breaches have harmed the business—a question which, with regard to the debate on bonus repayments, is more relevant than ever for many global players.
- Forty-six percent of businesses have implemented core elements of the compliance management system *only* at company HQ.[80]

Different Countries, Different Values

American anthropologist Clyde Kluckhohn once came up with a compact definition of values: "A conception...of the desirable..."[81]

Values differ depending on where we happen to be in the world, and psychology students learn that they are "aspects of the social construction of reality."[82] The guiding values of a three-hundred-strong community in rural Minnesota are different from those prevailing in a fashionable district in Oakland, California. In other words, you don't have to fly halfway around the world to find yourself in a place where different values apply. Nevertheless, in an international context, questions about values arise that play out way beyond our Western norms.

What Would You Do? Two Heavyweight Dilemmas

The head of a Eurostoxx 50 company in China, relatively new in the post, told us about two of his most difficult and memorable challenges concerning values.

First, some background information: In Chinese manufacturing companies, employees have to seek prior approval from their manager before taking time off to attend their own wedding or for socially related health reasons, because they are entitled to take one day additional leave.

After a happy and very positive discussion about her planned promotion, one young employee asked for a day to think things over and one day's leave which, of course, was approved. The day after her holiday, she came into the office of the China head, beaming with pride, and confirmed that she would gladly accept the promotion and was now able to commit 120 percent to the company. At the same time, she asked, retrospectively, for one-day special leave for her abortion. A promotion was more important for her than starting a family and she essentially considered it her duty to take this step, because the firm would now require even greater commitment from her in this new role.

How would you deal with such a situation? Are you ready and willing to face up to cases of conflicting values like this, or would you seek to delegate such a case? Anyone active in an international leadership role must be able to handle values dilemmas like this and, nevertheless, make the right decision. But what is "right" in this case? Perhaps you would like to put the book down for a moment and think it over.

Here is another equally dramatic example. A local manager at the Chinese subsidiary of a European company had misappropriated and gambled away around $150,000 in client funds and salaries. According to Chinese law, embezzlement on this scale is punishable by the death penalty. The European manager responsible for the local Chinese business called his boss, the Head of Region Asia and asked for advice. How should he deal with the situation? Should he report this employee to the authorities and perhaps be party to his execution? What would you have done in this situation? If one were to try and sweep the case under the carpet, the impression could be created within the company that you can get away with even bigger misdemeanors. After all, everyone in the organization knew about this case. On the other hand, reporting the true facts to the authorities could mean the death penalty. In this case, a hybrid solution was found in cooperation with the family of the employee concerned, some good lawyers, and the police. The family committed to repaying the money in installments, some of it was written off, and the employee went to prison for a few years.

There are, however, some situations that leave no room for such compromises. We know of two other cases involving joint venture companies where the Chinese partners—employer, HR department as well as employee representatives—insisted on the full force of the law being applied. Their argument was, "That is the law of the land here and you, too, must abide by our law. Nobody in the company would understand if it were any other way."

Does this make you feel a little uneasy? What does it mean for international managers? In our view, in such a situation, you can't simply turn your back on your responsibilities with a shrug of your shoulders saying "There is nothing I can do," and it is equally unrealistic to assume that the local organization just has to adapt to "our" values. You can only proceed on a case-by-case basis and judge for yourself, in the specific circumstances, what is doable and what price you are prepared to pay to protect your personal standpoint. If you take on responsibility for Latin America, Asia, the Middle East, or Africa, you must come extremely well-prepared and be ready and able, above all, to avoid cultural arrogance and self-righteousness. After all, are we keen to allow others to interfere with the way we do things when it's in our backyard, where we have jurisdiction? And are we really as "superior" as we sometimes believe? We get all hot under the collar about corruption elsewhere, yet smile indulgently about it when it happens close to home, laughing it off as a bit of harmless "you scratch my back and I'll scratch yours." Heinrich Pachl, a cabaret artist from Cologne in Germany, defended this practice rather cleverly: "The Klüngel [Cologne's version of local "relationship management"] is defined as securing public interests using private means, while corruption is defined as securing private interests using public means."[83]

Where does good cooperation end and corruption begin? Where is the boundary between "networking" and the "old boy network"? Is there really that big a difference between a business deal finalized during a round of golf and a traffic policeman at a busy intersection in Buenos Aires who waives issuing you a ticket for making an illegal turn in exchange for "a donation to the annual end-of-year tombola" or for the "Police Widows Fund"? This kind of "hidden" corruption is also much more subtle than most people brought up in a Westernized society realize. For instance, in Argentina, as in many other countries, there are no on-the-spot fines; the policeman must write a report, a system that was introduced to prevent corruption and stop cash payments. But of course, the policeman doesn't want to write a report and create all that paper, the result of which will be a written penalty for the offender, so instead he might suggest carrying out a full examination of the car, the driver's documents, and a list of other important aspects toward improving general road safety in Buenos Aires. He may even suspect that you have been drinking, in which case he would have to ask you to accompany him back to the police station for blood tests, all of which could last hours. And all you want to do is get home to your family after a long and tiring day at the office. This policeman has probably been waiting a long time to be assigned to the crossing near the offices of the many foreign-owned companies, where all the well-to-do expats work. He earns around three hundred dollars per month, has a family waiting for him at home, and has probably also had a long and tiring day—or has a long night shift ahead of him. So, who are we to cast judgment on his behavior? When are Western values unhelpful or even damaging, if they are in danger of closing our eyes to other "truths"?

At the end of the 1990s, the political scientist Samuel Huntington criticized the concept of "superior" Western democratic values being pushed to the fore, as if the associated economic growth gave these values a natural right to be preeminent and forecast a "Clash of Civilizations" in a book carrying the same name. A lot of what

Huntington writes turns out to have been prophetic and, in a world characterized by disruptive developments and fear, we are inevitably faced with questions about what our core values are and where we draw our "red lines."[84]

Even if you don't intend to travel as far away from home as our examples above involved, you would be well advised to be cautious and not assume unquestioningly that other, closer neighbors share a similar understanding of certain values. Christoph Barmeyer and Eric Davoine use "empowerment" to frame this point. Originally an American concept, in Britain and Germany it is perceived to be comparable to "self-responsibility," but in France, with its more hierarchical leadership culture, the idea just doesn't work. The two authors therefore have doubts about the widespread strategy of multinational corporations to seek integration by transposing common values from headquarters onto their overseas subsidiaries. Corporate values that have no connection to accepted local values have little impact and are, more often than not, simply misunderstood. What do the experts advise? Involve the overseas subsidiaries in the process of defining values, rather than prescribing them from a far-distant, ethnocentric viewpoint, and allow them space for national interpretation and variations—just like the Incas handled questions about religion five hundred years ago.[85]

And one final observation: The closer you look, the more variations in values you will find. There are values that are compulsory for all members of a certain culture, some that count as core values for particular states or regions, some that are specific to an organization, and finally the very specific construct of values for each individual. It is certainly helpful if you are clear and confident about your own personal values and act in accordance with them. A challenging but nevertheless illuminating exercise is, during a quiet moment, to draw up a list of all those values you consider important and then, in a second step, to reduce them down to the three or four that are absolutely indispensable for you. If you are honest with yourself, you will end up with a valuable and helpful aid to decision-making in difficult situations, whether at home or abroad.

Conflicting Values: Career or Family?

In the course of his career in a large international company, Paul Williams was twice offered new and attractive overseas postings, with the chance to head up the firm's subsidiary in Greece and then, shortly afterward, the Netherlands. Paul declined both offers for family reasons, despite significant pressure from senior executives to accept the opportunities. In the short term, this was difficult and painful for him, but in the long term it earned him the respect of many of his colleagues and superiors. The senior managers who had made the original offers, and had made it clear to him that they wanted him to go, were the very same who, at a later date, made sure he received other attractive development opportunities in the company which did not involve an international transfer. This was a good example of fair play and perhaps, as well, a degree of recognition for steadfastness when it came to adhering to personal values.

In summary, your own core values serve as the ultimate anchor in a fast-moving, diverse, and unpredictable (business) world. Where can you compromise, or at least come to terms with something and where, most definitely, can you not? No one else can make this decision for you.

Here is a cross-check on your personal values and those of the company or organization where you work.

A Stress Test for Your Values—and Those of Your Company

It starts with me. Or is that actually where it stops? It's hard to imagine being motivated, satisfied, and feeling good about yourself when your personal values are not closely aligned and compatible with the values of your company. If there is not a big overlap between the two, then at least one of these lists of values can only be "just pretending." The question then is, which one?

Your Personal Values Checklist

1. You are clear about what you stand for as an individual, what your values are, and what you base your decisions on. ☐

2. You know what your company stands for. The values of your company are largely in tune with your own values. ☐

3. These values are lived out to the full every day, by you and your company, including top management. ☐

4. You are able to apply these values (yours and those of the company) in everyday leadership situations (1:1, 1:10, 1:10,000, see Chapter 3) with conviction and credibility, and on a sustainable basis (consistently and continuously). ☐

5. If you cannot answer point 4 with an unequivocal "yes," then you are prepared (and it is realistic) to work at narrowing the gap between the stated values and daily practice. ☐

6. If this gap cannot be narrowed, then you are ready to face the consequences and either leave the company or pay the price demanded by compromise. ☐

Company/Organization Values Checklist

1. If you asked one of your employees what the values of the company/
   organization are, they would be able to name them. ☐

2. You take care to ensure that new hires share the values of the company. ☐

3. Apparent or perceived disregard of values or value conflicts are openly
   addressed in the course of everyday work. ☐

4. Serious breaches of values bring serious consequences for those
   concerned—at all levels of the organization! ☐

5. Investments, business partners, and customers are compatible with the
   company's values. ☐

6. Compliance is not just reduced to questions of legal liability but is
   viewed and accepted as a consensus concerning right and proper
   behavior. ☐

7. Managers assigned to international positions outside their respective
   native cultures are thoroughly and professionally prepared for potential
   values conflicts. ☐

INCA INSIGHTS

- Clear values, purposefully put into practice, make you stronger, not weaker.

- Anyone who considers themselves above the law is paving the way for their own and their company's downfall.

- Setting a good example may be seen by some as old-fashioned, but it remains important now and will continue to be important in the future.

"I was flabbergasted by two CEOs who had both left their old firms under difficult circumstances. In their respective new firms, they went on to develop a competing product, motivated solely by the desire to gain revenge on their old companies. And to make it worse, their 'I'll show them' attitude involved huge additional investments and the new products were only partly on strategy!"

—SENIOR EXECUTIVE (KNOWN TO US)

5 Tackling the Real Opponent

(or Are You Taking Your Eye off the Ball?)

Anyone who is under the impression that they're invincible will generally make the wrong decisions and speed up their own downfall as a result. The risk of failure is particularly high when the rules of the game are in flux, or during a period of "disruption" as we would call it today, and there is hardly a more poignant example of this than the fate of the Incas. On November 16, 1532, in the mountains near Cajamarca, two worlds collided as the Spanish conquistador Francisco Pizzaro, with just 180 soldiers and twenty-seven horsemen under his command, engaged the numerically vastly superior Inca army. Historians estimate the Incas had around twelve thousand men under arms and yet, apparently against all odds, the Spanish emerged victorious from the battle. A dynasty which over a few decades had built up a huge empire was shaken to its core by a handful of mercenaries and adventurers, with the story of the Incas' dramatic defeat at Cajamarca continuing to fascinate us to this day.

But that is only a small part of the tale. The ruling Inca Atahualpa's belief in his own invincibility was one of the main causes of his downfall, and this belief was so strong that the Incas approached the Spaniards completely unarmed. The Inca king had been convinced that the foreigners would be in awe of his divine appearance. He was handed a Bible, was at a loss to know what it was, and threw it to the ground, at which point the Spaniards opened fire. Atahualpa was taken prisoner and, just one year later, executed. Even after this devastating battle, a comeback might have been possible if the Incas had not been weakened by a bloody family feud. Since 1527, Atahualpa and his half-brother Huáscar had been battling for control of the empire, which their father Huayna Cápac had divided between them. The result was a civil war that split the empire down the middle, left countless dead, and created fertile ground for uprisings. Many local groups joined forces with the Spanish, hoping to shake off Inca rule, and the Spanish were quick to exploit this. To top it all off, diseases such as smallpox, flu, and measles, introduced by the Europeans, wiped out thousands of the natives and accelerated their decline.[86] To this day, there is a lake in Peru named *Yaguar Cocha* or Blood Lake, which serves as a gruesome reminder of one of the many battles that took place in the closing days of the empire.

The Inca king Atahualpa was convinced the newcomers would play according to his rules, a mistake which reminds us of the CEO of a large corporation, who listened to a start-up founder give a convincing presentation on his business concept before patronizingly wishing the young entrepreneur "Good luck!" The youngster thought for a moment, looked up, and calmly replied, "You too!" Seldom has a senior executive looked so surprised and taken aback.

In the history of business, there are countless examples of companies running into difficulty by becoming overconfident and spoiled by their own success. We looked at the story of Nokia in our introduction and have also highlighted other examples. When things get tough, a business needs to concentrate all its energy on remaining relevant in the market. It is even more disastrous if, at just this moment, a business becomes distracted by internal power struggles and side battles instead of facing up to the competition. If the Incas had stood up to the Spanish with the same determination they had shown when conquering the neighboring peoples and cultures decades earlier, we would probably have to rewrite the history of Latin America. There are many reasons why the Incas didn't counter the European invaders more forcefully: shock at seeing their divine leader taken prisoner with the wave of a hand, unfamiliar weapons such as cannons and guns, strange, frightening animals in the shape of horses and bloodhounds,[87] and, equally importantly, the challenge of being confronted with a completely different culture for the first time in their hitherto relatively isolated world. By comparison, the operating environment for our present-day business battles—or perhaps we should use the word competition here—is considerably friendlier.

Maybe that is the reason why, in such circumstances, we are sometimes too relaxed, too self-assured. How inflexible are we, how inward-looking are we, in many organizations? How often do we allow ourselves to be distracted, instead of focusing on the important questions and the real "enemy"? And, above all, why is all of this able to happen and how can we avoid it?

When Alphas Collide

What would you say is the "must-have" skill for someone who wants to get to the top in a large business, in a start-up, in public administration, in politics, or in an NGO? Intelligence? Creativity? Good communication? Are you shaking your head already? You should be. All of these are important skills, of course, but they count for nothing if you lack the magic ingredient: assertiveness. Nobody is swept to the top on a wave of warm sentiment and good will. You must stand out from your rivals, show determination, and, every now and then, elbow your way forward. You can't afford to lose sleep at night worrying about an unsuccessful rival who, at that very moment, might be drinking away his sorrows in the bar next door. If career success is about selection of the "fittest"—at least as far as assertiveness and resilience are concerned—then, sooner or later, the alpha personalities are going to clash in the corporate executive suites. They are the power-hungry movers and shakers, living and breathing their interpretation of success, for whom winning at virtually any cost is the ultimate motivation. This potentially explosive mixture helps explain many a conflict and their sometimes unbelievably trivial causes. Here, one of our interviewees recalls a striking example.

From Dr. Iris Löw-Friederich, Executive Vice President and Chief Medical Officer, UCB:

> In one of my earlier roles, the business was carrying out research into a fairly common disease. In the United States, big galas are routinely organized in such cases to raise donations. We were working in partnership with another company and, at this particular event, the CEOs of both companies sat at the same table. The president of a patient organization said a few words of thanks to open the event, but, at the beginning of her short speech, she named the "wrong" CEO first—at least according to some of our board members— namely, the CEO of the partner company. This ruined not only the rest of the evening, but also future business cooperation. From that moment onward, it just didn't work at a personal level anymore and all because of a few seemingly harmless welcoming words, which succeeded in rubbing two overinflated egos the wrong way. It was a huge storm in a tiny teacup.

If you think that is rather ridiculous, try parking your car once or twice "by mistake" in the CEO's parking space and see what happens. Steve Jobs is supposed to have fired a manager on the spot because he dared to add something to what Jobs had scribbled on a flipchart. And we know of a very experienced secretary who almost lost her job because she served her new boss his morning yogurt in its plastic container, rather than putting it in a glass bowl.

Such incidents demonstrate that many of the characteristics which are useful as you climb up the slippery pole, such as heightened self-confidence and a thick skin, can at some point become destructive. In his highly respected book, physician and psychotherapist Gerhard Dammann focuses his attention on the "narcissists, egomaniacs, and psychopaths in the executive suite." Dammann identifies some of the narcissistic characteristics that have a positive impact on career progression:

o Exaggerated sense of self-worth
o Tendency to overestimate yourself
o Addictive work behavior
o Ability to guide, influence, or manipulate others
o Cold-heartedness, lack of empathy
o Willingness to take risks[88]

Pathological narcissism is but one small step away, which for Dammann is characterized by, for example, feeling that you are "somebody special" without having actually done anything particularly special, constantly fantasizing about success and power, and scheming on ways to exploit personal relationships.[89] Where is the boundary between "high confidence" and an exaggerated belief in your own greatness? And how far does this boundary move after a series of successes? When "healthy" narcissism crosses over into something more extreme, failure is perceived as personal failure, screaming out for revenge. The result can sometimes be questionable investments, often into the millions of dollars, as we saw in the quote at the beginning of this chapter. Or it can come to haunt us when someone with this disposition gets into a position of power.

Office Madness: Tear Down this Wall!

In a well-known publishing house, the two joint managing directors were at such loggerheads that they literally sealed themselves off from one another. They avoided all contact and only met at the monthly management meeting, with all other communication between them being conducted via other employees. Then, they took things to the extreme and built a wall in the corridor between their respective offices! Access was only from the floor below, and even the shared roof terrace had to be divided. Their two assistants also allowed themselves to be sucked into the feud between their bosses and pursued their own internal war of attrition.

After a while, a real demarcation line had become established at the heart of the business, as well as in the minds of all the employees. We personally know the new managing director who was eventually brought in to succeed the two, and he told us what his first major action was in the new job: to tear down the wall!

Perhaps you were shaking your head in disbelief as you read about the two power-crazed Inca brothers prepared to provoke a civil war and risk an entire empire to satisfy their own personal and uncontrolled ambitions? That's understandable, and it's easy to fall into the trap of thinking that such behavior is a thing of the past—until hearing of current examples like the one above, at which point it becomes clear that our basic psychological makeup is pretty much the same as it was five hundred years ago. Conflicts at the upper levels of an organization are almost inevitable, because this is where the ambitious and aggressive leaders are gathered. Whether these conflicts turn out to be generally constructive, in the interest of the business, or destructive, where potentially negative impact on the company is simply ignored, depends largely on whether the right people have been promoted. Or, instead, those personalities whose thirst for power overwhelms all other considerations have found their way to the top.

The second category is the same group of highly ambitious people with no values that Jack Welch was referring to in his matrix (see Chapter

2, "Talent before Seniority"). Even if such reckless characters enjoy initial success, the end can never justify the means, and it should only be a matter of time until some kind of change of direction and corrective action concerning such behavior follows. Sadly, though, this often doesn't happen and nobody—or at least, nobody with the necessary authority—takes a stand against the unacceptable practices of the manager or managers in question. There have been far too many examples recently where boards have either intervened far too late in the process or, worse still, haven't intervened at all.

When Patriarchs Are Blind to the Future

Ninety-five percent of businesses in Germany are family-owned; we mentioned their importance in Chapter 2 and will go into more detail in Chapter 6. This type of company remains the backbone of the German economy, and some of these firms have a global presence. And they are often run by archetypal patriarchs. Once such example is Oetker. Before he died in 2007, Rudolf-August Oetker decreed that his eight children, from three marriages, should lead the family-owned business in "harmony and unity." It is entirely possible that Huayna Cápac said something similar to the two sons he had chosen as his successors. In the case of Oetker—one of the largest family-run consumer products businesses worldwide, with brands such as Ellios, Virtuoso, and Wilton in the United States, and more than thirteen billion dollars of annual revenue—simply the number of children involved multiplied the risk of conflict. Indeed, subsequent battles between the family heirs have captured the attention of the press and continue to fascinate, with some observers even speculating about the business conglomerate being broken up.[90]

"Companies run by siblings harbor the greatest risk for disputes and this risk is increased still further when the children are from multiple marriages," says Peter May, an expert in family businesses.

He attributes this to the antagonism of the older children toward the children of the woman who displaced their own mother.[91] And in another respect, the story of the Oetkers is typical. Almost two-thirds of family businesses fail between the third and fourth generations. By failure, we mean that either the family no longer runs the business itself, the business has been sold or partially sold, or the business no longer exists due to financial failure.[92] In the case of the Oetkers, the battle is now raging in the third generation, above all between August Oetker, chairman of the advisory board, and his youngest brother, Carl Friedrich Oetker. The list of examples where internal family feuds seriously damage or have already damaged businesses is almost endless, whether brother vs. brother, father vs. son, mother vs. daughter, uncle vs. nephew, brother vs. sister-in-law, or any other of the multitude of possible combinations.

Conflicts within and between different wings of a family often smolder for a long time before breaking out into the open. The causes are almost always the same. Typically, there is a patriarch who heads the business successfully for many years, but then delays his departure for too long. The firm is his life, and stepping down is a difficult choice to make. The succession has not been properly planned or thought through, so conflict is inevitable, and this behavior is in some respects understandable; nobody likes to face up to their own mortality. The problem is, the consequences can be extremely serious, with the well-being of a large business with thousands of employees at stake.

In addition, where there is a dominant patriarch, you rarely find a strong and autonomous management team. The urge to control everything and the fear that someone from outside the family could get things wrong is simply too great. This can work well for quite some time, but experience and a look at the history books teaches us that the success rarely, if ever, endures. Resilience turns into obstinacy, lack of foresight into existential threat, and continuity into inflexibility. So often, where leadership rests with one person over an extended period of time, important topics like the future development of the business, including necessary transformation and change, are neglected. And if, on top of all that, the next generation is tied up with internal disputes, then many organizations struggle to recover from such turbulent episodes. Throw in a portion of envy over the way the family inheritance is divided up, plus the absence of any well-structured mechanisms for dealing with disputes, and the fate of the business is sealed. Stable sales revenue and impressive business results are important, but they are only part of the overall puzzle in a volatile, complex, and fast-moving business world, and they have the unfortunate effect of lulling many family businesses into a false sense of security—just like Atahualpa at Cajamarca, who placed too much trust in what he believed to be the unquestionable superiority of his armed forces.

What is the solution? There are some obvious precautionary measures: timely succession planning (once the incumbent boss has reached fifty, then it is high time), a robust framework and accompanying processes for dealing with disputes (where differences are resolved rather than being left to fester), and willingness to involve external advisers, experts, coaches, and mediators if not enough progress is being made. In other words, making straightforward, practical preparations rather than pressing ahead blindly, engrossed only in the daily routine and the supposed immortality of the boss.

The most difficult call of all to make is picking the moment when the behavior of the patriarch or long-serving manager is no longer good for the future of the business. Later on, the question often arises: Were there warning signs that could have been seen and, if yes, when should they have been spotted? Unfortunately, there is no simple answer to this question, as it often only becomes clear after the event that something was actually going wrong. What can be helpful is the awareness that current success is a welcome but also fickle and untrustworthy companion and to not allow yourself to be dazzled by this success. While the truism "there is no long-term without short-term" is powerful, a series of short-term successes is no guarantee of longer-term survival. It is a very strong and very human temptation not to investigate things too closely when times are good, and most of us have experienced such a period at some point in our careers. If "the numbers are right," the pressure is generally lower, and recommendations and investment proposals are met with speedier, sometimes too speedy, approval; this applies at all levels of an organization. Who would have considered criticizing the leadership at Deutsche Bank while investment banking was generating billions in profits, or Enron's top management after *Fortune* magazine had just named it "America's most innovative company" for the sixth time in a row?

A confident patriarch, or for that matter a confident manager, should encourage dialogue and discussion, not stifle it. Both should surround themselves with people who are able to maintain a healthy distance from both the person and the problems and encourage these people to voice their feedback in a constructive and critical manner. This also applies to the relationship between management and board, between CEO and chairman and, if the position at the top is held by one person (e.g. in one-tier boards), then the corrective factor must be exercised by a third party. If the CEO and chairman get on well, operate on the same wavelength, and share similar values, then that can be of great benefit to the business. But at the same time, it presents a significant risk. After all, who is going to contradict the two most senior decision-makers in the business if they tend to agree on most things anyway? All the better, then, if there is a genuine commitment to listening to the unconventional thinkers, the contrarians, and the mavericks in your own organization! You can read more about how to create a culture of constructive criticism in Chapter 8 ("Ego beats Reality").

When the Problem Is in the System

As far as we are concerned, the real "enemy" for a business is its competition. Not everyone will be happy with using the word enemy here, but whether we say market player, market rival, business opponent, or just plain old competitor, it is all about being better, faster, and more successful than the rest, about winning and securing market share and creating long-lasting, sustainable value for customers. Any activity that doesn't directly help a business meet these objectives in the short to medium term and prevents it from consistently keeping its customers happy is nothing more than a sideshow. Classic examples of such distractions are the all-too-familiar departmental rivalries, with marketing vs. sales, sales vs. R&D, HQ vs. branch office or subsidiary, etc. Of course, there are some entirely understandable internal conflicts regarding functions that are an innate part of their differing responsibilities and shouldn't just be dismissed. R&D usually wants more time for further testing while, for equally good reasons, sales wants the product now. What is key, however, is whether the business culture encourages or hinders open communication and transparent solutions for internal conflicts, or leaves the field open to those who are most skilled in the art of office politics or those with the best connections to the people at the top. The very worst examples are those that follow the maxim "Divide and conquer," based on the mistaken assumption that internal competition is good for business. In the long term, these cultures allow precisely the wrong people to blossom: those with ambition and no values. Anyone with good options outside the company will probably leave—anyone who feels he has to stay keeps his head down, his nose clean, and never lives up to his full potential. Fear has never been a good basis for guidance and motivation.

A useful gauge of an organization's culture is to observe who is rising through the ranks and building a career there, and who isn't. What kind of behavior is actually rewarded? Is it smooth-talking flexibility or responsibly-minded clarity, overbearing dominance or appreciative dialogue, superficial busyness or a genuine focus on delivering results? Which unwritten rules and incentives really seem to matter?

Apart from the setting of undesirable examples by a culture of behaviors which actually go against the long-term interests of the company, the very structure of organizations can also be a fertile breeding ground for distractions and diversions. Large organizations are particularly adept at creating departments whose main "contribution" would appear to be toward operating costs and whose chief objective is to ensure their own continued survival.

When Departments Spring Up Like Flowers in the Rain

I (Andreas Krebs) had just taken up a position on the board of a company and was astonished when a colleague told me that his strategy paper was finished "in principle"; it just needed to pass through the Strategic Evaluation department. I had never heard of this department, but obviously someone had thought it a good idea to have important concepts reviewed by a third party which, at least on the surface, seemed fairly reasonable to me too. But what had started as a three-strong team of internal consultants had, meanwhile, grown into a 120-employee department where just about everything and anything was diligently analyzed and examined.

In a similar case, there was a sixty-strong internal SAP (systems, applications, and products) department, which programmed bespoke applications for different divisions in the company. This department had also, once upon a time, started small. But after word had spread that you could have standard software optimized to your own requirements, the department was swamped by inquiries and grew and grew. It all came to an abrupt halt when such "important and urgently required" enhancements had to be financed out of the respective departmental budgets, rather than from a central budget, as had been the case before.

Some readers are no doubt also well versed in "working" the system of cost allocation keys and drawing on other cost centers. There are more companies than you might think where 20 percent or more of costs are shunted around between different divisions and departments via such keys. What an enormous additional layer of bureaucracy—and interestingly, the masters of this dark art somehow seem to end up running the most "efficient" departments! I hesitate to commit these thoughts to paper but, as a young manager, I wasn't all that bad at playing this little game myself...

To put it bluntly, if it's available, it'll be used. Things haven't changed since the fifties, when Cyril Northcote Parkinson came up with his famous law: "Work expands so as to fill the time available for its completion." This is especially the case, at least for some, if it has the pleasant side effect of shifting some of the responsibility onto other shoulders. After all, if the "Strategic Evaluation" department has done its characteristically thorough analysis and subsequently waved through a concept paper, then the original author can start to relax, since any errors in the document are now no longer only their responsibility.

Staff and support functions are particularly prone to what might be called misguided expansion, triggered by the line functions around them. Many of the people in areas such as legal and IT, business planning or finance, market research and so forth, do excellent work and these functions are important to the effective running of most large businesses. What's not good is if the line functions make poorly considered demands on them just because they are there. For example, a product manager asks for a six-figure budget for market research, so that they can "better understand" the target group for their product. Instead of this, we would recommend that every product manager go out and about for a few days with a couple of their colleagues in sales, which will often make any formal market research unnecessary, or at least a lot cheaper.

Here is another example we've experienced. The new CEO of a Eurostoxx 50 company hires two financial controllers to report directly to him. Shortly afterward, the SVP for marketing and sales says he needs a controller as well, as he's also got "quite a lot of numbers" to deal with. The other VPs don't waste any time before arguing that they, too, need similar support. Before you know it, more than half a dozen financial controllers have appeared, all of them busy working on analyses for which they need detailed figures, which of course have to be generated by other colleagues, which costs them time and energy and distracts them from their core responsibilities. The additional documents and files generated are then sent back and forth, to be analyzed and commented on, creating a whole new wave of "work" and, before long, all the financial controllers urgently need assistants. (Cyril Parkinson would have been thrilled and amused by it all.) And then Human Resources needs to be consulted as to whether all these financial controllers should report directly to the senior financial controller or rather to the relevant functional vice president, or both, and whether this is shown by a dashed or a solid line (for the functional and/or the disciplinary reporting line on the organizational chart), and so on. The firm's competitors can only delight in this orgy of introspection and distraction!

In addition to the burgeoning of various departments, it is classic bureaucracy, which acts as a huge drag on business processes, costs time and money, and distracts from more important matters. It can lead to the most absurd situations, such as when every stationery order needs to be approved by seven different people. Under these circumstances, the ordering of a single pencil can cost the business ninety euros, according to the calculations of one consultant.[93] "Though this be madness, yet there is method in it," to quote Shakespeare. And even if the word "bureaucracy" has nowadays become almost a term of abuse, the original concept of a logical, rules-based, and transparent regulation of procedures[94] is still fundamentally right. The approach only becomes counterproductive if petty rules stand in the way of accountability and senseless regulations take up an unnecessary amount of time. A bureaucracy stands or falls on the quality of the rules on which it is based. The more rules, the more bureaucracy, and the longer someone has been working in such a bureaucracy, the less likely it is that this occurs to them. There are apparently some businesses where it costs as much again to check travel expenses as the travel expenses themselves. And a system based on excessive regulation is a sign of a business culture based on mistrust. The purchase of a new laptop may well justify several signatures, but is this really necessary for office materials with a value of a few dollars or euros?

In addition, there is a fatal link between excessive bureaucracy and a diminishing sense of responsibility. If there are rules for everything, then it makes life so much simpler to just stop thinking for yourself. Should problems arise from this self-generated erosion in personal responsibility, then a bureaucratic system reacts in the only way it knows and understands—with more rules. A downward spiral ensues and the business slides toward complete paralysis and is further distracted from the really important tasks. By contrast, a business culture based on trust makes micromanagement superfluous and broadens the scope of individual accountability. In a nutshell, if you want personal responsibility, you must allow independent action, and that requires trust. The same applies, by the way, to business headquarters that subject their branches or subsidiaries to more questions and controls than can possibly be good for the success of the business. Of course, there is always the occasional bad apple who abuses trust, but then these kinds of people have never paid much attention to rules anyway, so why hold back ninety-nine colleagues just because one might abuse the freedom granted?

A lot of organizations still spend months on "top-down/bottom-up" budget planning. It sometimes starts as early as April or May with broad guidance from top management, after which each of the country organizations and the central departments begin planning all their costs from scratch, although a simple extrapolation would normally suffice. This is then presented, discussed, negotiated, aggregated, and finally aligned and coordinated in regional meetings, middle management meetings, senior management meetings, and head office meetings, all with the sole purpose of making sure the numbers have been properly massaged before being presented at top management meetings. And then, in the middle of the process, top management intervenes with some additional top-down guidance (things have moved on in the meantime!) and it starts all over again, by which time it's October! But it doesn't have to be like this. The managing partner of a large European private equity company explained to us the difference between the corporate approach described above and their approach to this process: "For us, it's not about overly precise planning and then achieving the results of a monumental budget process. As long as the planned results match up with or exceed the guidance generated by our investment case, then we're happy. As soon as we are convinced of the company's strategy, the scaling possibilities, and the overall ability of its management to deliver, our motto is pretty straightforward: 'Be fairly right on strategy, but *execute* like hell!' "

A further organizational problem arises with a lack of robust governance, including poorly defined roles, responsibilities, and decision-making authority. Clear responsibilities provide the framework within which personal responsibility can flourish. Where there are no formal structures, informal ones develop, and wherever the source of decision-making power is not formally determined, an informal pecking order emerges sooner or later. Both situations are an ideal breeding ground for conflict and loss of productivity, with people concentrating on jostling for position rather than advancing the common good of the organization. It is easy to imagine this happening in firms, and most of us have probably witnessed this in our own company at some time or other: power battles, which consume huge amounts of energy, add no value at all, hamper the business, and strengthen the competition. But what about NGOs, charities, or other non-profit organizations? Unfortunately, here too, the scramble for power and status is an everyday occurrence according to some of our interviewees, almost as if doing something for a "good cause" grants a kind of moral absolution as far as questionable behavior is concerned.

All this reinforces the case that hierarchies, guidelines, and responsibilities should be clearly defined in order to make power battles, as far as is possible, unnecessary. This also explains the problem with matrix organizations, which not only require a high level of coordination but can also encourage inter-departmental disputes. Furthermore, they often favor those less-than-productive "corporate residents" who have found a nice little niche for themselves somewhere, know how to keep their heads down, and are experts at appearing extremely busy when additional work threatens.

How to Get a Six-Year Paid Holiday

It was the BBC which first broke the story in spring 2016, and there was hardly a newspaper which didn't pick up on it. A Spanish civil servant, who was meant to be supervising the construction of a sewage works, failed to turn up for work for six years without anyone noticing. Only when Joaquim G. was due to receive an award for "twenty years of loyal service" did it emerge that he only "occasionally" popped into the office. He spent most of his time at home reading books on philosophy. Diogenes would have been impressed! How could this happen? Very simple: poorly defined responsibilities. The water company assumed that Joaquim G. worked for the local authority, and the local authority assumed that he worked for the water company.[95]

Don't Underestimate the Power of Underestimation![96]

Anyone who is involved with the really major challenges faced by an organization cannot avoid the topic of risk management and, in particular, risk prevention. A lot of very good books have been written about the subject, yet it is often neglected. It seldom enjoys the detailed attention of senior management it requires, being dealt with just once or twice a year by the Tax & Audit Committee, and it is equally unusual to see it handled systematically and professionally in a company. Sure, it isn't much fun spending large amounts of time working through doomsday scenarios, but the reality is that risks are lurking everywhere. A large number of businesses have failed precisely because they paid too little attention to what preventative measures could be implemented, given their risk profile. They were not prepared when a possible risk became reality and had failed to conduct multiple scenario analyses, meaning not only scenarios involving the competition and the market, but also those looking at new regulations, natural disasters, cyberattacks and acts of sabotage.

Risk management is an elementary component of good business management, and it isn't enough just to work through a checklist of terms such as risk avoidance, risk reduction, risk aggregation, risk analysis, risk monitoring, etc. It starts much earlier, with risk awareness and the associated psychology of risk. The specialists who are allocated responsibility for risk management are often top-quality, rationally thinking individuals, which is, of course, fundamentally a good thing. The disadvantage is that soft factors and intangible risks are frequently neglected, simply because they are more difficult to identify and describe and are particularly difficult to quantify.

On top of this, we, as human beings, have a strong inclination to want to believe that we are actually doing everything, or nearly everything, right. The strategy is in place, implementation is in full swing, mistakes are being corrected as they arise. And we know our competition well enough too. In the course of our conversations, for example, it became apparent that many of us have not fully grasped or tend to underestimate the issue of innovation risk. We are proud of our products and our customer base, and it is hard for us to imagine that everything could suddenly be turned on its head, as was the case for Nokia. And innovation risk is not always a matter of a creeping threat, arising gradually from a product range ageing and becoming, almost invisibly, less competitive as each day passes. For Nokia, Apple was like a bolt out of the blue.

Not that long ago, the term "black swan" was used to describe a highly improbable event that nevertheless came to pass. More recently, the "VUCA" world (volatility, uncertainty, complexity, and ambiguity) has become a model to describe the current macro operating environment. Economics professor Klaus Schweinsberg recently extended the VUCA concept still further: "Today, this formula is too simple to describe the current framework and conditions. We are now dealing with a second set of dimensions, which further potentiate the already existing volatility, uncertainty, complexity, and ambiguity, and these are virtuality, infinity, cyber and artificial intelligence, VUCA 4.0 so to speak. This scenario poses enormous challenges for the economy as a whole, and in particular for small and medium-sized enterprises."[97] And we have not even touched upon completely unpredictable factors such as criminal activity from employees, customers, and business partners, political developments which can endanger the organization, or even natural disasters. It doesn't matter whether you work in a small or large organization, it is vital to be permanently alert to the warning signals. If you don't do this yourself, make sure there is someone else in your organization who is "thinking the unthinkable" and looking out for the changes going on around you, both the big "mega" trends as well as the smaller, slowly accumulating changes that often only become obvious once it is too late to change course.

Nik Gowing and Chris Langdon, in their excellent book *Thinking the Unthinkable*, state as one of their main findings the following: "The conformity which gets leaders to the top disqualifies most of them from gripping the scale of disruption and knowing what to do about it."[98] And they also coin the term "thinking the unpalatable," which they describe as "something that is known about, but too risky or dangerous or unattractive to think about or engage with."[99]

On that note, here is a practical question that you can ask yourself right now. Is it conceivable that just one employee or a small team of employees could bring your organization to its knees or even destroy it? Now that is undoubtedly an unpalatable thought, but it would be an illusion to think that isn't possible. A typical and very realistic example of such an individual could be the head of IT, for instance. In many family-owned businesses and community-based organizations, this person is the only one who knows the software and its inner workings. They may have even programmed much of the software themselves, and, if they suddenly disappear for whatever reason, then you have a real disaster. The same goes for people with key, critical business know-how who, without warning, are no longer there, move to the competition, or, even worse, start working outside the law. Unpalatable? Yes. But highly unlikely, surely. Presumably, that is also what the gentlemen at Barings Bank thought before their Singapore-based colleague, Nick Leeson, made a loss of $1.4 billion by speculating on risky interest rates and index derivatives. After two hundred years of successful trading, the bank was brought to its knees and eventually sold to ING for a symbolic one euro. So yes, these things, unfortunately, do happen.

These sorts of risks are by no means the exception. A good friend of ours, a supervisory board member of a large family-owned business, established early on in his new role that just one administrator in the finance department and his direct supervisor had complete access to the firm's six-hundred-million-euro cash reserves, thanks to a wide-ranging bank mandate. A potential "Nick Leeson 2.0!" Or take the example of the US-based Target retail group, which opted for a low-cost software supplier whose defective security software subsequently enabled a spectacularly successful cyberattack. More than a hundred million credit card and customer details, PINs, security codes, addresses, and more were stolen from Target. The Chief Information Officer was first to go, followed by CEO Gregg Steinhafel, and then many more senior executives.

And another anecdote to finish with. Paul Williams, then a young country manager and just a year and a half into his assignment in New Zealand, can still remember being asked by an experienced colleague whether he now had everything under control. Paul thought for a moment, smiled back confidently, and answered "Yes, I think I've got everything under control now. Nothing can go wrong!" Three days on and one metaphorical beat of a butterfly's wing later, chaos broke out. The authorities, quite unexpectedly, introduced new regulations with immediate and highly adverse consequences for Paul's division. He swore, on the spot, that he would never again say that he had "everything under control."

The Focused Organization

How much of your work time is really productive, by which we mean genuinely useful for the business? Ask this question at various levels throughout the organization and, assuming your company culture allows honest replies, you may be shocked by some of the answers. Or perhaps you won't be! Either way, almost all of those questioned will complain about endless meetings, bureaucratic processes, reports, and minutes of meetings which nobody reads, poor communication, floods of emails and "cc: madness," superfluous time-wasting activities, etc., etc., etc. In short, everyone will complain about a phenomenon that they themselves are instrumental in creating. That is the nature of complexity. The bigger a business is, the greater the need for coordination and alignment, the more complex the processes, the longer the decision paths, and the more rules and regulations spring up. And typically, as time goes on, new business units and acquired companies need to be integrated, and more and more products need to be managed. It is a bit like a house where a new room is added each year, every year. Eventually, you find yourself in a Byzantine labyrinth. And anyone who's been there long enough starts to think this maze is "normal."

Complexity Gone Mad: When Three Countries Check One Invoice

Large, publicly traded companies, including many who boast proudly about their values-driven management philosophies, are frequently unable to complete one simple administrative procedure: paying their bills on time. We often have to wait sixty, sometimes seventy, and occasionally up to one hundred days for payment. One of our "favorite" phone calls on this topic went something like this. The CEO's secretary, sympathetic and with a charming desire to be as helpful as possible, got back to us after we had sent yet another reminder (our payment was almost seventy days overdue) with some good news: we're almost there. Our invoice had "already" passed through the first check in their (outsourced) Shared Service Center in Slovenia, it had also been released for payment from another Shared Service Center in Romania, and all that was now missing was the final payment instruction. This would be processed in Hyderabad in India, but this last, vital step could only be a matter of days from now!

We couldn't help asking ourselves whether these types of constructions really save money, especially when you factor in the time taken for follow-up inquiries (by both parties) and misunderstandings.[100] And these same companies also talk about their "fair treatment of customers, suppliers, and other stakeholders" on their websites. Which raises the question, where does "values-based management" stop and "value-based management" begin?

There is a simple question that forces leaders to concentrate on what really matters. Imagine that, tomorrow, you are going to complete a management buyout of your business. What are the first things you would change? Based on our experience, typical change targets are those processes that most of the management team have considered unhelpful or even detrimental to the business for some time; older product lines, which are being sustained more out of tradition than for their commercial value; and the company offices—whether it be the overpriced building in a prime location in Paris or the cramped old production facility that has long since passed its prime. Why don't you try it out for yourself? Just think for a moment about the five most important things that you would immediately change if the company belonged to you. Another approach is to do it like Jeff Bezos at Amazon and look at the company from the outside, taking the customer's perspective and working your way into the organization from there. This sounds so obvious until you look at how many firms do their organizational and process designing in exactly the opposite direction, starting from within and finishing with the customer, who then probably feels like just what he or she is, namely an afterthought.

Ideally, a business should cultivate a culture of personal responsibility and efficiency, supported by a permanent change management process. Do we really need that? How can we do this more simply? What do we do out of habit and not because it drives our business objectives? It is worth making it part of your routine to ask these questions on a regular basis. Here are a couple more. Does X actually (still) contribute to our commercial success? What is really left of a project if you boil down the impressive PowerPoint slides into plain English? And do you penalize somebody for suggesting a commercially sensible downsizing of their own department by promptly downgrading their management level, or do you actually reward them for such altruistic behavior?

An explosion in complexity cannot be brought under control by occasional attempts at process optimization. It needs change to be part of the routine, backed up by a culture of cool-headed efficiency. Give the job to your more junior, and mostly still unspoiled, next-generation leaders, or a group of your high performers. Give them two to three days to work on a new company structure, on a management buyout plan or a cost-efficiency strategy. Arrange a suitable venue for their final presentation, one which reflects the importance you place in their work. Usually, the results are blindingly obvious, so not always easy to swallow for some members of senior management, but often immediately actionable and largely free of ulterior motives. These junior managers usually have little to lose and are perhaps less allergic to thinking about and describing the unpalatable. Or, alternatively, once a year, you can hold a one-day workshop for a small group of key managers to work through a "green field" scenario, where you build the business from scratch, or instigate regular "clear-out days" for all levels of the business. Fredmund Malik describes these days as "systematic rubbish removal" and simultaneously poses an elegant and challenging question: "What do we do today that we would not start doing if we were not already doing it?"[101] The wording of the question is deliberately forward-looking and is designed to discourage discussions focusing on retrospection and self-justification.

A focused business is constantly seeking to meet its goals in the most streamlined and efficient way. Normally, this involves pushing responsibility "down" the organization, reducing the number of decision-making bodies, removing bureaucratic barriers, maybe even slimming down the number of management levels. The more problems that are solved at the point where they arise and where the people are frequently the best qualified to solve them, the better. Think about Pull Leadership, which we wrote about in Chapter 3. A CEO can trigger a real cascade of increased personal responsibility in the business by handing over ambitious projects to the right people in management, who in turn must hand over responsibility to their direct reports. This requires the courage to let go and foster an atmosphere where making mistakes is allowed, which is, unfortunately, just about the opposite of the "safety first" culture which holds sway in many organizations. But it is precisely the working environment that the vast majority of employees, not least the digital natives, are looking for.

A Stress Test for Your Effectiveness

The more a business concentrates on its core tasks and the less it is distracted by internal conflicts, ballooning bureaucracy, and other side issues, the greater the likelihood that it will be able to respond quickly to external threats and sustain long-term commercial success.

Are your eyes on the ball? Let's find out! Yes or No?

1. The business is structured in such a way that at least 70 percent of work time is productive and geared toward meeting your goals. ☐

2. Even if your numbers look good, you regularly reflect on your strategy and its implementation. ☐

3. Courageous proposals for improvements to your organization that are not driven by self-interest are openly rewarded. ☐

4. Responsibilities and decision-making parameters are clearly defined. ☐

5. Risk management is handled professionally and is supported at the highest level. ☐

6. Departmental rivalries and silo thinking are kept in check. ☐

7. There are rules, but no ballooning bureaucracy based on petty and superfluous regulations. Efficiency has overriding importance. ☐

8. Managers with clear character flaws (lack of integrity, power-hungry self-interest) are not tolerated. ☐

9. Power battles within the organization are not tolerated and personal animosities are directly addressed and resolved. ☐

10. Were you to inherit the business tomorrow, you would see no need to take urgent action in core areas (people, product range, core processes, business culture). ☐

INCA INSIGHTS

- What is the greatest threat to your business right now? How much time do you devote to this threat?

- Just because we can't imagine something happening doesn't mean it won't actually happen. So, which "unimaginable" circumstances could pose a danger for you and your organization? How well-prepared are you for this scenario?

"You have to strike the right balance between incorporating the best features of the company being acquired and, at the same time, sticking with your own, clearly defined guiding principles."

—CHRISTINE WOLFF, MULTIPLE BOARD MEMBER

6 A Farsighted M&A Strategy
(or a License to Lose a Fortune?)

Our economic system is based on growth, and the ultimate indicator of success is "more": more turnover, more market share, more profit. Company takeovers and mergers are an integral component of this process and have become part of the routine in this continuous quest for more. And yet, while experts disagree on whether it's "only" half or actually more like two-thirds of mergers and acquisitions that fail,[102] the Incas, hundreds of years ago, managed to expand their "firm" over an extended period of time. If we think of their empire as a multinational business which acquired the knowledge and skills of a large number of regions and peoples, adopted and integrated these successfully and consolidated them into an ever more powerful entity, then it is fair to say that they provide an interesting example and plenty of food for thought for the leaders of today.

What's certain is that the Incas must have been doing plenty of things right five hundred years ago. For instance, despite their overall superiority in a number of fields, they placed great value on the know-how of the peoples they conquered and made full use of this new knowledge. As soon as they had acquired a new territory, they took a close look at how the skilled craftsmen and artisans worked and analyzed the farming methods. Whatever was good or better than the existing methods was used and, according to Nikolai Grube, an expert on pre-Columbian America, the Incas literally soaked up and absorbed the know-how and techniques as they found them.[103] In so doing, they utilized the knowledge of countless earlier cultures, for example the superiority of the Chimú in road-building, the highly developed pottery skills of the Moche and Nazca, the architectural prowess of the Tiwanaku, and the food storage techniques of the Huari.[104] Today, we can look back with amazement at the more than twenty-five thousand miles of roads built in the early Andean state, at the storage silos which reliably supplied food for a widespread empire, and at the monumental stone buildings, which defied earthquakes, in stark contrast to the later Spanish colonial buildings, which often didn't survive. The Incas really did manage to bring together "the best of all worlds."

A talent for strategic thinking also contributed to their success and, wherever possible, the Incas strove for what we, in today's language, would call a "friendly takeover." Before resorting to force, they gave their opponents the opportunity to agree to voluntary integration into their empire. This was underpinned by gifts, demonstration of their own skills and, of course, through openly flaunting their military superiority. If the focus of their interest, the "merger target," cooperated and chose the peaceful route, then there was a great shared celebration. The ruling elite of the acquired people were allowed to continue to exercise their regional power, now as local governors, and were further bound to the Inca nobility through the clever use of arranged marriages. This is how an empire came into being that had strong, centralized authority and, at the same time, allowed many functions to be carried out by regional governments, establishing a successful balance between integration and decentralization that was to remain stable for many years. How often do we manage that today?

At the same time, "Inca HQ" exported its own successful strategies to the regions, sending out soil and irrigation experts and administrators, and in so doing improved living conditions for the ordinary people. These were quick wins which helped to head off rebellions and kept "Inca Inc." at peace. We may condemn their harsh resettlement policy, the strict hierarchy, and the tight regulation of everyday life as dictatorial.[105] But that would be the twenty-first-century view of a culture which, centuries ago, managed to create something which so often eludes us today: taking different cultures, different operating units, and forging them into a sustainable whole, a functional and prosperous organization.

When talk turns to M&A, we tend to think first of the really big deals, the jumbo mergers, where billions of dollars are involved: Daimler/Chrysler, AOL/Time Warner, Bayer/Monsanto, to name but a few. These are the takeover battles that make the headlines and frequently continue to do so for many years thereafter, though not always for the right reasons. It always begins with the euphoric launch of the new enterprise, then, in the cases where it goes wrong, the first signs of crisis appear and finally, a few years later, following the confirmation of billion-dollar losses, the burial rites are read out. But the acquisition and integration of businesses is not just a topic for large corporations. Away from the glare of publicity, similar processes are taking place involving mid-sized companies, and in much greater numbers. Ninety-nine percent of all German businesses are classified as medium-sized, with fewer than five hundred employees and annual revenues of less than fifty million euros.[106] Furthermore, 95 percent of all German companies are family-owned and 85 percent of these are owner-managed. Around 1,300 of these businesses are so-called "Hidden Champions," highly successful world leaders in their respective product niches. By way of comparison, during the same period, there were around 360 such firms in the United States.[107]

The majority of the around forty-eight thousand M&A transactions which were completed globally in 2018 involved small and mid-sized businesses, and the drivers behind these deals varied widely.[108] Some were initiated because there was no successor from within the family, some to help grow and/or internationalize the business and to avoid becoming a takeover target, others to broaden their product portfolio or to take advantage of real or assumed synergies. So, while company mergers are a part of everyday business life, size does appear to matter here, in the sense that large companies can usually weather the fallout if a merger goes badly wrong, but for mid-sized companies, it can then be a question of life and death. Daimler survived Jürgen Schrempp's dalliance with the world of Chrysler, despite the billion-dollar losses that ensued. But whether J. Smith & Co will be able to hold out if its merger with F. Jones Ltd fails is another story altogether. This makes it all the more important to try and establish why mergers fail and to see if the history of the Incas is of any help to us in this regard. What we are interested in doing here is describing general principles that can be helpful for leaders and managers, rather than trying to create a detailed plan which will inevitably vary from case to case.

The Usual Merger Mania—and a Positive Example

At this point, you might expect us to take a closer look at the spectacular failure of one of the more prominent megamergers. However, we would like to take a different approach and highlight the case of a successful merger between two family-owned businesses, the IT consultancy firm Esprit and the management consultancy Agens, to create a powerful and hard-hitting new company called Q-Perior.

From Sailing Trip to Company Merger

It is 2004 and the IT consultants from Esprit are working with a team from Agens for a large client. Agens are specialists in the financial services sector and the two firms are highly complementary. The project is a success. Nevertheless, months after project completion, a dispute breaks out because Agens has poached one of Esprit's leading employees. Once he gets started at his new employer, the "defector" quickly establishes that not only do the two companies have a complementary product offering, but they also have a very similar business culture and general way of working. The ex-Esprit man reports this back to Rüdiger Lang, his former boss, and to the owner of Agens. A sailing trip for the partners of Agens and Esprit is arranged and they discuss the potential mutual benefits of working more closely together.

Fast forward to May 2009, and they have kept in touch after the introductory tour went well. In October 2010, a six-strong team of partners from both businesses are asked to examine in more depth the advantages of a merger. At this point, Agens has 140 employees and Esprit 240. Both firms are successful in their specialist areas and both are concerned that, in the longer term, they will not be able to keep pace with the larger consultancies. After a few weeks, the team of six gives the green light, the other twelve partners in both firms are brought into the picture, and detailed plans and timelines are worked out.

It is only in April 2011 that the senior executives inform all fifty managers at Agens and Esprit about their plans, and only once all of these have been persuaded of the merits of a merger are the employees told of the plans, simultaneously, at the end of May. On July 1, 2011, the Q-Perior business is formally launched with great fanfare at a big party. During the whole merger process, neither customers nor employees are unsettled, and business carries on smoothly as usual. The synergies sought from merging finance, accounting, HR, marketing, and support services are realized without any great delay[109].

Postscript: Q-Perior has continued to grow and now has around 1,100 employees in twelve locations in Europe and North America, with an annual revenue of €195 million.[110]

Looking closely at how these two mid-sized businesses came together, there are several lessons we can learn about how to go about ensuring a successful merger:

o Possible synergies are not simply assumed but are clearly identified, analyzed, and carefully evaluated in advance.

- The businesses are a good fit not just economically but also culturally, so that a new, unified entity can result with its own strong sense of identity.
- There is a genuine meeting of equals and the merger is seen as a shared project. One clear indicator is a new name for the merged business, with both companies agreeing to give up their old names.
- In the early days of the process, nothing is rushed, and senior management gives itself time to build trust between the two leadership teams. There is close personal contact between the respective CEOs and/or managing partners.
- Emotions are taken seriously, such as when the owner of Agens felt taken advantage of—and reacted accordingly—during discussions about the future ownership structure. Further discussion of this topic was adjourned and later renegotiated. The result: "At the end we came up with a fair solution."[111]
- Detailed preparations are made behind the scenes, ahead of the merger, in order to minimize any period of uncertainty for both customers and employees. Following a clandestine "engagement" period of one and a half years, where only a few senior managers are involved, it is then only a matter of a few weeks between all employees being officially informed and the establishment of the new business.
- After the merger, it is not a question of one side subordinating itself to the other; it really is the start of a completely new, common project. For example, new leadership and remuneration structures are introduced, integrating "the best of both worlds."[112]

The two companies were able to navigate their way around some of the typical rocks on which megamergers so often founder: cultural differences are underestimated or ignored, synergies are overestimated or imagined, the true costs in both time and money of a merger are not properly taken into account, and the top performers, unsettled by long transition periods, decide to seek their fortunes elsewhere. After all, it's hardly a state secret that the best talent is usually the first to leave in such circumstances. If we look at the recent history of mega-deals, there is no shortage of examples where all of this has happened, so here is a small selection:

AOL/Time Warner—AOL's takeover of Time Warner in 2000 for a headline price of $182 billion was one of the biggest deals of all time. The hoped-for synergies between "old" and "new" media failed to materialize, however, and in 2009 the merger was reversed, by which point Time Warner's share price had fallen by more than 80 percent. With the bursting of the dot-com bubble, the whole project was, if nothing else, a victim of very unfortunate timing.[113]

Daimler/Chrysler—In 1998, Daimler paid thirty-eight billion dollars to the American Chrysler Group, which, compared to the AOL/Time Warner deal, looked like something of a bargain. In 2007, the two companies went their separate ways again. At the time of the merger, Jürgen Schrempp promised it would be one of the most innovative and profitable companies in the world, but according to McKinsey, during his period as CEO (1995–2005), he destroyed seventy-four billion dollars in value. Over the ten years, that works out to more than twenty million dollars per day! Nowadays, external observers largely agree on why this came about. Mutual distrust between the two management teams was never successfully tackled, which was due in part to the company maintaining for two years the "lie that this was a marriage of equals," before officially acknowledging that it was actually a takeover of Chrysler by Daimler.[114] On top of this, the cultural differences between the two businesses could not be bridged. The culture shock began with a fundamentally different understanding of the product. There are a million miles between the quality- and status-oriented Mercedes dealer and customer and the more pragmatic perception of what a car is in the United States. In addition, senior executives viewed the car industry from completely different perspectives. Compounding all of this, national cultural differences appear to be a blind spot for many business leaders, and a common error is when superficial similarities with their own country's culture leads these managers into making the mistake of thinking they understand the other culture much better than is actually the case.

Another of our interviewees told us about a failed foray into the United States.

From Rüdiger Lentz, Director of the Aspen Institute:

> *I worked for more than thirty years as a journalist, including three years as the Managing Director of "German TV" in the United States. This was a business whose objective was to bring German television (a joint venture between the two national broadcasters ARD and ZDF and the international Deutsche Welle) to the American market. This enterprise was planned as a German business and was thus, from the outset, misconceived. We tried to introduce a national German television channel into a market dominated by local television and radio stations. It was not the first time that I had seen something like this happen, where Germans try to do business in the United States and think as Germans and their reference point is Germany and so they end up completely underestimating the unique character and peculiarities of the market.*

Porsche/Volkswagen—On October 26, 2008, the Porsche boss, Wendelin Wiedeking, made an announcement directly contradicting what had been explicitly stated in a press release from March of the same year. Porsche Automobil Holding intended to increase its shareholding in VW to 75 percent in a de facto takeover of Volkswagen. The company already owned 43 percent of shares but ended up completely overextending itself with the financing of the deal and, all of a sudden, the tables were turned. VW then had to rescue Porsche and took over the sports car manufacturer. Furthermore, Porsche's muddled and murky tactics resulted in public prosecutors launching proceedings against Porsche managers, with billion-dollar lawsuits from institutional investors adding to the misery.[115]

Pfizer/Astra Zeneca—Pharmaceutical companies are constantly under pressure to innovate. Patents for their existing drugs expire and cheaper generics come onto the market, and one of their favored strategies to counter this is to acquire competitors. Over recent years, among others, Viagra manufacturer Pfizer has been featured in the headlines. In 2014, the American company tried to become the world number one by acquiring its British competitor, Astra Zeneca. The management of Astra Zeneca rejected all offers and the hostile takeover attempt failed. AZ was confident of significantly increasing revenue over the coming years without a merger. The business press criticized Pfizer for pursuing a strategy "with a crowbar" and for its "inability to grow organically" (FAZ). American magazine *Forbes* compared the company to one of the most feared marine predators in an article entitled "The Shark That Can't Stop Feeding." But the search for acquisition targets didn't stop there, and, while it is easy to take issue with this approach, from a strategic point of view it made quite a lot of sense, with Pfizer pursuing a hybrid strategy combining internal research with externally acquired revenue and product pipeline. In April 2016, Pfizer's $160 billion offer for Allergan collapsed, even though merger talks were well advanced. The deal was also built around anticipated tax savings, as Allergan had its head office in Ireland and the new, combined firm would also have been based in Ireland. At the proverbial last minute, the US tax authority changed its rules and, in so doing, negated just about all the anticipated tax savings. At this point, questions were raised in the media about how such a deal could collapse solely because hoped-for tax advantages could no longer be realized.[116] That's an understandable point, but undoubtedly oversimplified the situation. To be fair to Pfizer, we assume that they tried hard to realize the deal and, following intensive due diligence, came to the conclusion that the final deal was not as compelling as originally planned and no longer made sense. They chose to walk away at a late stage in the negotiations, which also takes courage, and they have done very well since then.

But, in spite of all of the examples above and the many others not mentioned here but that you may be aware of, this doesn't seem to discourage other businesses from pursuing growth at all costs. Here is a recent example:

Valeant—"From Analysts' Darling to Investors' Nightmare"[117]

The story of Valeant has now become a case study at Harvard Business School. The tale of how a small Canadian generics firm grew to be a pharmaceutical giant at breakneck speed is quickly told and constitutes a lesson in modern capitalism. In 2009, the company had an annual revenue of around five hundred million dollars and was no more than a regional player. Twenty-three takeovers, with acquisition costs of more than thirty billion dollars, later, the company had secured its place among the international big hitters. Its market capitalization rocketed, and everyone watched with amazement as the share price, which until 2009 had traded in a narrow range between twenty and thirty dollars, suddenly shot up to more than $250 in 2015. The media, markets, banks, hedge funds, private equity firms, other stakeholders, almost everyone was delighted! "Financial experts," in particular, applauded the company, but health care insiders could not fathom it. What was their secret? What did Valeant top management know that nobody else did?

These were the questions that Andreas Krebs and Philip Burchard, CEO of Merz, also asked themselves at the leading investor conference for the industry, which takes place in January every year in San Francisco. This was where, in 2013, the head of Valeant, Michael Pearson, addressed more than a thousand CEOs, chairmen, and board members from the pharmaceutical and financial services industries in the largest auditorium available at the congress center and told them how their business worked. He had a simple formula: acquire companies, ideally 100 percent debt-financed, keep R&D expenditure to the absolute minimum, close down administrative functions and anything creating costs, immediately generating cash flow and profit. What about innovation through research and product development? Come on, guys, that's old school!

Innovations need to be bought in from the outside. And everything else is just ballast.

"We were speechless," Andreas Krebs recalls. "Weren't acquired products and company acquisitions much more expensive than a good mix of internally generated and in-licensed innovations? Or was Pearson somehow taking advantage of market forces that we didn't know about? And the arrogance of the speaker, who was telling some of the most important figures from the industry how to do their job, was just staggering. Later, in a private conversation, Michael Pearson repeated his insistence that his was the superior strategy. He was obviously completely convinced of it."

Well, you either already know what happened next or, if not, you can sense it. The success story came to an abrupt and painful end. The shortcomings of the strategy started to become clearer and the forces that normally drive the capital markets took over once again, as the accumulated burden of debt brought the company under pressure. After Valeant failed to complete a contested takeover attempt of Allergan, analysts decided to have a closer look. The share price collapsed from $250 to less than ten dollars and is now around twenty. A lot of people lost a great deal of money. Others had already lost their jobs following earlier takeovers, company values were ignored, business value was destroyed, and a trail of destruction was left behind. Of course, there were winners too, such as the shareholders of the firms taken over for astronomically high prices, plus investment bankers and lawyers who picked up hefty advisory fees, and not forgetting Valeant executives, who collected big bonuses for several years. In July 2018, they chose to drop the Valeant name altogether, which only served to cause still further frustration and head-shaking in the market.

We are left asking the question: Who allowed all this to happen? Where was the board of directors? Is it possible that the board and shareholders consciously or subconsciously ignored the warning signals due to their thirst for "more"? Valeant is a classic example of the destructive force of over-powerful CEOs, when nobody bothers to keep a close eye on them (see Chapter 8 on the topic of "Ego"). And Valeant is also a sad example of a short-sighted M&A strategy, where no attention whatsoever is paid to the longer-term sustainability of all that is happening.

At the end of the day, the Incas, too, pushed their ambitious expansion policy to the limits of what was possible. But unlike Pearson, the former CEO of Valeant, they didn't just consider their newly integrated regions and peoples as bounty to be plundered and exploited. They were acquiring know-how while at the same time introducing their own accumulated knowledge. They sought to achieve a balance between conquering and developing. By contrast, Pearson pursued a destructive strategy which was not geared toward creating long-term value but was exclusively focused on maximizing profits. This approach seems more reminiscent of colonialism than a farsighted M&A strategy, not to mention the negative impact on R&D and the consequences this had on innovation. After some early successes, Pearson fell victim to the illusion of invincibility, but he was not alone in succumbing to this. "The more successful a business is, the more dangerous it becomes. Anyone who, up until then, has only enjoyed success, often fails to subject a planned takeover to sufficient scrutiny" warns the M&A expert Jost Harmann.[118]

We are the first to acknowledge that mergers and takeovers are a highly complex undertaking, and the bigger the entities involved, the more difficult it is to form a new functioning unit out of a collection of organizations which are already difficult enough to manage. There are good reasons why armies of analysts, number-crunchers, and consultants specialize in this area. Every project is different, standardized approaches are unlikely to work, and anyone who criticizes with the benefit of hindsight is quickly labelled a know-it-all. As we can see in the case of Valeant, though, a careful analysis can reveal some general mistakes from which businesses of all sizes can learn, and we'll go into some of the most important of these in the next section.

A Master Plan—or All Based on Hope?

Let's take another look at what happened five hundred years ago. Even if contemporary eyewitness accounts are a little thin on the ground, all the evidence points to the Incas always following exactly the same approach when on the campaign trail. In short, it looked like this: stage a show of strength, make a ("friendly") takeover offer, demonstrate clearly the advantages of cooperation, remove the provincial lords in the case of resistance or integrate them into the Inca hierarchy in the case of acceptance. Continue by examining the new region carefully, adopt the local practices which look successful, and introduce your own tried-and-tested procedures where necessary. By following this approach, the Inca managers became masters of efficiency, drawing on their extensive experience of continuous expansion. Put another way, the Incas had plenty of practice, whereas for most companies, major M&A projects are by definition a one-off event. For the economists Maximilian Dreher and Dietmar Ernst, experience is also the "most important factor" in executing a successful M&A project. "The more transactions a business is involved with, the better its ability generally to evaluate potential M&A projects, to structure and carry out due diligence, to complete post-merger integration and so realize the anticipated synergies."[119]

Of course, you can't practice a takeover five times in order to be successful on the sixth attempt, but you can benefit from the experience of others by:

- Not underestimating the complexity and time required to complete the process.
- Being crystal clear about the overall objective and methodically assessing how realistic or achievable this objective is. "Global, Inc." or "Being Number One" are marketing slogans, not real objectives which drive a specific action plan.

- Carefully thinking through and planning each step of the process in advance, at every relevant level (business units, processes, people).
- Recognizing the importance of psychological and emotional factors (see the next section entitled "Rational? You Must Be Joking!") and robust change management.

There have been plenty of papers, books, and other publications written about the main elements and processes involved in M&A activities.[120] Despite this, according to a study conducted by a leading European university in which two hundred mergers were analyzed since the year 2000, only 10 percent of businesses have a clear concept of how to go about merging the newly acquired business at the moment when contracts are actually signed.[121] This means that, when the other 90 percent of businesses embark on a project that, if it fails, could threaten the very existence of the company (as we saw earlier), their main or only strategy is hope! Ironic indeed, since experience suggests that it is strongly advisable to draw up the most detailed plans possible in the run-up to a transaction, without risking unsettling the various stakeholders. Put simply, by doubling the preparation time, you halve the time needed for implementation and, if any further argument for this approach is needed, it has been shown that the shorter the transition from the old to the new business form, the better.[122]

Lengthy periods of uncertainty not only demotivate employees, they also increase the risk of key people leaving the business and expose the organization to the risk of being taken over by the competition. With this in mind, Winfried Berner and his colleagues at The Implementation Consultancy speak about the "window of vulnerability."[123] In the transition phase, during which employees at all levels of the organization are chiefly preoccupied with their own personal fears and plans for the future, the normal daily business falters. There is a "high degree of introspection" accompanied by an increase in the number of rumors. Competitors can take advantage of this to poach top performers, to persuade customers or suppliers they are the more reliable partner, to launch competing products, or to move in on sales and distribution channels.

A high-profile example is the downfall of the once proud Hoechst AG, which under CEO Jürgen Dormann merged with its French rival Rhône-Poulenc in 1999 to form Aventis. Since 1996, Dormann had pursued several merger opportunities, but without success, and had sold off a number of business units. Employee representatives went on the warpath and competitors such as Bayer, among others, took full advantage of the paralysis in this long-established company by winning over market share from Hoechst. To add insult to injury, a large number of key staff, fed up with the years of uncertainty about the future of the company, left to join the competition.

Even experienced managers with many years of success behind them often dramatically underestimate the "collateral damage" which can result from M&A activities. In 2001, a book was published in the United States, giving advice on how to best take advantage of a competitor distracted by M&A activity: *Capitalize on Merger Chaos: Six Ways to Profit from Your Competitors' Consolidation and Your Own* by Thomas M. Grubb and Robert B. Lamb. The front cover shows a lonely manager in a pool of sharks and, to avoid becoming a victim of your own M&A project, the authors recommend "firstly, to keep the window of vulnerability as small as possible and, secondly, to close this window again as soon as you possibly can."[124]

However, the smartest strategy in the world can't offer complete protection from the vagaries of the global economy. How much better could the AOL/Time Warner merger have been if the dot-com bubble hadn't burst and Wall Street analysts had been more positive about the whole project? Would Porsche have succeeded in its, well, let's call it daring attempt to take over VW if the 2008 banking crisis had not unnerved the banks to such an extent that, in early 2009, they refused to grant any more credit to Porsche, bringing the business to the brink of insolvency?[125]

We want the numbers, love the data, have to see the analyses. And yet, sometimes, the sheer volume of it all lulls us into a false sense of security. While plans alone are not everything, without a plan behind it, the insight gained from all this information is worth nothing. And every project on the scale of those mentioned above needs an exit strategy, an escape route, a Plan B for the unexpected. And a plan C, of course, for the unthinkable.

As leaders and managers, we have good reason to be more sensitive to risks. After all, the improbable only remains improbable until it happens. One of our interviewees has direct personal experience of just such an event when, in 2002, Arthur Andersen, then one of the top five global auditors, was caught up in the Enron scandal, lost a large number of clients within a few weeks, and was subsequently dismantled under the burden of a series of massive lawsuits.

From Gerd Stürz, Head of Life Sciences (DACH) at EY:

> *The experience proved to be an enormous help to me in my continuing professional career because, since then, I have a completely different understanding of risk. Up to that point, I felt secure, because I was confident that our risk management system could handle any eventuality. But then came an event which you could liken to a large aircraft crash-landing on top of a nuclear power station: something you cannot plan for. The probability of such an event occurring was so minuscule, coming so far after the decimal point, that you could hardly decipher it. All my personal capital was invested in that business and it left a permanent impression. The company I now work for has shown continuous expansion in recent years and we look at risks in a different fashion today, where in the past we assessed*

the probability as highly unlikely. If you just do the calculation
(probability multiplied by the value of the risk), then you get a
relatively small number. I disregard the probability, though, and
make provision for the maximum risk. To this day, that is the way this
organization operates.

Vince Ebert, physicist and cabaret artist, and, in his first life, a management consultant in data analytics, regularly generates lots of laughs during his talks to managers when he uses amusing examples to highlight the limitations of predictability.[126] We met Ebert in 2014 at the Alpensymposium in Interlaken and, in his parting words, he said something particularly interesting:

"Be careful with algorithms. All they illustrate are correlations, not causalities. Despite this, we trust them, in our daily lives, in lots of situations. Remember, computers calculate, humans comprehend." One of his most popular books is entitled *Unpredictable* (2016) and we can thoroughly recommend it.

Against the background of this type of thinking and the example of Valeant, which we outlined above, megamergers provide plenty of food for thought. Is the philosophy "Eat or be eaten" viable in the long term? Is "bigger" really automatically "better"? At what point does an organization cease to be manageable?

From Gerd Stürz, Head of Life Sciences (DACH) at EY:

Sooner rather than later, I believe that a broad discussion about
company size will become unavoidable and I question whether large
organizations will be able to justify their existence in the long term.
Agility in business processes requires much quicker reaction times
than big organizations can manage. In the medium term, we'll have
to evaluate how much we still have to do in-house and how much

innovation can be integrated by, for instance, taking over start-ups with innovative and complementary know-how.

Gerd Stürz is addressing a dilemma for which the Incas were able to find a workable and long-lasting solution. How can you ensure that a large organization is manageable over the long term and thus capable of surviving and/or remaining profitable? The Inca strategists' answer was to establish a clever network of regional and central authorities, where authority was distributed and spread. If it made sense for a decision to be made locally, that's where it was made, not at HQ in Cuzco. The Swiss management expert, Albert Stähli, is an admirer of the Inca approach and writes, "The Incas understood how to build up an organization in which a central imperial administration worked alongside relatively autonomous provinces."[127] This division of authority encouraged and facilitated the integration of local rulers into the government machinery of the Incas, on the pragmatic assumption that those who continue to have a say in something tend to be less inclined to rebel against it. In this respect, the Incas were smarter than many of today's executives, who persist in ignoring the impact of emotional factors as well as cultural barriers on M&A activities.

Another of our interview partners had a positive experience with a leading US company which risked a radical restructuring, moving away from a regional to a business-unit structure and, in so doing, did away with its traditional and deeply embedded regional structures covering Europe, the Middle East, Africa, Latin America, and Asia. Its new maxim went like this: Whatever the organization cannot deliver globally with a high level of efficiency and standardization will be managed locally. As a result, there were no more triplicated functions, and superfluous and often inefficient intermediary structures that had grown up over time were eliminated. In their place came, on the one hand, more freedom for local initiatives, and, on the other hand, a framework of globally applicable values and objectives, a clear and binding worldwide brand and corporate identity, as well as other non-negotiable global elements, such as compliance processes.

When it comes to M&A activity, decision-makers are well advised to ask themselves these questions: How much integration does each business area really need? How much autonomy do we want to allow? What aspects of a potential integration are most useful for the business as a whole, and what would ensure that it remains innovative and able to act decisively? How do we stay close to our markets and our customers? How do we hold on to the best people? The smarter the answers to these questions, the more efficient and profitable an organization will be in the long term, with or without a merger.

Rational? You Must Be Joking!

One of the biggest myths about daily business life is that, when it comes to decision-making, cool, calm, hard-headed logic rules the roost, and emotions, perceptions, and personal perspectives play little or no part. Individual feelings and sensitivities are brushed aside as "kids' stuff," people are swift to appeal for the use of sound reasoning and common sense, especially in controversial meetings, and others are readily told not to take things "personally." But this veneer of rationality quickly starts to peel away when the issue is not *other* people's emotions but our own, which, let's be honest, is not easy to admit to and even tougher to deal with.

Psychologists can only smile about the myth of rationality, and, over the last few decades, neurological research has amassed a large body of evidence which shows that emotions are key drivers for our decisions and actions.[128] And this applies just as much to senior executives as to everyone else. Does anyone seriously believe that Ferdinand Piëch's Phaeton adventure into the luxury car sector, Wendelin Wiedeking's attempted takeover of VW, or Michael Pearson's billion-dollar purchasing spree in the pharmaceutical sector were driven by hard numbers? Hans-Olaf Henkel, former Head of Europe at IBM, didn't hold back when he commented in the press, "It seems to me that the presence of an egomaniacal macho is one of the more frequent explanations for failed megamergers."[129] We will look at how to avoid falling into the "ego trap" in our final chapter.

Many mergers start with numbers and finish because of emotions, and one of the most powerful of these emotions is fear. Uncertainty worries the majority of people, and changes in an organization are always accompanied by periods of uncertainty. Managers so often believe that all it takes are some nice slides and a good story and their people will deal with the changes. How wrong they can be— particularly those who are closely involved in an M&A activity can easily overlook the reactions of those employees directly affected by the announcement of a corporate restructuring. Christine Wolff considers this one of her biggest failings when looking back on her impressive career.

From Christine Wolff, Multiple Board Member:

> I worked in a large American company and we were constantly on the acquisition trail and handling change on a daily basis. Good leaders can handle change; they love it. But most people are very afraid of change, preferring to stick with what is familiar. I got a flavor of this when I went into one of our newly acquired companies. I was quite euphoric and basically said: We've bought this company, here are your new colleagues, and now we are all one big family. Suddenly, all I could see was fear in everyone's eyes. The feedback we received was also clear that it just didn't work like that. And then situations arose where desks were decorated with the logo and flag and the coffee cups of the "old" company. I exaggerate slightly, but sometimes I had the impression that many of the people in the company we had taken over would rather die than drink coffee from a mug with the logo of the

new company on it! It is in the small details like this that you discover quite how much fear and insecurity there really is. What did I take away from this all? With a big acquisition, you must integrate very quickly and, at the same time, invest a lot of time to bring everyone on board. I was involved with many acquisitions and completed them successfully because I dedicated a huge amount of time to the integration process. And I often wished I'd have received more support from the "post-merger team."

The approach to integration recommended by Christine Wolff is much more than just cosmetic hand-holding. It is all about serving and supporting the hard-nosed economic interests of the business by installing professional change management processes that address the so-called softer issues of the people involved and affected. Here is an example of what happens when this is not done properly. Toward the end of 2016, the airline Tuifly made headlines when hundreds of pilots and countless cabin crew members phoned in sick, pretty well paralyzing the airline for a whole day. *Handelsblatt* reported, "Many employees are worried about what the future holds in store for them as a result of the planned merger between Tuifly and Air Berlin."[130] Representatives from the cabin crew union claimed that the firm's "dreadful communications policy" was responsible for causing the psychological stress which, presumably, had led to the wave of illness.[131] Politicians were sharply critical of the company because it was customers who ended up having to suffer the consequences of an internal company dispute, and thousands of customers indeed chose to lodge complaints.[132] All in all, it was an absolute PR disaster.

Seldom are the consequences of employee frustration made so public, and many employees go a step further in such circumstances and, at least in their heads and hearts, quietly resign. The Gallup Institute calculates the economic costs of this type of employee disengagement at between seventy-five and ninety-nine billion euros per year due to the fact that, among other reasons, employees with no emotional attachment to their company are almost twice as likely to be sick as those that are still motivated.[133]

You can't get away from the feeling that, in this discipline, the Incas had a better understanding of psychology than many of today's business leaders. At least they seemed to have been aware that it was worthwhile proactively courting "takeover candidates" to demonstrate to the rulers ("management") and the general population ("employees") the benefits of a merger and not to provoke unnecessary divisions between the acquirer and the acquired. Fundamentally, in the case of a friendly takeover, there is always a realistic chance that the management of the target company is prepared to cooperate and counter any possible skepticism among their employees with genuine enthusiasm, so it's certainly best to start by winning over their hearts and minds before expecting them to cascade the process down through the organization. The biggest resisters and obstacles to change, at least in larger organizations, are often to be found in that frequently rather opaque ecological niche known as "middle management," once referred to critically by former Siemens boss Peter Löscher as the "layer of paralysis." At the time he said that people were up in arms. However, given the reluctance to change demonstrated by so many managers at this level, Löscher could easily have been even less diplomatic in his choice of words.

What are the criteria for a solid pre- and post-merger management process? Here are some suggestions:

o A properly thought-through communications strategy. Who finds out what, when, and from whom? It still happens that employees hear that their company is a takeover candidate through the press, even though (or perhaps precisely because) top management has long been involved in negotiations. The huge erosion in trust which results from such incidents is almost impossible to repair. Of course, finding the right moment to make announcements is often a delicate balancing act, and considerations such as insider knowledge and the need to comply with corporate law make finding a good solution challenging, to say the least. But "as soon as professionally possible" is probably a good guiding thought.

o The quickest possible integration process. The smaller the window of vulnerability and the shorter the period of uncertainty, the better. Any extended period where things are still open brings with it the danger that the best people leave the organization and competitors use the transitional period to their own advantage.

o A precise set of objectives that is clearly derived from a high-caliber due diligence done in advance. How deep should integration go, how much regional power is to be permitted? Where are the synergies (cost reductions or productivity improvements) going to be achieved? Which sections should be merged, which should continue unchanged?

o Realistic human resources planning. Who is in charge of the integration process? Which managers and employees are dedicated to the project? How do you make sure that normal business continues without interruption during this challenging period? Which key knowledge holders in the target company are essential for the post-merger phase?

o A structured integration plan for key functions (technical operations, sales and marketing, R&D, IT, HR, legal, accounting, and finance) to make sure the underlying business remains fully operational and normal business continues without interruption.

o A speedy clarification of open personnel questions, in particular how senior positions and key functions are to be filled and possible job cuts. Inevitably and understandably, everyone involved wonders, "What is going to happen to me?" before thinking about the future of the business. The sooner this question is answered, the better.

o Setting up a leadership team which supports the M&A project. This also means parting company with managers who act as a drag or do not meet the expected standards. Experience has frequently and successfully shown that you should replace a third of the management with hires from outside, keep another third in place, and replace a third using internal talent.

o Constructive cooperation with employee representatives, trade unions, and works councils, where present. This is a very important and frequently underestimated element of successful M&A processes. Many managers have relatively little experience in this area and are thus poorly equipped, although it doesn't need to be as difficult as it may seem. Agreeing on a set of clear rules and sticking to them is a good start. Then, just like everywhere else, ensuring proactive communication, respect for your negotiating partners, and the right level of detailed preparation are all a great help too. Many managers fail to appreciate the constraints within which elected employee representatives are forced to operate. After all, they are the ones who are actually most directly confronted with the concerns and demands of their voters. Often, managers who whine about this important part of their job are simply those who have failed to do their homework and some good and proactive stakeholder management!

o Identification of problem areas and points of resistance, robust and disciplined implementation of decisions, and systematic action to remove people who quite clearly do not want to come along on the journey. In this respect, we can learn—at least to some extent—from the intransigence of the Incas, who went about executing their plans with ruthless determination.

o And last but not least, a clear communication plan for interacting with the customers. Let them know whether they will be impacted and, if so, in what way, and make sure they are aware of why the merger is a good thing for them. Above all, ensure that the company is driving the merger story from its own and its customers' perspectives. Otherwise, competitors and other critical stakeholders, who are less interested in seeing the whole project being successful, will fill the information vacuum.

Does this all sound self-evident and rather obvious to you? That may well be, but then why do we still see so much incredibly bad merger management? For example, when, during one of his talks, Andreas Krebs asks who in the audience has already been involved in a merger, a lot of hands usually go up. When he then asks, "And how many of you found out very quickly whether you were secure in your job or not?" almost all the hands go down again. It would be nice if what we all hold to be self-evident would simply be taken on board and done. Management consultant Michael Hirt recommends that all important integration measures should be fully implemented within three to six months of the formal takeover and closing of the transaction. After this, "integration fatigue" sets in and the chance of overall success diminishes rapidly.[134] A challenging timescale, yes, but Hirt's concerns are fully justified. Employees will only find their peace with the new organization and start to engage constructively with it when the turf wars have stopped. Change expert Winfried Berner has a clear warning: "As long as structural and organizational issues have not been resolved, people who, on a personal level, could actually get along very well with each other, will remain vulnerable to falling back into the mindset of opposition to the merger."[135] Future task allocation, key locations, production facilities, division of responsibilities, and more: these cannot be determined soon enough.

On top of all this, there is one thing you can do which is more effective at breaking down the barriers between the different camps than the most heart-rending speeches at town hall meetings can ever be: Get people working together on a challenging project. Most of us are well aware that empathy is a necessary prerequisite for good cooperation, but it also works the other way around. Cooperation (preferably voluntary, but if need be, with an appropriate degree of, let's call it forceful encouragement) is the best way to evoke genuine empathy, or at least mutual understanding. This is the basic principle that lies behind countless outdoor training exercises and team-building courses that we've all had the dubious pleasure of attending at some time or another, but the real adventure is, or can be, in our day-to-day business. People can grow together much more effectively and consistently by doing enjoyable and successful work together and being given appropriate recognition for the results of that work than by abseiling down a cliff, grazing their knees on a climbing wall, or hugging a tree together.

The Best of All Worlds—or The Tyranny of the Victor?

If the Incas had not taken the time and trouble to drink wisely from the pool of experience offered to them by the peoples they acquired along the way, then their empire would never have blossomed the way it did. This concept is as fascinating as it is illuminating. We can move a step closer to invincibility through integrating what is new and foreign to us, but only if we take the time to stop, open our eyes, and have the humility to recognize and appreciate what they, the conquered, do better than us. This concept operates in the world of M&A too; the idea is to bring together the best of two worlds. But how often does this really happen? Usually it remains just an empty wish or statement, even when a "merger of equals" is boldly proclaimed. Underneath the cover of objectivity and reasoning, most mergers are all about egos, position, and power. In practice, how often does the leader of the smaller or "target" partner rise to the top of the new organization? How often are the practices of the acquiring company put under the microscope because the acquired company actually has the more effective processes? The best of all worlds means doing what is right, not just what is enforceable. This means putting all aspects of both organizations to the same test. Not everyone has the independence of thought and vision or, more importantly, the mature self-confidence to pull this off.

When looked at dispassionately, there is a lot to be said for positioning yourself as a partner and not a colonialist:

1. A "best of" merger offers the opportunity to select the best brains, the best concepts, the most successful products, and the most efficient processes from a bigger pool, and so increase the profitability of the (new) business.

2. A "best of" merger reduces emotional resistance from smaller or weaker partners and speeds up the integration process. You can buy a business, but this does not automatically mean that its employees will cooperate willingly, and you can't buy their commitment or trust. All this must be earned or won over, and this has a direct impact on productivity. Anyone going in like a victorious general will provoke resistance rather than unifying and will foster frustration rather than encouraging cooperation.

3. A "best of" merger meets the needs of the many employees who are looking for the familiar, something to cling to early on, something in the new setup that still feels at least a bit like home. Organizations don't only survive by having visionary leaders and ambitious managers. They also rely on people who are reliable, are grounded, and just get on with doing their daily business without any great fanfare. When these employees see that some of their old managers, existing working methods, and/or products have been carried over, on merit, into the new business, then it is much easier for them to identify with the new organization. Earlier on, Christine Wolff graphically demonstrated how strong the need for at least a degree of familiarity is for people in times of change. For some, it is already a big step to have to drink out of a cup with the new

firm's logo printed on it. We can only assume that, for a large part of their history, the Incas knew exactly what they were doing in their quest for expansion and integration. Yes, they demanded subservience to the Inca Sun God from all, but at the same time they acknowledged local deities and incorporated them into their own established culture.[136]

The prerequisite for a "best of" strategy is to be able, early in the due diligence process, to clearly identify the people, departments, processes, and products with a positive prognosis and then to measure these against an internal benchmark in the subsequent integration process. This takes time, requires a fair amount of effort, and won't always completely succeed, so a balance needs to be struck between thoroughness and speed. The key point is to demonstrate, very quickly, that the promised cooperation among equals is more than just a short-term sedative, soon to be followed by an autocratic takeover. All it takes are a few key decisions, which will then be acknowledged and interpreted by the smaller partner as credible signals that equals really means equals.

Our final example shows that you really can learn from one another.

A Clever Buyer: Sometimes, the Old Ways Are the Best

In 2010, Israeli pharmaceutical manufacturer Teva took over Ratiopharm, which was number two in the German generics market at the time, and this move enabled Teva to continue its expansion in Europe. About a year and a half later, Ratiopharm spoke openly about the project with the business magazine *Brand eins* and revealed that the takeover was turning out to be broadly positive. This was helped, for instance, by the management at Teva not having tried to impose a new culture on the business, with the company kindergarten being allowed to carry on as usual, free mineral water still being made available, and the modern art collection being left to hang undisturbed on the walls of the corridors. What may appear to be of little importance to those inhabiting the top floor of a company can often have strong meaning, symbolic or otherwise, for those working closer to the coal face, as was the case here. On occasion, just getting rid of the free chocolate biscuits in meetings is enough to get the rumor mill turning at full speed.

Even more important was Teva's explicit acknowledgment of, and respect for, the skills of their German colleagues. For example, the former head of production at Ratiopharm was promoted to Head of European Production. In addition, Teva adopted aspects of Ratiopharm's central storage and logistics, a system that avoided delivery bottlenecks at subsidiaries and reduced storage costs. And in a move to achieve a more flexible production schedule, adjustments were made that were clearly based on the methods being used by the smaller business.

Of course, as the magazine article pointed out, following the merger, a lot had changed at Ratiopharm as well; the pace of the business had been stepped up and there was a much stronger emphasis on performance. As in any takeover, when faced with duplication of responsibilities, managers were compared head-to-head with their counterparts from the new business, with the best-suited person taking over complete responsibility, irrespective of how long he or she had been with the company. But then that is the logical consequence of a "best of" approach, if it's consistently applied. There are no preferential rights for previous incumbents, with the philosophy being that the best is always the enemy of the good.[137]

Indeed, up until about three years ago, this motto seemed to be fully applicable to Teva: The company was growing very quickly organically, was aggressively buying companies and paying high prices for them, and seemed to be going from strength to strength. If you're beginning to sense parallels to the Valeant story, then you're absolutely right. Although Teva was, for a number of years, much smarter at integrating companies, as the Ratiopharm takeover showed, the company had significantly overstretched itself, with a huge debt burden and cashflow problems becoming overwhelming, not to mention the challenge of managing over three hundred manufacturing sites around the world. The stock price has since fallen from over seventy dollars in 2015 to under ten dollars in 2019, and the company is now undergoing major restructuring, a process which is likely to go on for some years to come. But in spite of all this, their approach to integrating a smaller partner, as described above, remains a valid and very positive example.

A Stress Test for Your M&A Planning

Since all sectors and businesses are different, and the amalgamation of various businesses becomes ever more complex, it seems almost presumptuous to pull together important ideas into one summary. Nevertheless, we will give it a try.

Merger Test. Yes or No?

1. Merger plans are consistent with overall business strategy and are not primarily driven by power, status, or influence.

2. Due diligence was carefully carried out. The "hope for the best" approach is not the main driver, but rather a critical analysis of numbers, data, and facts takes place. Potential synergies are clearly identified and not just assumed (most synergies from M&A activity are never realized).

3. The business cultures of the entities concerned are compatible. (Before you can assess this, you must be aware of the specific cultural details of the target company.)

4. There is sufficient leadership and project management capacity to ensure an orderly integration of the company. (If that is not the case, you at least know where you are going to get this capacity from.)

5. It is clear which external service providers are to be involved with the project (consultants, lawyers, other experts, and advisers) and to what extent.

6. You have already examined whether antitrust issues could arise.

7. You have a concept for the structure of the new organization. How much is to be centralized, how much decentralized? What will be delivered by global, regional, and local departments? Is there a clear governance process in place?

8. You plan to implement a process which ensures that the know-how and best practices of both parties are identified and transferred into the new organization ("best of all worlds").

9. There is a detailed integration blueprint (for post-merger integration) and change management process, with timelines, first steps, and clear priorities. ☐

10. Worst-case scenarios are simulated, and there is a plan B in case the improbable comes to pass, including a last-minute failure of the merger. ☐

11. Your communication and information policy is designed to be proactive and unambiguous, and to build trust among your employees, customers, investors, and other key stakeholders. ☐

12. The fastest possible integration is assured. How large will you allow the "window of vulnerability" to be? ☐

INCA INSIGHTS

Three important things for a successful M&A:

- **Early and sincere offers of cooperation to the other negotiating side to help build trust and accelerate the process.**

- **A crystal-clear and compelling strategy that convinces employees, investors, and the potential partner of the merits of the project.**

- **A recognizable openness to best practices and a "best-of-both-worlds" approach, creating mutual respect between key stakeholders on both sides of the deal.**

"Flying high and flying low, respected leaders are not only brilliant strategists, but being close to the trenches is also part of their DNA. Knowing the best sales managers who tell them what is really going on, conducting customer visits which are not preplanned milk runs, sending an employee home to take care of a sick family member—these are actions that make people at all levels feel comfortable about creating a shared reality together, and as a nice side effect, it builds loyalty!"

—ROLF HOFFMANN, EXECUTIVE AND GENERAL MANAGER IN VARIOUS COUNTRIES FROM 1994–2016

7 Sound Judgment?
(Look Who's Telling the Story!)

Peter F. Drucker once said that "a manager is responsible for the application and performance of knowledge."[138] In the course of a career, you can't be consistently successful without accurate information, but how often do you ask yourself which version of "reality" you have just had presented to you? Let's look at the question like this. Just imagine an empire that has been waging war for centuries. In a series of bloody battles, followers of a different religion are continuously oppressed and forced back. Neither the plague nor peasants' revolts have any influence on the despotic activities of the rich and powerful. With the aim of unifying the empire, arranged marriages are forged, brutal torture and grisly executions are daily occurrences, and a special authority is created which is deemed to be "holy" and therefore infallible and above the law. As soon as the country has been brought back under control, the military expansion continues into other continents, using a combination of superior weaponry and brutal subjugation. While the ruling nobility lives a life of luxury, the general population gets ever poorer and is threatened with starvation until, finally, even grain has to be imported from neighboring countries.

This is what was happening in Spain, while, at the same time 5,500 miles away, the Inca Empire was expanding rapidly toward becoming an imperial giant: the Reconquista (the Spanish reconquering of the land occupied by the Moors from North Africa), the Inquisition, the unification of the Houses of Castile and Aragon, the subsequent expulsion of the Moors, countless military confrontations, and, in 1557, state bankruptcy.[139] Spain was marked by religious fanaticism, economic ruin, and an insatiable thirst for power, and, yet, despite all this, the country, or at least its elite, considered itself morally vastly superior to the Incas. There were reports of human sacrifices in the Inca Empire, which did occur, but they were grossly exaggerated by the Spanish. For instance, stories about the massacre of twenty thousand prisoners, and the brutality with which this was supposedly carried out, were invented.[140] The reasons for this are clear. The more the Spaniards succeeded in portraying the Incas as a primitive and barbaric people, the easier it was to justify colonization and the process of Christianization. Plundering an advanced civilization? That's quite difficult to communicate. But taking gold and silver from a hoard of uncouth savages and, in return, guiding them along the taxing and testing path toward the one true faith? Now we're talking about a legitimate and, indeed, sacred campaign in the name of God. A much easier sell.

It is well known that history books are written by the victors, and, in this respect, the Incas were no better than their Spanish conquerors. In early chronicles, such as those of the Inca nobleman Garcilaso de la Vega from 1609, they justify the subjugation of other indigenous peoples with the claim that they brought the blessings of their culture to the neighbors who, up to then, had been living "like wild animals."[141] We human beings are extremely adept at presenting facts in a way that suits our standpoint, attitudes, and intentions. In the age of social media, the boundaries between facts, ideologically colored statements, and outright lies become ever more blurred. It is time to get worried when major election campaigns are influenced by fake news and presidential advisers reframe and elevate blatant lies to the "level" of alternative facts.[142] But aside from these worrying and admittedly extreme examples, we are all prone to being a little economical with the truth from time to time. And this brings us back to the day-to-day business of management. How often do you think you really hear the "whole truth" from your employees/direct reports/peers/boss/organization, and so forth, before having to make a decision? In your company, how often are strategic initiatives or action plans based on numbers which, while not false, are at least somewhat selective, or perhaps even biased? How often have you found yourself "fine-tuning" the description of a situation in your favor? You may wish to reflect on this for a moment. If you answer "never" to this question, then we can't help suspecting that you maybe haven't thought about it for long enough. Or you're the first Business Saint we've ever encountered!

In the Hall of Mirrors of the Executive Suite

In 1997, the top manager Daniel Gouedevert published an unorthodox book entitled *Like a Bird in the Aquarium*, which went straight onto the bestseller lists and sold well over a hundred thousand copies. A native Frenchman, Gouedevert was managing director of Ford in Germany over an eight-year period in the 1980s and then sat on the board of VW until 1993. His revealing and unfiltered collection of stories and insights from the C-suite level is completely different from the usual, self-congratulatory volumes that are handed out to business partners and customers, only to end up unread and gathering dust on a corporate bookshelf somewhere. Gouedevert's description of how information flows (or often doesn't flow) up to the top of an organization is not just interesting to read but is still relevant today. "If you manage to rise up through the ranks of a company, as far as CEO or Managing Director, then you usually find yourself on the top floor of the building. And fascinatingly, the further you climb, the more the windows turn into mirrors. And once you have reached the very top, you are not only completely alone, but you don't have any more windows either. Your view to the outside world is blocked and all you can see is yourself. And the people with whom you interact are also constantly holding up that mirror, saying, "Look, boss, you are the best." Even if you try to contradict them or to engage in an open and critical discussion, you rarely get any kind of reaction or a stimulating response that could get you thinking."[143]

When described as candidly as above, it becomes clear that the image many of us have of the all-powerful CEO is actually not particularly accurate. Often distanced and isolated from the daily machinations of the "real world" organization, they are almost completely reliant on others to deliver what they have asked for, while at the same time being kept under the closest scrutiny by a large number of stakeholders, all checking that they are doing their duty correctly and acting in their best interests. It may well also be that, as a result of recent corporate scandals, financial crises, and public debates about salaries and bonuses, people at this level were held in much higher esteem twenty years ago than they are today. However, the core problem which Gouedevert highlights remains as before, and also applies to the levels below the C-executives, which is how to ensure that you are not being fed solely information that has been filtered by self-interest or by the desire to avoid conflict. How can you possibly make informed decisions if you don't have reliable information? In the next section ("The Map Is not the Territory"), we set out some possible escape routes from this dilemma.

Gouedevert is describing a structural and institutionalized detachment from reality which is not limited to senior executives but also applies to other positions of authority and responsibility. Take politicians, for example, who rather revealingly often talk about "the general public and/or the ordinary people out there" as if they themselves were hovering above us all in some kind of manned drone or, worse still, giant spaceship. It starts to get really dangerous if, on top of the already murky and "managed" information flow, the person is of the conviction (entirely human, by the way) that they have superior insight precisely *because* of their position. But then, sometimes, daily business reality has the refreshing ability to bring the hierarchy right back down to earth with a bump, as the following story rather elegantly and amusingly (at least for onlookers) shows.

We're Not Taking Off Until You Pay!

A large American company undertook a major project to outsource a number of administrative functions, such as customer and supplier accounting, invoice control, and other financial controlling services. It implemented the project on a global basis, against the recommendation of some members of the board, who considered the project to be, in many respects, overblown and were also concerned about the potential loss of customer contact and orientation. The project was in full swing when more and more spanners seemed to be getting thrown into the works. Suppliers complained that they were not being paid in full, some bills were either being paid twice or not being paid at all, service providers refused to continue working, and the whole process seemed to be a mess. This is not unusual with projects of this magnitude, but this time, the sheer volume of complaints was dramatic. Several of his best executive board members had tried pointing all this out to the CEO, but he had made this into his project and would not countenance any criticism. And, to be fair to him, there were strong advocates from the financial and procurement departments for the project, and the external consultants had put up a very good case. Furthermore, the CEO was under strong cost pressure, wanted to set an example, and interpreted the comments of his closest colleagues as a sign of concern rather than a signal to completely rethink the project.

And then, it happened. Some members of the board, as is relatively common in corporate America, were scheduled to travel by helicopter to a meeting about a hundred miles away from headquarters. At the departure point, a small regional airport, with everyone huddled up on board, the aviation service provider refused to refuel the helicopter. Despite having been a supplier of the firm for many years, three unpaid invoices totaling seventy-two thousand dollars was simply too much to bear. The CEO got out of the helicopter and had a quiet word with the owner of the service company and, then, he pulled out his credit card. Even for people at his salary level, credit card limits are not that high, but his card was gracefully and gratefully accepted and, after a phone call to the credit card company, the helicopter could finally take on fuel. Helicopters are pretty loud inside, but the ten-minute embarrassed silence following takeoff could be "heard" by all, as the CEO reflected on how this absurd situation could have arisen.

And the incident had consequences. The board member responsible had to go, as well as the responsible consultants, and the project was scaled back to a more sensible and manageable scale. And most importantly, everyone could get back to focusing on what really mattered: the underlying business and the customers.

There are three aspects to the challenge of ensuring you receive sound information upon which you can exercise balanced judgment. First of all, leaders are at risk of having a hall of mirrors built around them by their organization. This prevents unfiltered information from reaching the leaders, and the "reflections" they see in the mirrors are actually carefully crafted packets of flattery being fed in by the people around them. And the higher they climb, the worse it gets. Secondly, if the senior manager also has a domineering and authoritative leadership style, with the tendency to shoot the bearer of bad news, then any information will be cleansed still further before it reaches them, to the point of being both germ- and fact-free! The third danger is of another layer of mirrors being erected if the manager has a self-centered, smug, and overly self-confident attitude, not entirely unheard of at this level, which may result in them distancing themselves even further from reality. And if things then don't work out as they thought they should, the manager is at a complete loss to understand why.

The Map Is Not the Territory[144]

A sales rep gets direct customer feedback every single day about their company's products and services. Their boss, the regional manager, relies mainly on reports from the reps reporting to them, plus their colleagues in the sales department and assorted sales statistics and summaries. The sales and marketing director relies on reports from national sales management and data from the finance department. Finally, the CEO completes their jigsaw puzzle of business performance using even more distilled, edited, and filtered information. His or her picture is much broader than that of the representatives on the ground, but at the same time its resolution or granularity is not as high. It's like a map, where the scale gets bigger and bigger while the area covered gets ever larger. No, the map is not the territory, and it is an important skill for any manager to understand the difference between the two and actively compensate if, at their level, they usually only have the larger scale map in their hand. The advantage remains with those executives who maintain some direct contact with customers and the competitive environment.

So how can you, in a senior position, actively compensate for the inherent differences between the map and the actual territory? Well, every now and then, leave the spaceship occupied by the inner top management circle and go and listen to the views and experiences of employees, customers, and other stakeholders. For many senior managers, this is actually quite a stressful thought, even though they would never want to admit it, because the spaceship is also a haven, a shelter, offering protection from unexpected interactions. Many senior executives are worried about engaging in conversations with key customers for fear of making a fool of themselves because they are so far removed from day-to-day business and the company's products. Other leaders find it difficult to approach ordinary employees because this means stepping out of their comfort zone, leaving the familiarity of the daily discussions with their peers in top management. But if you really want to find out what the territory looks like, rather than relying on the map you usually use to navigate your way through the day, then there is no avoiding these forays into the real business world that is your organization. Ideally, it is part of your management DNA to regularly carry out reality checks on issues that normally land on your desk in the significantly more abstract form of a concept, draft resolution, status report, presentation, or numbers in a spreadsheet.

From Dr. Iris Löw-Friedrich, Executive Vice President and Chief Medical Officer, UCB:

When I consider how we go about taking decisions on the Board and how far down into detail we want to or are able to go, then that certainly gives me food for thought. A little knowledge must be recognized as such. Of course, you have to speak with someone you trust and who knows what they are talking about and then make a judgment and ideally you speak with several completely independent sources. After all, we all bring certain prejudices to the table, so you should strive to gain a complete, 360-degree picture, even if it is sometimes uncomfortable.

"Breakfast with Andreas Krebs" was the name given to the bimonthly meeting to which ten to twelve employees from all levels were invited. As the newly appointed managing director, Andreas wanted to get to know the organization and hear what was on people's minds. He invited them for breakfast in his office, and they were encouraged to prepare two questions each; we mentioned the idea in the chapter on leadership. And, of course, members of the management team had to follow up and answer any questions from their areas of responsibility that could not be answered on the spot. People quickly realized that it was possible, and even encouraged, to openly air their grievances and to question whether specific shortcomings in the way the company operated were really deliberate decisions by management or had simply become routine practice, regardless of whether they really made sense. But, please, don't think that the job is completed by organizing one or two breakfast meetings or a short series of similar events. It takes a long time, sometimes six to twelve months, before word spreads that, at these meetings, an employee can speak directly and openly and ask the really tough and awkward questions. This requires trust, and this is only secured if you show that you take the meetings seriously, that you genuinely want to get a proper and complete all-around picture, that you follow up on suggestions and criticism, and then keep the employees informed about concrete results. And above all, you don't ever penalize anyone in any way, shape, or form, for being courageous enough to ask a tough or unpopular question.

Alongside these types of events, you can also practice the well-known technique of "management by walking around." This involves being out and about regularly in various departments within the organization, including all the way into the production line and, most importantly, ensuring that you are approachable, meaning that you are not surrounded by an entourage of lieutenants and minders. And again, this only works when you do it on an ongoing basis, you are genuinely interested in the concerns and issues people raise, and you speak with them directly, openly, and honestly. The major hotels around the world set a good example here, where, as a young trainee, you learn very early on that a hotel manager should spend at least one to two hours a day making the rounds in their hotel, rubbing elbows and interacting with the guests and staff alike. The good ones do just that throughout their careers, and it works.

Be Visible—and See for Yourself!

Andreas Krebs was able to spend a day with Jürgen Baumhoff who, at the time, was director of a five-star hotel in Hong Kong and observe how he practiced management in its purest form by walking around. Baumhoff could walk into a ballroom filled with a thousand guests and tell straightaway whether everything was running smoothly or there was a problem with the service. He could sense immediately the mood of the guests, whether they were happy or whether any parts of the room were dissatisfied. He explained, "The moment we let our service standards slip, we start to lose money. One empty wine glass is a momentary oversight by a waiter, a hundred empty glasses is a considerable loss of business opportunity." The sheer presence of the (very popular) hotel director, just passing by to get an impression of how things were going, lifted performance and gave him the opportunity to stay close to the customers and his staff. And what really counts is not just "having a quick look," but to have a regular routine to ensure that you are in touch with and visible across the various parts of your organization.

Incentive events provide some of the most effective opportunities for senior managers, including CEOs, to find out what is really going on in their organizations. Celebrations honoring the best performers, whether in sales or technical departments, or employees of the month in other areas, give you a fantastic chance to hear an uncensored version of where the real problems are in your company. When your best people open up to you, they are not doing it because they want to moan—these types of people are seldom moaners anyway—they are doing it because they want to help the organization improve. These events are also fun, so please don't be afraid to use them! You can also bolster your standing in the market with attractive customer events, where you get the chance to speak directly with the people who buy and use, or don't buy and don't use, your products, and all that within the bounds of good compliance, similar to the way airlines connect with their frequent flyers.

Every leader benefits from having critical sparring partners in their inner circle. Sometimes, this can be uncomfortable, but in the long term it is vitally important. Winston Churchill summed it up quite succinctly: "If two people always have the same opinion, one of them is superfluous." Can people contradict you without being punished in some way or another? You can be pretty sure that all those working immediately around you watch very carefully how you deal with people who are honest and confident enough to express their own opinion. Not many people are courageous enough to do this, so if you do discourage them, you will end up being surrounded by "yes men" in no time at all.

If, despite your willingness to enter into meaningful and critical discussions, you encounter too much uniformity within a particular group or concerning a specific topic, then one option is to look to the Oxford Union Debate as a model to break the silence. The Oxford Union Society, established in 1823, is the debating club at Oxford University. Debates are organized with a clear separation of roles between proposers and opponents of a so-called motion, with the proceedings presided over by a chairman or moderator. During a debate, some of the participants are given the opportunity to adopt a position that directly contradicts their original opinion.[145] The idea of forcing people to consider a wider perspective in the context of, essentially, a role-play is long-established and was practiced in the monasteries of old in the form of a "scholastic dispute." The Prior chose two monks, one to represent a thesis and another the antithesis, and then they had to defend the viewpoints allocated to them. The real trick was not just that of changing the roles, but before giving their response, every participant had to repeat, very precisely, what their opponent had said. So, both the debate and the scholastic dispute also force the participants to focus on their listening skills, an extremely challenging but very effective and revealing exercise, especially for many top managers. Give it a try and find out for yourself.

Paul Williams uses these techniques when coaching executive teams and the results are striking, every time. Issues are brought to the fore which would otherwise be hushed up. Topics that were identified behind closed doors as taboo are brought out into the open and, at the end, there are no elephants left anywhere in the room. Focused listening, forcing people to look at issues from a different viewpoint, and the openness, honesty, and (not to forget) humor which are made possible by the fact that it is only a role-play, that we are "just playing," break down barriers and facilitate a genuine exchange of views. The contrast to the more typical exchange of blows in a classical, confrontational meeting, where politics, power, and personal positions override all attempts to achieve a constructive discourse, is impressive. Drawing on the title of this section, methods such as these enable adversaries to swap maps with each other and, in so doing, reach higher-quality conclusions and decisions, rather than following the normal route of arguing about who's got the better map.

"Man Errs as Long as He Doth Strive"

…says none other than "The Lord" himself in the prologue to Goethe's famous play, *Faust, Part One*. When you look back at the decisions you have made, how many would you say were exactly right, how many more or less okay, and how many were clearly wrong? After thinking about this for a few moments, you'll probably come to the conclusion that giving a clear answer to the question is difficult if not impossible, simply because, in many cases, you will never know how things would have turned out if you had decided differently. A lot of decisions are made on the basis of limited information and/or in the face of differing expert opinions and recommendations. If we had absolute certainty regarding the situation in question, then the decision would no longer be a decision; it would be perfectly obvious what needed to be done. And what about expert opinions? We have had the privilege of working with a number of quite brilliant thought leaders in their respective fields. Nevertheless, it is vital to ensure that you have sufficient general understanding of a particular topic to be able to judge whether an expert is still completely up to date or, perhaps, already past their best. At what stage is it permissible, or indeed necessary, to challenge the opinions of an expert? How can you prevent decisions being made based on outdated know-how or on theories that worked well in the past, but no longer apply? The half-life of ideas, methods, approaches, and solutions is getting shorter every day. Presumably the Inca Atahualpa asked his most trusted advisers and priests how he should deal with the arrival of the newcomers, but, in the end, it would appear that he single-mindedly led his empire toward its destruction, and with it, his own demise too.

Winston Churchill benefited from countless expert opinions as chancellor of the exchequer, home secretary and prime minister. He made the wry observation, "An expert is someone who, after the event, can tell you exactly why his advice was wrong." But no longer asking experts for their opinion is also not the solution. There is much to be gained by remembering that every expert views the world through the established map in their own head, the narrow window of their particular specialization. And no map tells you everything about the area in question. In a difficult situation, it can undoubtedly help to seek the differing opinions of more than one expert, and, in a period of upheaval, it can help to ask for deliberately contrasting opinions to avoid possibly being seduced into making a decision based on what is actually only a fleeting fad, not a sustainable trend or full-blown paradigm shift. It can also help to carry out a "reality check" within the organization by speaking with those directly affected by perceived changes in the market and those who will have to carry out your decisions, once you've made them. The computer pioneer and US Navy officer, Admiral Grace Hopper, said, "One accurate measurement is worth a thousand expert opinions." This was certainly confirmed by the planning and development department of a local authority. It mandated experts to build a new hospital and left them to get on with it. The result? They now have doors so narrow that it is very difficult to move beds through them, and the distances between the patient wards and operating rooms are vast. To make matters worse, the hospital was built on marshland, and walls and windows are now cracking as a result. Local farmers tried to warn the decision-makers, but the "experts" knew better.[146]

Experts can make mistakes, and experts are also as prone as the rest of us to groupthink. And most of us tend to prefer the warm comfort of affirmation to the message that we need to make changes to our opinions and actions. We pay more attention to things that match our views than to evidence that suggests these views may be wrong. We are much slower to reverse bad decisions after we have already invested a large amount of time, effort, and reputation into them than those decisions where implementation is yet to get underway; the financial and intangible implications of this "close your eyes and hope for the best" strategy can be horrendous. And we live in an ever more complex world where more and more people are looking for simple truths and solutions. With this comes an increasing tendency to cling to a convenient lie rather than face up to the less convenient facts. We certainly hope that the majority of decision-makers are prepared to make a stand against the post-truth Zeitgeist. Incidentally, *postfaktisch*, the German translation of post-truth, was voted Germany's "word of the year" in 2016, but people have been prone to self-deception and selective blindness for as long as we have been on this earth and have regularly paid a very high price for being so. In one of his many fascinating books, the evolutionary biologist and geographer Jared Diamond addressed the question, "Why Societies Survive or Disappear."[147] In one chapter, he examines a particularly fascinating aspect: "Why do some societies take catastrophic decisions?" You don't need to make a giant leap of imagination to apply the observations and conclusions of this Pulitzer Prize winner to companies. Here's a brief summary of some of the things he says, including some additional thoughts from us.

Why Societies (and Businesses) Make Disastrous Decisions (Jared Diamond)

1. A problem is not anticipated

For example, the first settlers in Australia introduced rabbits. Ever since then, the country has suffered from a plague of rabbits. The reasons:

a. No experience with the phenomenon (introducing species to new environments).
b. Drawing false analogies. For instance, our example of the Incas, who approached the Spanish as if they were just another regional rival.

2. A problem is not perceived as such

For example, soil exhaustion before the existence of modern analytical techniques. The reasons:

a. Basically, the problem is invisible (see soil exhaustion).
b. The responsible decision-makers are physically too far away from the problem (for example, issues in overseas subsidiaries).
c. "Creeping normality": The problem is concealed by a slow, variable, and therefore difficult-to-observe trend (see climate change).

3. You recognize a problem, but don't set about solving it
The reasons:

a. "Rational behavior": What is good for the individual may be bad for society. For example, enjoying owning a powerful car while being aware of and concerned about the problems of high emissions.
b. "The tragedy of common ownership": If I don't do it, someone else will. For example, overfishing of the oceans and generating business through bribery.
c. The inability to let go of traditional, long-established behaviors and attitudes. For example, the deforestation of whole islands and regions.
d. Thinking that you have already invested too much. This is the "sunk-cost effect"; for instance, selling declining shares too late.
e. The person or people who highlight the problem are ignored, as well as any remedy they might suggest. For example, the suggestions for improvement made by "junior" merger partners.
f. "Irrational conflict between short- and long-term motives." For example, see the dynamite fishing practiced by poor fishermen[148], who are thereby destroying the basis of their long-term livelihood.
g. "Groupthink": This arises, above all, when a small group "is under

pressure, in difficult circumstances, to reach a decision." Stress and the need for affirmation can lead to the suppression of counterarguments, doubts, and criticism. For example, Kennedy and the Bay of Pigs invasion.

h. Denial: Particularly painful perceptions are suppressed. For example, the phenomenon that people living below a large dam are those least afraid of the dam breaking. Or the idea of not wanting to "think the unpalatable" mentioned in Chapter 5.

4. An attempt is made to solve a problem, but it's not successful

The reasons:

a. Attempts to tackle problems come too late. For example, the Nokia story.
b. The attempts are too half-hearted. For example, the endless debates on necessary reforms of state pension systems in a number of European countries.
c. The attempts are counterproductive. For example, the effort in Australia to control insects by bringing toads to the country. Now, it's the toads that are the problem.[149]

A look at this summary is insightful and unsettling at the same time. As we can see, there are more than enough reasons and temptations to look away from problems, and you encounter all of these excuses in business life, too. Quite clearly, it remains a core task for anyone in a position of responsibility in an organization to critically question their own judgment on a continuous basis. As a closing thought, we particularly like something that a much-loved German humorist of the 1950s, Heinz Erhard, once said: "Don't believe everything you think!"

Riots in Berlin! Who Really Is Objective?

"The Inca Empire was maligned as an exploitative regime or celebrated as a socialist paradise, because of its comprehensive redistribution network," wrote the respected journalist, Michael Zick.[150] Which view is correct? What is fact and what is fiction? Whether it was the first Inca chroniclers of the sixteenth and seventeenth centuries, or the Spanish priests or soldiers, or the early adventurers and researchers, such as Hiram Bingham, who claimed to have discovered Machu Picchu in 1911, each portrayed their own "truth" and, we assume, was totally convinced of their own objectivity at the time.

We judge the world based on our own personal convictions, which have been formed by education, experience, cultural influences, and inherited character traits. In our heads, we have clear ideas about how the world is and how it should be. This is the basis on which we perceive, judge, and interpret what goes on around us. We "construct" our reality, as described by constructivist philosophers such as Paul Watzlawick, Heinz von Foerster, or Ernst von Glasersfeld. Cultural differences are often the most obvious and visible factor to help illustrate and explain the variations in these constructions. For example, many Europeans struggle to understand the relationship of some Americans to the seemingly extensive possession of firearms.[151] But equally, if an American sat down in a pub in Germany and suggested that imposing a speed limit on the Autobahns might make sense for safety and ecological reasons, they'd witness a similar lack of understanding! And the exception proves the rule in both cases. By no means does every American keep a gun at home, of course. And not all Germans get a kick out of driving 140 mph down the highway. When Andreas Krebs was serving on the board of a big US company, every year, toward the end of April, he'd receive an advisory message from the Corporate Security Department with the headline "Travel Warning—Germany": all this because of the traditional street riots in Berlin-Kreuzberg on May 1. "Riots in Berlin" were to be expected and the city should be avoided. Every attempt by him to put this complete overreaction into context failed, due to Corporate Security's perception of the "dangerous world" out there.

Yes, we live on the same planet but in different worlds, and while there is of course plenty of overlap between your view of the world and that of your colleagues, there are also plenty of differences. Your own perception of how the (your) world works and how it should be dealt with is influenced by whether you grew up in a well-off family or a working-class household, whether your parents were lawyers or musicians, or whether you were born and brought up in London or Sontra, a little town in rural Germany. We all have our blind spots when it comes to how we see ourselves and others, and one of the most unsettling thoughts for most of us is not knowing that we don't know something. These blind spots are an important aspect of self-leadership and frequently a topic in management coaching. For example, a typical gripe from executives: "I never find out anything from my people, even though I'm such an approachable guy!" Gentle questioning reveals that this same person is conveniently overlooking the fact that their perpetual state of being in a hurry and on the way to somewhere else, their often impulsive and negative reaction to being spoken to when they do actually venture outside their office, not to mention their loyal and protective assistant, means they are anything but approachable.

In the cold light of day, nobody can be completely objective, even if we consciously attempt to block out biases, actively try to avoid omitting important factors, and remain suspicious of correlations and other potential pitfalls. So how can you reduce the risk of becoming the victim of half-truths or downright deceptions? Well, here are a couple of basic but potentially effective ideas:

○ Go back and ask again, to make sure that you have really understood the message and argumentation. As we saw in Chapter 2 ("Talent before Seniority"), the ability to listen carefully often diminishes the further you climb up the corporate ladder. Just remembering that we have two ears but only one mouth will generally enable you to make better decisions.

- Get a second opinion and be cautious in your response if you have a bad feeling about something. Intuitive reactions, our "gut feelings," are often correct. After all, they are the result of the bundling of our life experiences, sorted, networked and cross-connected in our brains, which can enable a valuable analytical shortcut.
- Resist artificially generated time pressure. The word "deadline" should be used with greater care and preferably only when missing a timeline would have genuinely serious consequences for the organization.
- Be prepared to take a closer look, below the surface, and don't be put off by the thought that you might find something you really don't like. The stronger your reputation becomes as someone who doesn't allow others to pull the wool over their eyes, the less likely that people will try and do exactly that. One of our interviewees has a clear stance on this.

From Gerd Stürz, Head of Life Sciences (DACH) at EY:

Everyone can probably name examples of where they were presented with just one aspect of the truth. If someone openly claims to be impartial, they are probably just the opposite. If, for example, I hear someone say "I am completely unbiased on this," then all my alarm bells go off. And if I have the feeling that someone is giving me carefully edited information with the intention of getting me to do something for the wrong reasons, then I give them a piece of my mind.

A Stress Test for your Judgment

Do you really have a full 360-degree view or do you have, at best, only partial knowledge of the true facts? Is your map of the business still up to date, or is it time to take a fresh look at the territory? You can never know exactly, but there are always things you can do to sharpen up your powers of judgment. Then again, this is of course just our own personal view of things!

True Insight or a Stab in the Dark? Let's find out!
Yes or No?

1. You regularly engage in conversation with employees at all levels in your organization.

2. You don't only listen to the same three or four advisers.

3. You also talk directly with your firm's customers or participate in client meetings.

4. You recognize potentially important information and check whether it is plausible and credible.

5. You also consider the arguments of people you don't really like.

6. You make an effort to overcome the blind spots in your own perceptions by, for example, seeking honest feedback from a trusted colleague or an experienced coach.

7. You know that your views on something will not necessarily be shared by colleagues, advisers, or business partners. You try to understand *why* there are differences before rushing to make a judgment.

8. You don't rely on just one expert when it comes to important, in-depth questions.

9. You assume positive intent, but accept that one of the main human motivators is self-interest. You don't fundamentally condemn this, but bear it in mind, sound it out, and head it off whenever it appears to be against the best interests of the organization.

10. You know that you don't know everything and make decisions to the best of your knowledge and good conscience.

INCA INSIGHTS

- **Today's certainties can be preparing the ground for tomorrow's failures.**

- **Who is telling me what and why? This question can protect you from deception, disappointment and even disaster.**

"I have often been caught out by my ego, overestimating my abilities and then having the problem of how to sort things out again. Those who demand a lot from themselves also have an increased risk of failure. One of the reasons I rarely failed is that others helped me out at the right moment and I then managed to turn things around in time."

—RÜDIGER LENTZ, DIRECTOR OF THE ASPEN INSTITUTE

8 Ego Beats Reality

(For Whom or for What Am I Doing This?)

It is particularly tragic when a painful defeat is not due to external circumstances but is caused by one's own blindness. This is the scenario upon which many of the great dramas of world literature are based, and economic history is similarly rich in such examples. In the case of the Incas, the fall of the empire was accompanied by a bitter war between two half-brothers which accelerated its decline. From the death of the Inca Huayna Cápac in 1527 to the arrival of the Spaniards in 1532, the Incas' story reads like a never-ending tale of death and destruction. Following Huayna Cápac's fatal decision[152] to divide the succession between two of his sons, Huáscar and Atahualpa, murder and widespread slaughter ensued without regard for the consequences. The trouble began when Huáscar, ruling south of Cuzco, had another brother executed for conspiracy, while Atahualpa, in the north, was assembling an army of ethnic groups who were hostile to the southern Incas due to earlier conquests. Huáscar made the decision to eliminate all of his brothers and rivals for good and invited them to Cuzco under false pretenses. Atahualpa was forewarned of this plan and sent messengers in his place. These messengers suffered gruesome fates and this triggered the escalation of a war in which different tribes sided with different brothers. Atahualpa's generals devastated vast tracts of land and killed anyone suspected of making pacts with the opposing side.

Finally, Huáscar and his entire family were captured and killed, securing Atahualpa's reign. Though this left Atahualpa free to proclaim himself the "sole Inca," various ethnic groups remained hostile to him, and Huáscar's supporters never regarded Atahualpa as their legitimate ruler. Even after his capture by the Spaniards in November 1532 and his execution almost a year later, many local rulers were still allying themselves with the foreign invaders in the hope of shaking off the Inca occupation. That actually succeeded, but at what price? In 1571, after a series of rearguard actions and renewed advances, the last ruler of the Incas, Tupac Amaro, was beheaded in Cuzco. The mightiest empire ever seen on the South American continent was history; the colonial power of Spain had triumphed.[153]

It was during this war between brothers that the strengths and virtues of the Incas revealed their gruesome flip side: The claim to power became a bloodthirsty lust, tenacity became destructive fury, the ability to endure pain and deprivation became a never-ending bloodbath. Together, these factors pushed the Incas toward the abyss. Five hundred years later, we can only speculate on the motivations of the rival brothers, though they were unlikely to include concern for the once-prosperous kingdom. After all, if you really want the best for your country, you don't normally leave scorched earth and massacres in your wake. We are not professional historians and are thus not bound by the limitations of academic caution, so we will allow ourselves to speculate that Atahualpa and Huáscar became victims of their own uncontrolled egos. Their personal claims to power became more important to them than the good of the empire. They were driven by the same qualities that, to a certain extent, enabled them to rule their people in the first place: the desire for power, determination, decisiveness, and the willingness to make great sacrifices.

We don't have to go as far as the modern theaters of war to discover parallels. Even though they fight bloodless battles, strong business leaders face a similar dilemma in that the characteristics that empower them to lead—an almost obsessive belief in their own convictions and the willingness to prevail against resistance—are also their Achilles heel, with the constant risk that a strong ego will at some point turn into self-possessed arrogance. "Some executives crave moments of indulgence for their egos, be it VIP boxes in football stadiums, first-class travel, or corporate jets, like the air they need to breathe, and this becomes increasingly dangerous for the company the further and higher these people advance," in the words of one colleague. It's an interesting and revealing question to ask yourself: Who are you doing it for? For the company, for the issue at hand, or for yourself? That's what this chapter is all about.

Indiana Jones Makes a Hard-Earned Appearance

Dr. Henry Walton "Indiana" Jones Jr. is one of the best-loved figures in popular culture today. Since 1981, the college professor and self-styled archaeologist has undertaken four expeditions, each time in pursuit of spectacular finds, mysterious temples, precious stones and, in his most thrilling adventure to date, an alleged crystal skull of the Incas. In line with the classic blockbuster storyline, Indy's adventures always end in success, but not before the customary serving of crash, bang, and wallop as he heroically succeeds in leaving a dusty trail of devastation in his wake. Treasure recovered, temple(s) and all other irreplaceable monuments destroyed forever! The films thus bear little resemblance to the painstaking excavation work of real archaeologists, who are armed not with a whip and revolver but with tweezers and a brush—and yet, maybe even precisely for this reason, fans are already eagerly anticipating the next installment. Paul Williams isn't ashamed to admit that *Raiders of the Lost Ark* is the only movie he has ever chosen to see twice. On the same day!

Indiana Jones is an adventurer to whom personal triumph means everything and the bone-dry toil of academic archaeology very little. So long as his quest concludes with a mysterious find and the sensation that goes with it, there is no manner of destruction his ego cannot justify. The vast majority of moviegoers can identify with his daredevil charm. And no wonder, since we have all had our Indiana Jones moments, where personal success matters more than the real task at hand or the bigger picture. Not surprisingly, Harrison Ford's most famous character is inspired by a real historical figure: US archaeologist Hiram Bingham, who undertook six expeditions to South America between 1908 and 1924 and later allowed himself to be celebrated as the sole discoverer of Machu Picchu, though this interpretation remains highly controversial to this day.[154] He wasn't too particular about the truth on other occasions either,[155] so long as his version of the story served to increase his renown.

Andreas Krebs still recalls vividly how once upon a time his ego took control…

Belize: Andreas on the Trail of Indiana Jones

As a young country manager in Guatemala, Andreas had the idea of setting up a sales office in neighboring Belize, although a local distribution agreement would have been perfectly adequate. For those who are not familiar with the country of Belize, it has beautiful beaches, a coral reef on its doorstep, lush vegetation, and a population of around 375,000—about the same number of inhabitants as Bakersfield or Bradford. The company's Head of Central America was against the plan, but with the tenacity, enthusiasm, and general chutzpah of youth, Andreas saw to it that his (ad)venture was seen through. The investment was substantial, the return…well, modest would be a generous description. Nonetheless, and fortunately for Andreas, the project was actually seen as a partial success. But what had driven him to do this? The singular and honorable ambition to push the regional business forward? Or was it really the desire to be the first to enter *terra incognita* and make an indelible mark on the history of the company as the intrepid discoverer of new worlds? Well, let's be honest: there are worse places to travel to than Belize...

The beauty of human intelligence is that we are very creative when it comes to finding rational reasons for irrational behavior. We drive an SUV in the smoothly tarmacked city purely for reasons of safety, buy astronomically expensive watches solely as an investment, and make sure our office tower is taller than the rival's building next door only because we need the extra space. If we are honest with ourselves, ego and status play a major role in all of this—from the boardroom right through to the suburbs, where the neighbor always seems to have a slightly newer car than our own. The desire to impress and outdo others appears to be part of human nature, in some of us less, in some of us more.

It is not without reason that some large corporations have developed a system of status-related insignia that would put a royal household to shame. Who has only a basic desk and chair? Who has an office with a sofa? Who has three windows, and who's got that ultimate status symbol, the corner office? Some managerial careers resemble a never-ending ego trip: bigger and faster company cars, ever more luxurious hotels, dinner after dinner in exclusive restaurants and first-class flights in between, all of which can lead to a dangerous loss of contact with reality. Having said that, everyone starts small.

Some years ago, in a large Eurostoxx company, Andreas Krebs succeeded in being promoted from a square meeting table to a round meeting table, long before his official promotion to so-called senior executive, the level at which he would be entitled to such luxuries. The "table system" had previously been explained to Andreas by the facility manager in the broadest of local accents and, as Andreas had been thoroughly trained at the Latin American school of ground-level stakeholder management, he began building a relationship with this valuable colleague. A few months later, the moment arrived when Andreas felt it was worth testing the water regarding a potential furniture upgrade and, lo and behold, he got lucky. The facility manager, by now a personal friend, was just in the process of moving the furniture from a retired senior vice president's office down to the basement, and it would be absolutely no problem to divert one or two items along the way to Andreas's office. A round wooden colossus was thus carefully transported to the fourth floor and, as it made its way along the corridor, his colleagues poured out of their offices to come and congratulate Andreas—not on the magnificent table, but on the promotion! To them, a round table could only mean one thing.

Ego-driven behavior can be very expensive for a business, since it doesn't always turn out as well as the Belize adventure. Risk factors include board members who seek revenge on their old company by developing and launching an economically pointless competitor product (see Chapter 5: "Tackling the Real Opponent") or PPPs ("President's Pet Projects") at the top levels of management. One example of such a project was the Bugatti Veyron, a thousand-horsepower car costing millions of euros that was developed by VW at the personal request of Ferdinand Piëch. "It was clear to all concerned that, from a business point of view, the idea was complete nonsense," commented one of our interviewees. According to the press, Piëch, the CEO at the time and later chairman of the board, still has one of these gas-guzzling creations in his own garage today.[156] Ego gets the better of most executives at some point along the way, for the simple reason that a strong ego is usually conducive to a successful career. Rarely is it described in such a charming combination of honesty and tongue-in-cheek humor as by the following interviewee:

As I took on the new position, I "inherited" six season tickets for the VIP lounge at one of the top Premier league soccer clubs from

my predecessor. Of course, I couldn't possibly just hand them back.
I mean, there are year-long waiting lists for these things. But six?
So, I made a cool-headed, cost-driven management decision and
cut the number of tickets down brutally...to four. Four seemed to
be a good number and my US boss gave me an excellent tip along
the way, which helped ensure that the remaining tickets were
documented completely according to company compliance standards:
He recommended listing them under "Retention and Motivation of
Key Staff."

You might want to put the book aside for a moment and consider
when you yourself became a victim of your ego. When was your
personal Indiana Jones moment or moments? Has everything you
have pushed for and initiated been motivated purely by "objective"
reasons, or have you occasionally given in to the urge for fame,
status, power, or revenge and done things that benefited you, but not
necessarily the company? Before you dismiss such acts as legitimate
compensation for all the hard effort involved in climbing the ranks,
a warning: Anyone who surrenders too readily and too openly to
their ego becomes vulnerable to manipulation. A streetwise colleague
or opponent can quickly sense vanity and recognize which buttons
to press to get what they want from you. More on that later in this
chapter, but for the moment let's take a look at the dramatic downfall
of a senior executive whose overblown ego led ultimately to his
expulsion from the firm.

CEO Today, Gone Tomorrow

When the American magazine *Forbes* got wind of a tragedy of
Shakespearean proportions, it conducted over a hundred interviews
and spent months on its research. There is scarcely a manager whose
fate is as well documented as that of Jeff Kindler, whose rise and fall are
a prototype for CEOs and managing directors in a range of industries.

Kindler joined Pfizer in 2002 as Executive Vice President and General Counsel, led the company as CEO from 2006 to 2010, and was fired by the board on December 4, 2010, in a brief meeting convened specially for this purpose.[157] Like Shakespeare's Macbeth or King Lear, Kindler's downfall also resulted from a fatal miscalculation of his situation; he believed until the last moment that he could convince the board of his merits. His story can be summed up as follows.

In 2006, Kindler succeeded Henry (Hank) McKinnell, CEO since 2001 and responsible for a 47 percent drop in Pfizer's stock. An internal power struggle had already erupted around the issue of succession and had split the company into two camps, with Kindler's emergence as victor being a surprise to many, partly because he had been at Pfizer a relatively short time and the company was known for normally having long-serving employees take over the reins, and partly because he was a trained lawyer and unfamiliar with the pharmaceutical business. Former CEO William (Bill) Steere, who had led Pfizer in the glory days of Lipitor and Viagra and who continued to pull the strings as the gray eminence and Pfizer "adviser" in the background, played a key role in Kindler's appointment. All of this meant that Kindler was taking on a very difficult challenge, and Kindler himself was already known as being anything but easy to get along with.

His appointment was, in the words of *Forbes* magazine, "a shock," and one of his closest future colleagues, a lawyer and twenty-six-year veteran of the company, resigned a day later. "At the end of the day, you have to have some level of respect for the person you are working for," George Evans told *Forbes*. "Having watched Jeff in action over a number of years, I just couldn't work for a company that had him as its CEO." You could dismiss this as personal animosity, except that other voices expressed similar concerns. Kindler was notorious for his rough manner, often cross-examining his employees as he had previously done with witnesses and opponents in court. He called them at any time of the day or night, sometimes to shout at and insult them, only to offer a verbose apology a day later. He trusted no one, took charge of even the smallest details himself, and expected immediate answers to questions, no matter where the respondent was or how important or mundane the matter.

Meanwhile, the company was desperately looking for a new blockbuster, a drug to serve as a potential successor to Lipitor or Viagra. Kindler wore out three R&D bosses in four and a half years and other senior executives also left the company.[158] Kindler sought the advice of external consultants and former colleagues, restructured, purchased, restructured again, but the company was on the decline. He also hired Mary McLeod as global head of HR, who had been dismissed by her previous company because of doubts about her integrity and character issues. McLeod had no problem commuting from Delaware to New York by helicopter almost daily while organizing the job cuts of thousands of employees. Even putting aside these disastrous warning signs, her performance failed to convince: An external audit later branded her as simply "incompetent." But she was unconditionally loyal to Jeff Kindler, controlled access to him, defamed other executives, and took home earnings that made her one of Pfizer's five highest-paid employees. The whole story and the corporate players within would have indeed provided more than enough material for a modern-day tragedy!

The stock price continued to decline and other key employees considered leaving or retiring—until the board slammed on the brakes, ordered Kindler to Florida and, despite a long defense plea, simply threw him out. It should have served as a warning to Kindler that his predecessor Hank McKinnell had also been fired, having awarded himself a salary increase of 72 percent despite the drastic decrease in company value over which he had presided. The higher up in the organization, the more prevalent and dangerous the illusion of invincibility would seem to be.

Andreas Krebs attended an international leadership conference some time later in which three CEOs, who had all been in similar situations to Kindler, discussed their learnings and reflected on what had happened to them in a session about the hiring and firing of CEOs. They shared their experiences with ruthless, unflinching honesty, later sharing additional details in one-on-one discussions. Their key messages, as recounted from memory, were as follows:

- "My fundamental mistrust was a huge mistake. I mistrusted anyone and everyone, especially ex-confidants of my predecessor. But a lot of these people were in truth very good."
- "As a trained attorney, I thought I could do anything. Lawyers tend to think like that. I'd already had to deal with practically every issue you can think of; why should things be any different now that I was CEO?"
- "I sought out a narrow circle of confidants of my own and favored loyalty over quality—a big mistake."
- "I wasn't prepared for the task. After all, who is when they become a CEO for the first time? But I also failed to look for sparring partners—colleagues in similar situations, experienced CEOs, whom I could have talked to openly about what to look out for."
- "I created a kind of isolated inner circle. The few confidants I had barely let anyone approach me without their say-so. I had hardly any one-on-one conversations with colleagues outside of this circle and, if I did, the contents of the conversation were checked and filtered in advance. People had a briefing on what to discuss with me and what not. I realized that much too late."
- "I was blinded by the red-carpet universe. A visit to the Brazil organization, for example, involved a delegation of at least fifteen to twenty-five people plus bodyguards. Several corporate jets were taken on the trip. How on earth was I supposed to maintain a connection to reality?"

○ "This inner circle eventually sealed my fate when the board accused me of inappropriate concessions to close confidants."

Two of the CEOs went so far as to say that it was absolutely right to fire them, and you have to give all three great credit for being able to look back with such poise and describe their learnings so openly. Not everyone is able to do that! The examples above are also typical for the degree of inflated self-esteem and hubris that sooner or later is likely to lead to downfall. The person becomes increasingly blind to danger and ever more ruthless, creating personal enemies and, by focusing more and more on themselves, vulnerable to making the wrong decisions for the organization. How prone do you think you are to this? We asked a few executives to take stock of their management experience and compiled a list of warning signs:

The Egometer—How Big Is Your Ego?

Hand on heart, which of the following thoughts have ever gone through your mind?

"What would the company be without me?!" ☐

"The rules that apply to everyone else don't necessarily apply to me." ☐

"I'm just better; I'm playing in a different league." ☐

"It's best if I just do it myself!" ☐

"What could possibly happen to me?" ☐

"If you're not with me, you're against me!" ☐

"You can't really trust anyone." ☐

"For me, only the best is good enough—and I've earned the right to say so." ☐

"The more, the better! The sky is the limit." ☐

"You can't make an omelet without breaking eggs." ☐

"Loyalty is more important than performance and knowledge!" ☐

"I expect unconditional support, not so-called pragmatists and people who think they know better." ☐

It goes without saying that the Egometer is not intended to be taken too seriously and is by no means scientific. However, if you've ticked more than two or three boxes, you'll almost certainly benefit from reading on!

On the Drip Feed of Admiration

Why is it that some managers become blind to the dangers they face, deaf to all warnings they hear, and insensitive to the needs of others, and just keep plowing on, driven by pure ego, to their eventual demise? We touched upon it in Chapter 5, noting that the line between healthy self-confidence and destructive self-obsession is very fine. Anyone in a leadership position needs to be resilient and must be able to deal with pushback and make unpopular decisions. Understandably, most people who have led teams or organizations successfully over an extended period of time will inevitably cultivate some of these traits which, after all, have helped them achieve that success. Add to this the fact that critical and dissenting voices get quieter and quieter the higher someone climbs and the more influential they become until, finally, they reach the "hall of mirrors" on the Executive Floor, as described in Chapter 7. Once there, everyone assures them how marvelous they are, unless they manage to break out of the cage and find sparring partners prepared to be open and honest. The mistakes described above are not only to be found in large corporations and public companies. You can also find many a patriarch in family businesses brimming over with confidence based on past successes, which can prove very dangerous for their organizations, simply because they can no longer imagine ever being wrong.

Happily, not everyone who has had a successful career succumbs to egomania, but it happens often enough for it to have been the subject of some very interesting publications, such as the book *The Neuroses of the Bosses* that psychologists Jürgen Hesse and Hans Christian Schrader wrote some years ago.[159] They looked at early childhood influences such as a loveless or very performance-oriented upbringing as possible causes for a later excessive craving for recognition, the tendency to block out criticism, or a lack of empathetic emotion, but we are not psychologists and don't intend to dig down that deep. And just because someone doesn't behave particularly selflessly or cooperatively doesn't automatically mean that they have a personality disorder of some kind! Nevertheless, the job of a manager carries with it the inherent risk of *déformation professionnelle*, of slipping into the *Indiana Jones* mode, which is good for neither the person nor their surroundings. So, how can you manage your ego? How do you successfully tread the fine line between robust self-esteem and dangerous overconfidence? How do you avoid blind obstinacy and dangerous hubris? And how do you protect other people and your organization from the side effects of your ego?

The key to answering these questions is understanding more about your self-esteem and what it is based on. What we mean by self-esteem or self-worth is the degree to which we value and appreciate ourselves. How much respect do you have for yourself, to what extent are you content within yourself? Above all, what influences your self-worth? In his coaching sessions, Paul Williams sometimes works with a simple model, the self-esteem tank. Picture your sense of self-worth as a tank or small barrel, with an opening at the top and an outlet at the bottom, which is controlled by a tap. Both the inlet and the outlet of the tank are accessible to everyone. Every day we pour self-esteem marbles into the tank and every day we lose some of these little marbles. Sometimes the inflow of self-worth comes from external influences, such as praise and recognition, material rewards, titles, status symbols, and in all these cases, we are relying either exclusively or to a large extent on other people for topping up our self-esteem marbles, in the form of their reactions and their behaviors toward us. Alternatively, sometimes our self-worth tank is topped up from within, such as when we are on our own and immerse ourselves in a task, occasionally even to the point of achieving a so-called "flow," when we reach a goal which means a great deal to us alone, with no outside help. The interesting part is that the latter, internal route toward topping up the self-esteem marbles is entirely self-contained and under our individual control, whereas the external route relies, as mentioned above, on other people's reactions and these can, of course, also be negative, in the form of unfair criticism, disrespect, or other variations of mistreatment. And all of these reactions will open the lower tap and drain self-worth marbles from the tank.

Most of us have a preference for one of the two methods to increase self-worth, the external or the internal, and it is important to work out for yourself which one works best for you, finding out how you "tick." The more extroverted leaders and managers—those who, interestingly, are often viewed as classic leadership material—are frequently reliant on external affirmation. Indeed, sometimes they appear almost addicted to praise and admiration. This is a dangerous situation as, by doing this, they have essentially delegated control over their own happiness and self-esteem to other people. Staying with the tank model, this means that lots of people can also come along, open up the tap, and drain away a lot of those marbles! If that happens, the manager must strive all the more to replace these "losses" and typically does this by seeking still further recognition, feeding a kind of addiction with higher and higher doses of external praise. This not only leads to a treadmill effect but can also push the manager further and further into the ego trap, as they surround themselves with "yes men" and uncritical admirers (praise givers) and divides the world into friends and enemies. This can also cause the person to do things (or not do things) for the recognition of the gallery rather than in the interests of the company. This at least partly explains why glitzy new company buildings get constructed even though they are neither necessary nor affordable, or why pointless prestige projects are pursued even though they can never be profitable. And there are undoubtedly mergers and acquisitions that have been started, and even completed, based largely on the fantasy of becoming Number One, even when the business case is weak and likely to fail. What's more, let's not forget to mention what we talked about in Chapter 1—that being Number One is seldom a good guide for sensible behavior.

On the other side, you have the more introverted people, often the "tinkering" types or experts, who are usually extremely happy if they are just left alone to get on with things and do what they are good at and enjoy. Their self-worth is far less reliant on the recognition of other people and, even when it is, the self-respect they earn from the positive feedback of a recognized expert or peer in their own field is much more important than broader public recognition. A quiet pat on the back is usually more than enough, and this makes them less reliant on the judgment and feedback of others. And, as ever, the exception proves the rule here too.

The first level of protection against one way of falling into the ego trap is to understand and be honest with yourself about what drives your own sense of self-worth. If you notice, or someone else who knows you well notices, that the admiration of others is becoming rather too important to you, then it would be a clever move to try and counter this and, in so doing, protect that lower drainage tap from others getting their hands on it. A good way to practice what this feels like is to find environments, ideally outside your organization, which enhance your self-worth without you having to impress other people and where your status and rank in the company is unimportant or of no relevance at all. Finding satisfaction and success outside your business environment is not just good fun, but also very good practice for later on. After all, if your work is your life, and your life is your work, then what is left in your life when you are no longer working? If your ego and your position in the company are so closely linked that they become one entity, then this is particularly dangerous for an organization, especially when the person concerned is at the very top. As a rule, this type of person will battle for the position and not for the business. They want to look good and be feted by the media, and the result is activity for activity's sake and often at the shareholders' or employees' expense. Smart senior executives keep this in mind when making hiring decisions for top positions, as illustrated in the following example.

From Dr. Christoph Straub, CEO of BARMER:

> *After I was appointed to a board position for the very first time, and once I had gotten started, I asked one of the decision-makers why he was so convinced that I should get the job. I had only been at the business three years and had been, up until then, head of business development. He answered, "because you were the only one here who didn't desperately want the job." He was right.*

That has echoes of Machiavelli and his shrewd observation: "It is not titles that honor men, but men that honor titles." Christoph Straub drew our attention to another aspect which is linked to the question of ego: the physical embodiment of power.

> *At the end of the day, the right to make a show of power goes hand in hand with leadership. This is not something I am comfortable doing, which is not necessarily positive, because leaders can use this to strengthen their ability to get things done. In so doing, they make it clear that they are the ones who call the shots and simultaneously sends the signal "I'm not really that interested in the rest of you. I'm going to get on and do my thing whatever."*

A boss who orders a Mercedes Maybach as his company car while at the same time pushing through a tough cost-cutting program in the organization takes this power game too far, and the same applies to a board member who, in similar circumstances, commutes to work by helicopter. The Maybach example is a true story from a Eurostoxx-listed business. It is all a question of dosage and degree, and the important thing is to be conscious about what you are doing and the associated messages you are sending. There is a big difference between deliberately putting your mark on the organization and making excessive and eccentric demands, purely based on the fact that you think you are entitled to do this, regardless of what is happening around you in the real world. Angela Maier and Christoph Nesshoever summed it up nicely in their recent article in a major European business journal: "It's like so often: Success makes you complacent. And the best, whether elsewhere in business, sport or other organizations, become the biggest risks themselves at the end of their careers."

And now to our final thoughts on this topic. A healthy ego requires a healthy distance from the demands of professional life. Anybody who devotes themselves body and soul to his company is living just as dangerously as the person who uses the company as a vehicle to quench their thirst for recognition. Jim Collins has been looking at outstanding management success for decades and, among the great figures in leadership, he has observed a paradoxical mixture of "ambition" and "humility."[160] This enables the person to set and achieve ambitious targets and drive dynamic activity, while at the same time never forgetting the ever-present risk of personal failure. This, again, protects against both the illusion of invincibility and the dangers of basing an entire ego on the attainment and maintenance of a specific hierarchical status.

Sparring Partners, Not Court Toadies

To this day, almost every child knows Hans Christian Andersen's fairy tale "The Emperor's New Clothes." The pomp-obsessed Emperor falls for two fraudsters who convince him that they can weave the most unbelievably beautiful clothes. These fine garments are, however, invisible to those who cannot live up to the demands of high office. The Emperor is enthused, procures gold and the finest silk, and the fraudsters set to work on their tailors' hoax. By and by, ministers come by to monitor the progress of the work; none of them can see anything, but each one of them assures the Emperor that the new garments look quite magnificent! The Emperor elevates the scoundrels to court weavers, decorates them with medals and then, ahead of the grand ceremonial procession, they "dress" him and he praises them for how feather-light his magnificent new cloak is. The crowds lining the street play along with the charade too until, finally, a small child shouts out, "But the Emperor hasn't got any clothes on!" The rest of the assembled crowds join in and laugh out loud at his naked embarrassment. "I've got to get through this somehow," the Emperor thinks as he plows bravely on. Andersen finishes off with, "And the court chamberlains carried on walking, bearing the cloak which was not there."[161]

Children love this story because, finally, they get to be smarter than the grown-ups. Many adults, on the other hand, react with slight unease. Would you have had the courage to speak up or would you, like the ministers, have carried on the pretense? What Andersen describes is not that far from the reality of many businesses. A vain executive or patriarch comes up with a dubious idea. Anyone who dares to speak out is automatically considered incompetent and disloyal and must expect to pay the price for their cheek. So, everyone carries on as though they think it is a tremendous idea, even after it has been exposed as complete nonsense.

The VW Phaeton, named confidently after the son of the sun god Helios, with which Ferdinand Piëch once wanted to take on and beat the luxury limousines of Mercedes or BMW, turned out to be a huge flop and VW didn't even come close to meeting its sale targets.[162] Was there nobody in the army of VW managers prepared to warn that "Volkswagen" and "Luxury" were, from a branding and marketing perspective, uneasy bedfellows? Just as with the Emperor and his new clothes, when the last Phaeton came off the production line in the glass halls in Dresden, certain members of VW senior management still seemed convinced the whole project had been an excellent idea. VW headquarters issued a statement saying, "The Phaeton is and remains an important project for Volkswagen. It is critical for Volkswagen's brand positioning and showcasing our technical capabilities."[163] We are reminded of the marvelous rhyming couplet from the German poet Christian Morgenstern: "And thus in their considered view, what did not suit could not be true!"

Those who reduce highly qualified, experienced, and well-paid employees to the level of court toadies hurt themselves, first and foremost, because they no longer get the benefit of what they are paying for: the employees' specialist knowledge, experience, and ideas. A number of our interviewees had stories to tell about this. Here are a couple of examples.

From Dr. Iris Löw-Friedrich, Executive Vice President and Chief Medical Officer, UCB:

> And then we have the issue of ignorance, which goes like this: "I know everything better anyway and I can't be bothered to take a closer look either." I think this phenomenon also relates to how I choose my team. Am I brave enough to not just put up with people who express different opinions and respect them, but also to consciously bring these types of people on board? The urge to conform is often a strong one.

*How open am I to different opinions, how willing am I to encourage
alternative approaches and then to run with them?*

From Werner Spinner, former board member at Bayer and President
of FC Cologne (2012-2019):

*You enter a new environment, take football as an example, and
suddenly you are faced with people who are afraid. Based on their
previous experience with management, they are so afraid that the only
answers you get have been sterilized at maximum heat. It is not easy
to change this culture because you need people who are not afraid,
who step up to the mark and are fearless in their decision-making.*

The best way to prevent yourself falling into the ego trap is to
surround yourself with genuine sparring partners. Do you really have
a culture of openness in your management team? Can you show a
colleague (or they you) a metaphorical "yellow ego card" if one of you
is in the process of rushing off in the wrong direction? If no one has
contradicted you or openly pushed back on an issue for a long time
it is, of course, possible that this is because you are such a fantastic
leader and have such a brilliant mind and never make mistakes. But
it is much more likely that you have either surrounded yourself with
the wrong people or have succeeded in sealing the lips of the team
around you. All your alarm bells should be ringing if key performers
unexpectedly resign and you are surprised because you actually
thought that everything was running smoothly. Don't be offended,
put your pride to one side and ask them what the real reasons are for
choosing to go. We are always surprised at how many colleagues don't
include exit interviews as a formal part (and sadly the last part!) of
their HR hiring and development process. This is the final opportunity
to ask open questions and get honest answers, provided, of course,
that you have already provided them with a good reference. Are you
prepared to listen to a few critical and uncomfortable truths about
yourself and your organization?

Trusted and critical colleagues are therefore invaluable for giving feedback, enabling self-reflection and, in certain circumstances, preventing bad decisions from being made. But if you haven't got such a colleague handy right now, you can also do this on your own with a couple of helpful questions:

o If I achieve my objectives, what are the positives for me, for my colleagues, and for the organization?
o If I achieve my objectives, what are the negatives for me, for my colleagues, and for the organization?

If you answer these questions honestly, you will quickly find out whether your objectives are driven by the interests of the business or by your ego, and whether the potential price to be paid, if it's the latter, is worth it.

Another good way to keep your feet on the ground is to take on roles where you are not the most important person. Look for opportunities where you are simply "X" and not the CEO, the head of department, or the boss. Surround yourself with positive, honest, and grounded people, those who work hard and play hard, in free interpretation of Colin Powell's quote earlier in the book. A strong life partner or a good friend can also be a big help. They sometimes know our weaknesses better than we do ourselves and can highlight difficult issues with sensitivity. Many people swear by the apparently simple but often very challenging exercise of explaining to their eight-year-old child what they actually do all day long. After the third "why?" they have usually come down to earth with a bump. Another good exercise in modesty and humility is to learn something new, something fun to do, whether a sport, music making, or some other type of artistic pursuit: anything where you currently have a relatively low level of competence and no special status due to acquired privileges. And finally, let's not forget how important it is to learn lessons from making bad decisions as a result of falling victim to your ego along the way.

Paul Williams encountered his Indiana Jones moment while he was still a student.

"You Can Only Pull a Rabbit out of the Hat if You've Put One in There First!" —Paul on the Trail of Indiana Jones

My ego moment happened early on, before I actually started in a proper job. I was at the University of London, enjoying student life and living in a hall of residence with 130 other young guys. The hall had a management committee, which was chosen by the other residents and, in my second year, I was elected deputy senior student. So far, so good.

Every May, the hall of residence had an annual dinner, where everyone could invite a guest and all the students got dressed up for the evening and dined together in a more formal atmosphere. And, for some unknown reason, I volunteered to make a speech at the event. I didn't have to do this—the senior student was expected to give some sort of address, but not his deputy. But I clearly fancied the chance of demonstrating to a wider audience my brilliant rhetorical skills and lightning wit, so without giving it a great deal of thought, I confidently assumed I would come up with some hilarious stories, side-splitting anecdotes, and razor-sharp satire to the entertainment and amusement of all present. I was wrong.

The evening approached, and I kept putting off writing a concept for the structure and content of the speech, as it slowly dawned on me that I had no real clue what I wanted to say. But I was too proud to admit this to anyone and still felt fairly confident that "it'll be alright on the night." Eventually I managed to put together a few jokes and tried to string these together in some sort of cohesive story, but felt uncomfortable and unprepared. The speech was a disaster. It was dull, boring, without a message and I got only a few weak laughs. I was nervous the whole time and suffered a thousand deaths while giving it. It was self-serving, vain, and unnecessary—a classic Indiana Jones ego moment!

So, what did the "personal temple" look like that I had destroyed? Well, gone was a fair amount of self-confidence and ego. Gone was the desire to stand up and make any kind of speech at a similar gathering in the foreseeable future, and gone was part of a hard-earned reputation and standing among my peers.

In short, I had caused a mid-sized trauma to my self-esteem. But happily, there was a positive side to the whole fiasco, though it took a while for me to realize this. Among other aspects, it led me to become a fanatical preparer of things, to the point of almost panicking if I had the feeling that I hadn't done enough preparation, regardless of the task. Only in more recent years have I learned to channel this and prepare to an appropriate level, where the input is in keeping with the desired output and the occasion. So, the whole episode had its good side in the long run, but cost me a lot of energy between the time it happened and the point where I started turning it into a positive influence on how I work and manage myself. I wouldn't dream of saying it cured me of the ego trap forever, but it certainly helped sensitize me to the importance of watching out for it more closely in the future.

A Stress Test for Your Ego

Do you have your ego under control? This is such a prickly topic that some years ago, in the *Harvard Business Manager*, a proposal was made for a "Hippocratic oath for managers" including: "I promise that I will not advance my personal interests at the expense of my enterprise or society.... I recognize that my behavior must set an example of integrity, eliciting trust and esteem from those I serve."[164] Hmm, so far it doesn't seem to have completely caught on. Let's finish off with a few last thoughts on ego.

Fighter for the Cause or Just Another Ego-shooter?

Who or what are you really doing it for?

1. There are people in your immediate circle who tell you openly and honestly what they really think about you and what you're doing.

2. It has not been that long since you admitted to making a mistake.

---

3. Someone in your circle of friends outside of work has, at some point, warned you about your ego. ☐

4. You don't confuse loyalty with flattery or blind agreement. ☐

5. When it comes to important projects, you weigh up who is going to derive the greatest advantage from it and who, if anyone, is going to have to pay for it. ☐

6. When things go wrong, you don't automatically assume the blame lies elsewhere. ☐

7. As far as you are concerned, status symbols are just part of the job but have no real intrinsic value. ☐

8. You can look back, self-critically, to occasions when your ego has played tricks on you or bitten through the leash and taken over. ☐

9. You are not terrified by the thought of what might become of you if you were to lose your job tomorrow. ☐

10. You are well aware that you, too, can fail. ☐

INCA INSIGHTS

- **Those who can't imagine failing simply have too little imagination.**

- **Real leaders are not egomaniacs but fighters for the cause.**

- **Those who can combine ambition with critical self-awareness can achieve truly great things!**

A Closing Word

This is where our tour of the management world ends. Along the way, we took you back into the world of the Incas, those inspirational experts in organization, innovation, and integration, whose Andean empire ultimately failed so tragically and yet who reflect our situation today in so many ways. If this book has opened your eyes to some of the possible pitfalls in your own day-to-day work as a manager and leader and has shown you some potential ways to avoid these, then it has served its purpose.

The catalyst for the book was a comment made by a guide during a tour of Tipón, Peru, one of the Incas' first agricultural research sites. Unlike the vast majority of other conquerors, the Incas succeeded in uniting "the best of all worlds," integrating and applying knowledge from the conquered regions to achieve impressive levels of mastery in architecture, agriculture, animal husbandry, and many other fields. This is why the Inca buildings survived almost every earthquake while the churches of the Spaniards often collapsed. Our spontaneous comments on the parallels between the world of the Incas and the world of management and leadership in organizations today brought a smile to the lips of our small group of friends at the time, but were meant to be light-hearted. However, this quickly changed as we looked more deeply into the story of the Incas—their know-how and their social and economic system—and were surprised to find that, in many ways, they were smarter than we are today. Even their dramatic decline showed striking parallels with some of the crash landings of today's so-called leaders. We hope the lessons and stories in this book will encourage you to reflect on your own strengths and weaknesses and to reconsider positively some of the key elements of the ideas behind values-based leadership, both for yourself and for your organization. Perhaps we've been able to provide some insights for your future selection of people, your human resources development strategy, the promotion of future talent, or the timely identification and nurturing of a capable successor.

For us, our encounter with the Incas provided a number of enlightening moments, not least in the area of ego, with the realization of how important a healthy ego is to being successful in an organization, and yet how dangerous such an ego can become if it is allowed to take over and lead us into the ego trap. This trap was not only dangerous for the rival Inca rulers Huáscar and Atahualpa, the ambitious archeologist Hiram Bingham, and his fictitious alter ego "Indiana Jones"; it has also reared its ugly head in our lives, to the detriment of ourselves and, far worse, of those around us.

In times in which we appear to be surrounded by egomaniacs in companies and organizations, but also at the highest governmental level, it is undeniable that clear-headedness, personal integrity, and a firm grasp on reality are more important than ever. If reading this book has made you a little more sensitive to the temptations of egocentric goals, meaningless side battles, false and empty values, verbose visions that inspire nobody, and the unshakeable belief in your own importance—in short, if it has helped immunize you against the illusion of invincibility—then our efforts were worthwhile. And if you ever catch yourself thinking, "I'm the only one who can fix it!" then might we respectfully suggest you take a cold shower, a cool beer, or just pick up our book again and reconsider that statement for a minute or two. The world, or at the very least your organization, your boss, your colleagues and employees, your partner, children, and friends will probably be grateful, as, indeed, would we!

Andreas Krebs and Paul Williams, Langenfeld, Germany
www.inca-inc.com

Epilogue: A Message from Peru
by Dr. Max Hernandez

Former executive director of the Acuerdo National (National Round Table), Peru

Paul Williams and Andreas Krebs became friends of Peru at first sight. No, wait, let me correct what I have just written: Paul Williams and Andreas Krebs's friendship with Peru began at first sight, yes, but only deepened after they learned something about the Incas. They became interested in the history of the Incas and were eager to understand what archeologists, historians, ethnohistorians, and anthropologists had published. They visited the area around Cuzco, the ancient Inca capital, "the navel of the world," a number of times and gained a firsthand view of the setting and the physical and cultural elements of the Inca Empire that have persisted through the centuries. Their fascination grew and was one of the key sparks for their decision to write their book.

They became acquainted with the work of the likes of Raúl Porras, María Rostworowski, John Murra, and Franklin Pease, to name just some of the most important authors and researchers to have studied the sociopolitical organization of the Tawantinsuyu and the manner in which, without the assistance of a phonetic alphabet and hence of writing, nor the wheel, nor draft animals, the Incas managed to rule over such an enormous territory. By talking to both experts on the Inca nation and members of modern Peruvian society, Paul Williams and Andreas Krebs succeeded in combining the insights gathered from their knowledge and experience of the world of business with their interest in the history and the social makeup of the Incas and Peru.

This book is the result of their inquiry into some of the reasons for the success of the Inca "enterprise." They include what they have learned about the importance of reciprocity, of the values embedded in the daily salute *Ama Sua* (Don't steal), *Ama Llulla* (Don't lie) *y Ama Quella* (Don't be lazy)—now principles adopted by the United Nations— or about the advanced way in which the Incas handled matters of succession. Originally inspired by their observation about how the Incas dealt with the people they conquered, how they respected and maintained many of their customs and adopted and integrated the best of their skills, and how this could be transferred into the modern world, Williams and Krebs have now successfully extended this connection into other areas and turned this all into this one piece of work: *The Illusion of Invincibility: The Rise and Fall of Organizations— Inspired by the Incas of Peru.*

In this period of a continuous flow of challenges, it is a truism that entrepreneurs and business leaders have to go beyond the usual core activities of controlling, monitoring, organizing, and planning and be prepared to face how change occurs in complex social systems. This is not a problem that can be solved simply, with a single stroke of insightful thought, but is a multifactorial challenge to be worked through slowly, step by step, piece by piece. As part of this process, the importance of making the right decisions and recommendations, based on a clear and common understanding of which values are important, is an indispensable starting point toward improving the structure, dynamics, and leadership of organizations today.

It is the contention of Krebs and Williams that, in the difficult task of formulating frameworks broad and flexible enough to allow the coexistence of business effectiveness and ethical values, the ancient and practical wisdom of those remarkable leaders and politicians that were the Incas may well prove to be an example and inspiration for the creation of the conditions that can help us to navigate more wisely the realities of businesses and organizations today and in the future.

To close, let me recount the last question the two gentlemen asked me when we met during their visit to Lima in 2016: "Is it legitimate to use the Incas as an inspiration and analogy for modern business life?" Well, I told them I believed that this was something that every individual should be free to decide for themselves—both as an author and as a reader. But since they had asked me, I was happy to give them an answer, roughly as follows: "The Incas faced coming to terms with a difficult environment, with extreme conditions and challenges, and had to deal with these as best they could, which led them to develop some resourceful solutions. And maybe they dealt with some of these challenges better than other cultures, which is perhaps why they were the dominant people in the region for some time. What better inspiration and analogy for the modern business world would you wish to find?"

Dr. Max Hernandez
Lima, Peru

Endnotes

1 Company.nokia.com and NZZ.

2 Erdle 2014 and www.itopnews.de/2013/04. Last accessed 10/15/2016.

3 Ankenbrand/Nienhaus 2011.

4 Froitzheim 2012, p. 63.

5 *Manager Magazin*, 06/2018, FAZ Online. Last accessed 6/20/2018.

6 n-tv from 01.03.2016.

7 *Spiegel* 34/2013.

8 *Manager Magazin* 04/19.

9 Probst/Raisch. www.researchgate.net/profile/Gilbert_Probst/publication/285635057_Organizational_Crisis_-_The_Logic_of_Failure/links/5a997b7aa6fdcc3cbac91a64/Organizational-Crisis-The-Logic-of-Failure.pdf.

10 Ibid.

11 Collins 2009.

12 www.cnbc.com/2018/11/15/bezos-tells-employees-one-day-amazon-will-fail-and-to-stay-hungry.html. Last accessed 5/22/2019.

13 Probst/Raisch. www.researchgate.net/profile/Gilbert_Probst/publication/285635057_Organizational_Crisis_-_The_Logic_of_Failure/links/5a997b7aa6fdcc3cbac91a64/Organizational-Crisis-The-Logic-of-Failure.pdf.

14 Goede Montalván (2013), p. 208, Kurella (2013), p. 46 ff., Schulz (2014), p. 44, Wikipedia, Artikel "Inka", p. 11 and 23.

15 Panmore.com/google-vision-statement-mission-statement.

16 Tietz 2011, p. 87.

17 This refers to a well-known Jobs-quotation: "We're gambling on our vision, and we would rather do that than make 'me too' products. Let some other companies do that. For us, it's always the next dream." en.wikiquote.org/wiki/Steve_Jobs. Last accessed on 8/22/2017.

18 Cited in business-wissen.de: "What Vision and Mission can Cause in the Enterprise"; www.business-wissen.de. Last accessed 9/12/2016.

19 www.amazon.jobs/de/working/working-amazon.

20 www.youtube.com/watch?v=pbemFDRcyyg ("Mercedes-Benz: Das Beste oder nichts").

21 www.mercedes-benz.com/de/mercedes-benz/classic/markenclubs/gottlieb-daimler-gedaechtnisstaette/.

22 www.db.com/ir/en/download/Code_of_Business_Conduct_and_Ethics_for_ Deutsche_Bank_Group.pdf, www2.basf.us/careers/pdfs/Vision_Values_Principles_e.pdf, www.henkel.de/unternehmen/unternehmenskultur/vision-und-werte, www.rewe-group.com/de/unternehmen/leitbild. Last accessed 09/09/2016.

23 www.unicef.de/ueber-uns/leitbild, www.amnesty.de/kontakt, www.ikea.com/ ms/de_DE/this-is-ikea/about-the-ikeagroup/index.html, www.youtube.com/ watch?v=SGPcSnGvf44(Syngenta), www.presseportal.de/pm/57334/3247706, www.google.de/about/company, www.southwest.com/html/about-southwest/ careers/culture.html. Last accessed 09/9/2016.

24 Startwithwhy.com/.

25 Collins/Porras (2004), p. 91 A short definition by Collins can be found here: www.jimcollins.com/concepts.html. Last accessed 9/20/2016.

26 "Toyota bleibt größter Autobauer der Welt," *Handelsblatt*, 1/27/2016.

27 Download of survey results for (2015) at www.gallup.de/183104/engagement-index-deutschland.aspx.

28 www.gallup.com.

29 *Brand eins* (2015, p. 115).

30 Stähli 2013, p. 113.

31 Stähli 2013, p. 114.

32 IfM 2012, p. 6 f. A transfer to a daughter is an option in 32 percent of cases; 26 percent have "several children" in mind, 7.4 percent "other family members," 5.9 percent spouse.

33 Schwartz/Gerstenberger 2015, p. 1.

34 Grimberg 2010.

35 Ibid.

36 Cited in Krohn 2009.

37 Langenscheidt/May 2014, p. 95.

38 Rosenthal-Effekt see: www.stangl-taller.at/TESTEXPERIMENT/experimentbsprosenthal.html. Last accessed 10/21/2016.

39 Quellen: karrierebibel.de/koerpergroesse. Last accessed 10/24/2016.

40 Hartmann (2013).

41 *Lexicon of Psychology*, "Errors of judgement"; www.spektrum.de. Last accessed 10/19/2016. Thormann 2016 provides a compact overview of perception errors.

42 Probst/Raisch. www.researchgate.net/profile/Gilbert_Probst/publication/285635057_Organizational_Crisis_-_The_Logic_of_Failure/

links/5a997b7aa6fdcc3cbac91a64/Organizational-Crisis-The-Logic-of-Failure. pdf.

43 Gasche 2016, p. 59.

44 Collins 2011, p. 59 ff.

45 govleaders.org/powell.htm. Last accessed 10/17/2016.

46 Botelho et al. 2017.

47 Cappelli/Tavis 2016.

48 www.managementpotenzial.de. Last accessed 10/21/2016).

49 Stähli 2013, p. 129.

50 The "Development over time of the Engagement Index 2001–2015" www.gallup.de/183104/engagement-index-deutschland.aspx.

51 Herzberg 1959.

52 Sprenger 2014.

53 www.wiwo.de/erfolg/beruf/ranking-die-beliebtesten-arbeitgeber-deutschlands/11682336.html. Last accessed 12/14/2016.

54 Vgl. Neuberger 2002, Who gave his book the title *Führen und führen lassen*.

55 Mayer-Kuckuk 2016.

56 Explanation/background: Europe, Middle East, Africa; approx. 8,000 employees, at that time, a turnover of approx. 6 billion US dollars.

57 For a concise description, see Blanchard et al. 2015.

58 Investors.southwest.com/news-and-events/news-releases/2018/01-25-2018-113046083.

59 www.brainyquote.com/quotes/authors/h/herb_kelleher.html.

60 Pundt/Nerdinger 2012.

61 Gerpott/Voelpel 2014.

62 Wikipedia "Inka," p. 15. Last accessed 08/29/2016; Schulz 2013, p. 152; Noack 2013, p. 146.

63 Stähli 2013, p. 78 f. Last accessed 11/9/2016.

64 Press release from 4/7/2016: "Creation of social values becomes part of a company's success," download at www.pwc.de. Title of the study: "Government and the Global CEO" (19th Annual Global CEO Survey 2016) www.pwc.com/ceosurvey. Last accessed 11/10/2016.

65 www.pwc.com/gr/en/publications/19th-ceo-survey-government.pdf.

66 www.wertekommission.de/wp-content/uploads/2018/06/Führungskräftebefragung-2018.pdf.

67 Rochus Mummert 2012.

68 de.m.wikipedia.org/wiki/Siemens#Korruptionsaffäre, Cf. Handelsblatt of 12.07.2016: "Heinrich von Pierer: Trial against ex-Siemens managers fails at first attempt"; Handelsblatt 5/27/2014 "Siemens bribe money affair: The big ones ones get away" (www.handelsblatt.com), and *Spiegel* online 06.09.2016: "Bribery scandal Siemens: Federal High Court overturns acquittal of Ex-CEO."

69 Dahlkamp et al. 2008, p. 81.

70 Collins 1995, Rochus Mummert 2012.

71 friedhelmwachs.de/buch-evangelisch-erfolgreich-wirtschaften/.

72 www.accounting-degree.org/scandals/.

73 Heinrich von Pierer, *Zwischen Profit und Moral* (*Between Profit and Morality*); Pierer, Heinrich von/Homann, Karl/Lübbe-Wolf, Gertrude: *Zwischen Profit und Moral: Für eine menschliche Wirtschaft.* München: Hanser 2003, p. 7 ff. and: p. 7 f. and 12.

74 Revenue 2018 2,34b€ www.dussmanngroup.com/dussmann-group/zahlen-fakten/ Last accessed 05/23/2019.

75 There is a film about Catherine Fürstenberg-Dussmann's undercover experiment to be found here: www.swr.de/betrifft/catherine-fuerstenberg-dussmann-undercov/-/id=98466/did=7481992/nid=98466/zvgix9/index.html. Last accessed 7/17/2017.

76 Dahlkamp et al., p. 88.

77 www.db.com/cr/en/concrete-cultural-change.htm?kid=werte.inter.redirect#tab_corporate-values.

78 Hetzer 2014.

79 Bertelsmann Stiftung 2016, p. 11 (31 percent have confidence in listed companies.)

80 Ernst & Young 2016, p. 24, 51, 53, 55.

81 viaconflict.wordpress.com/2015/11/30/managing-conflict-with-the-values-orientation-theory/.

82 www.uni-kassel.de/fb4/psychologie/personal/lantermann/sozial08/werte.pdf. Last accessed 11/14/2016.

83 Brüser 2002.

84 Huntington 1997.

85 Barmeyer/Davoine 2014, S. 37 et. seq.

86 Goede Montalván 2013 (a), S. 198 ff. and (b), p. 207 et. seq. as well as the documentary "Das Blut des Sonnengottes" at www.youtube.com/watch?v=C-CWkTfAi97Y.

87 Goede Montalván (b), p. 208.

88 Dammann 2007, p. 40.

89 Ibid., p. 43.

90 Focus 38/2016.

91 Schuster 2016, p. 60.

92 Krämer 2012. ("Only 10 to 15 percent of family businesses make it into the fourth generation.")

93 Uehlecke 2006.

94 wirtschaftslexikon.gabler.de/Definition/buerokratie.html.

95 *Spiegel* online 2/12/2016 "Civil servant doesn't come to work for six years—

and nobody notices" Last accessed 11/23/2016.

96 Izey Victoria Odiase, www.goodreads.com/quotes/tag/underestimate.

97 *Manager Magazin* 04/19.

98 *Thinking the Unthinkable* by Nik Gowing & Chris Langdon, 2018, p. 20.

99 *Thinking the Unthinkable* by Nik Gowing & Chris Langdon, 2018, p. 45.

100 It's not always due to bureaucracy; there is often a deliberate and systematic approach to late payments. Receivables are mainly due via monthly and quarterly payments. The cash flow from operating activities is used at the end of the quarter to optimize cash management. What sounds like clever financial management is actually an abuse of the supplier's money and remains a violation of the contract conditions. And, of course, a violation of the publicly stated values that most companies are committed to.

101 Malik 2013, p. 360.

102 f.ex. Berner o. J. (a)("more than two thirds of all mergers fail,") Dreher/ Ernst 2016, p. 5 ("around 56 percent of all mergers and acquisitions [turn out to be] failures".)

103 Grube 2014, p. 23.

104 Zick 2011, p. 146 et.seq.

105 Willmann 2013.

106 As of 2013.

107 This comparison refers to the year 2012. Source for all data: Turner/Ernst 2016, p. 42.

108 de.statista.com/themen/1370/mergers-und-acquisitions/.

109 Gaide 2012, p. 124 et.seq.

110 www.q-perior.com.

111 Gaide 2012, p. 126.

112 Ibid., p. 127.

113 *Manager Magazin* (2014): "Five Reasons Why Mergers Can End in a Fiasco," www.manager-magazin.de. Last accessed 09/15/2016.

114 Büschemann 2013.

115 Hägler 2014.

116 "Pfizer stops Astra-Zeneca takeover—for the time being," *Handelsblatt*, 5/26/2014; Roland Lindner, "Pfizer mit der Brechstange," *Frankfurter Allgemeine Zeitung*, 4/28/2014; John LaMattina, "Pfizer, The Shark That Can't Stop Feeding," *Forbes* 6/5/2014; Astrid Dörner/Axel Postinett, "Pfizer gets cold feet," *Handelsblatt*, 4/6/2016.

117 ...the conclusion of the *Manager Magazin* (Lange/Schürmann 2016).

118 *Manager Magazin* (2014): "Fünf Gründe, weshalb Fusionen im Fiasko enden."

119 Dreher/Ernst 2016, p. 33.

120 Dreher/Ernst 2016; Gerds/Schewe 2014, Hirt 2015.

121 Döhle 2011, p. 22.

122 In order to precisely examine mergers in advance without revealing sensitive internal company information, consulting firms have developed the concept of the "clean team," a neutral mediator who confidentially evaluates data supplied by both sides, questions it and transmits it to the other side only after explicitly approval (for an example, see Friemel 2004).

123 www.umsetzungsberatung.de.

124 Berner o. J. (a).

125 See the chronicle of events in the *Manager Magazin* article "The Hottest Deal Ever" (2013).

126 Ebert 2014.

127 Stähli 2013, p. 80.

128 See f.ex. Antonio R. Damasio, Descartes' Irrtum. Fühlen, Denken und das menschliche Gehirn. München: List, 6. edition. 2010, or Gerald Hüther, Biologie der Angst, Göttingen: Vandenhoeck & Ruprecht, 8. edition 2007.

129 Henkel (2010).

130 Exuzidis/Raschke 2016.

131 "Kollektive Krankmeldungen sind ein schlaues Mittel," *Spiegel* online, 10/6/2016.

132 Ibid.

133 Gallup 2016, p. 13 f.

134 Hirt 2015, p. 108.

135 Berner o. J. (b).

136 Stähli 2013, p. 78 et.seq.

137 Even though we are reporting on a success story here, Teva has slipped in its expansion strategy. In the summer of 2017, parts of the 40-billion-Actavis acquisition had to be depreciated, and the company has lost more than two thirds of its market capitalization since 2015. See also www.handelsblatt.com/unternehmen/industrie/ratiopharmmutter-in-the-crisis-miese-prices-no-recorrection/20149000.html. Last accessed 8/22/2017.

138 www.newlearningonline.com. Last accessed 5/11/2019.

139 www.tu-chemnitz.de/phil/europastudien/swandel/projekte/madrid/erinnerung/zeittafelneu.htm. Last accessed 7/17/2017.

140 Grube 2014, p. 22.

141 De la Vega 1609 ("The Origin of the Inca Kings of Peru.")

142 www.heute.de/alternative-fakten-trumps-top-beraterin-conway-erfindet-anschlag-46476104.html. Last accessed 5/31/2017. We're referring to Kellyanne Conway, who false assertion that Trump's inauguration involved more people vs. Obama's, spoke of "alternative facts."

143 Gouedevert 1996, p. 180.

144 Alfred Korzybski; Wiki. Last accessed 5/11/2019.

145 Brief descriptions of the methodology can be found on the Internet, for example here: www.iynn.org/sub3/3_2.pdf (Han-Rog Kan, "What is an Oxford Style Debate?") Last accessed 11/28/2016.

146 From the report of an affected employee.

147 This is the subtitle of his book *Kollaps* (2005).

148 Jared Diamond's book; Also: www.nytimes.com/2018/06/15/world/asia/philippines-dynamite-fishing-coral.html; www.thewaterchannel.tv/media-gallery/6546-dynamite-fishing-tanzania.

149 This is a short summary of Diamond's remarks 2005, p. 517–543.

150 Zick 2011, p. 18.

151 www.n-tv.de/mediathek/sendungen/auslandsreport/US-Amerikaner-kaufen-mehr-Waffen-denn-je-article16587186.html. Last accessed 12/1/2016.

152 This decision is assumed today by many researchers; others see either Huáscar or Atahualpa as legitimate successor. The fact is that the rule of the Inca empire was shared after Huayna Cápac's death (cf. Goede Montalván 2013 (a), p. 199).

153 Goede Montalván 2013 (a), p. 199 et.seq., ibid. (b), S. 208 et.seq.

154 www.smithsonianmag.com/history/who-discovered-machu-picchu-52654657/. Last accessed 5/14/2019.

155 Riese 2012, p. 11–27.

156 www.manager-magazin.de/fotostrecke/sportwagen-dieprominentesten-bugatti-veyron-besitzer-fotostrecke-124148-2.html. Last accessed 12/6/2016.

157 Elkind/Reingold 2011.

158 Ibid. (Sequence "The Blockbuster Pipeline Dries Up").

159 Hesse/Schrader 1994.

160 www.jimcollins.com/concepts.html ("Level 5 Leadership") Last accessed 12/7/2016.

161 You can read the whole fairy tale at gutenberg.spiegel.de/book/-1227/71.

162 www.spiegel.de/auto/fahrkultur/60-deutsche-autos-der-vwpha-eton-a-626753.html. Last accessed 12/8/2016.); Also: www.welt.de/wirtschaft/article153445218/Derletzte-Phaeton-verlaesst-die-Glaeserne-Manu-faktur.html. Last accessed 12/8/2016.

163 Khurana/Nohria 2009, p. 29.

164 Ibid.

Bibliography

Aktienchart Nokia: www.boerse.de.

Ankenbrand, Hendrik / Nienhaus, Lisa: »Das finnische Wunder ist zu Ende«, in: Frankfurter Allgemeine Zeitung vom 14.02.2011; im Internet unter www.faz.net (Zugriff am 24.07.2016).

Barmeyer, Christoph / Davoine, Eric: »Werte in multinationalen Unternehmen – Transfer mit Hindernissen«; in: Wirtschaftspsychologie aktuell 4/2014, S. 37 ff.

Barrenstein, Peter / Huber, Wolfgang / Wachs, Friedhelm (Hrsg.): Evangelisch. Erfolgreich. Wirtschaften. Leipzig: Evangelische Verlagsanstalt 2016 (edition chrismon).

Berner, Winfried und Kollegen o. J. (a): »Verwundbarkeit: Die Phase der Wehrlosigkeit möglichst kurz halten«, im Internet unter www.umsetzungsberatung.de (Zugriff am 31.08.2016).

Berner, Winfried und Kollegen o. J. (b): »Fusion, Übernahme, Post-Merger-Integration«, im Internet unter www.umsetzungsberatung. de (Zugriff am 31.08.2016).

Blanchard, Kenneth / Zigarmi, Patricia / Zigarmi, Drea: Der Minuten-Manager: Führungsstile. Situationsbezogenes Führen (Vollständig überarbeitete Ausgabe für die Manager von heute). Reinbek bei Hamburg: Rowohlt, 3. Aufl. 2015.

Botelho, Lytkina Elena / Rosenkoetter Powell, Kim / Kincaid, Stephen / Wang, Dina: »What Sets Successful CEOs Apart«; in: Harvard Business Review Mai/Juni 2017, S. 70ff.; im Internet unter https://hbr.org/2017/05/what-sets-successful-ceos-apart (Zugriff am 29.05.2017).

Brüser, Wolfgang: »Die Kölner und das Klüngeln oder die Leichtigkeit des Unrechts«; in: Kölner Stadtanzeiger vom 08.03.2002; im Internet unter www.ksta.de (Zugriff am 14.11.2016).

Büschemann, Karl-Heinz: »Pleite nach Lehrbuch«, in: Süddeutsche Zeitung vom 07.05.2013; im Internet unter www.sueddeutsche.de

(Zugriff am 24.07.2016).

Bertelsmann Stiftung: Trau, schau, wem! Unternehmen in Deutschland. Gütersloh 2016 (Download im Internet unter www.bertelsmann-stiftung.de/de/publikationen/publikation/did/trau-schau-wem-unternehmen-in-deutschland/) (Zugriff am 11.11.2016).

Cappelli, Peter/Tavis, Anna: »Assessing Performance: The Performance Management Revolution«, in: Harvard Business Review October 2016; im Internet unter https://hbr.org/2016/10/the-performance-management-revolution (Zugriff am 12.10.2016).

Charan, Ram/Drotter, Stephen/Noel, James: The Leadership Pipeline: How to Build the Leadership Powered Company. San Francisco: John Wiley (Jossey-Bass), 2. Aufl. 2011.

Collins, Jim: »Building Companies to Last« (1995); Download im Internet unter www.jimcollins.com/article_topics/articles/building-companies.html (Zugriff am 10.09.2016).

Collins, Jim/Porras, Jerry I.: Built to Last. Successful Habits of Visionary Companies. New York: HarperCollins, 3. Aufl. 2004 (dt.: Immer erfolgreich).

Collins, Jim: »How the Mighty Fall«, in: Business Week Mai 2009; im Internet unter http://jimcollins.com/books/how-the-mighty-fall.html (Zugriff am 01.09.2016).

Collins, Jim: Der Weg zu den Besten. Die sieben Management-Prinzipien für dauerhaften Unternehmenserfolg. Frankfurt a.M.: Campus 2011.

Dahlkamp, Jürgen/Deckstein, Dinah/Schmitt, Jörg: »Die Firma«; in: Der Spiegel 16/2008, S. 76ff.

»Daimler und Chrysler: Hochzeit des Grauens«, in: Süddeutsche Zeitung vom 17.05.2010; im Internet unter www.sueddeutsche.de.

Dammann, Gerhard: Narzissten, Egomanen, Psychopathen in der Führungsetage. Bern: Haupt 2007.

De la Vega, Garcilaso: »The Origin of the Inca Kings of Peru«; in: Ders.: Royal Commentaries of the Incas (1609), Download im Internet unter http://images.classwell.com/mcd_xhtml_ebooks/2005_world_history/pdf/WHS05_016_461_PS.pdf (Zugriff am 28.11.2016).

Diamond, Jared: Kollaps. Warum Gesellschaften überleben oder untergehen. Frankfurt a.M.: Büchergilde Gutenberg 2005.

Döhle, Patricia: »Preußisch, mit langer Leine«, in: Brand eins 09/2011, S. 19ff.

Dreher, Maximilian/Ernst, Dietmar: Mergers & Acquisitions, 2., überarbeitete Auflage Konstanz: UVK/Lucius 2016 (= utb 4203).

Ebert, Vince: »Teurer Spaß« (Interview), in: Brand eins 08/2014,

S. 54 ff.

Ebert, Vince: Unberechenbar. Warum das Leben zu komplex ist, um es perfekt zu planen. Reinbek bei Hamburg: Rowohlt 2016.

Elkind, Peter / Reingold, Jennifer: »Inside Pfizer's Palace Coup«; in: Fortune vom 15.08.2011; Download unter http://fortune.com/2011/07/28/inside-pfizers-palace-coup/ (Zugriff am 06.12.2016).

Erdle, Frank: »Die Geschichte von Nokia«, in: Connect vom 21.08.2014; im Internet unter www.connect.de (Zugriff am 02.04.2016).

Ernst & Young (EY): »Existing Practice in Compliance 2016« (Download unter www.ey.com/Publication/vwLUAssets/ey-existing-practice-in-compliance-2016-survey/$FILE/ey-existing-practice-in-compliance-2016-survey.pdf) (Zugriff am 08.11.2016).

Exuzidis, Leonidas / Raschke, Michael: »Die kranke Airline«, in: Handelsblatt vom 07.10.2016; im Internet unter www.handelsblatt.com (Zugriff am 10.10.2016).

Friemel, Kerstin: »Saubere Sache«, in: McK Wissen 11 (»Das Magazin von McKinsey«), Dezember 2004, S. 96 ff. (Download im Internet unter www.brandeins.de/uploads/tx_b4/mck_12_17_Saubere_Sache.pdf).

Froitzheim, Ulf J.: »Alles auf Anfang«, in: Brand eins 11/2012, S. 60 ff.

Gaide, Peter: »Manchmal ist Illoyalität gut – für einen Neuanfang«, in: Brand eins 05/2012, S. 124 ff.

Gallup Inc. 2016: »Engagement Index Deutschland 2015« (Präsentation). Download im Internet unter www.gallup.de/183104/engagement-index-deutschland.aspx (Zugriff am 19.09.2016).

Gasche, Ralf: So geht Führung! 7 Gesetze, die Sie im Führungsalltag wirklich weiterbringen. Wiesbaden: Springer Gabler 2016.

Gerds, Johannes / Schewe, Gerhard: Post Merger Integration. Unternehmenserfolg durch Integration Excellence. Wiesbaden: Springer Gabler, 5. Aufl. 2014.

Gerpott, Fabiola H. / Voelpel, Sven C.: »Zurück auf Los! Warum ein Überdenken des transformationalen Führungsansatzes notwendig ist«; in: Personalführung 4/2014, S. 17 ff.

Glück, Thomas R, »Strategisches (Wissens)Management« (1999); Download im Internet unter www.wissensqualitaet.de/wissenschaftlich/nicht-wissen.pdf (Zugriff am 28.11.2016).

Goede Montalván, Peggy (a): »Huayna Capac und die unklare Erbfolge – das Reich zerfällt«; in: Kurella, Doris / de Castro, Inés (Hrsg.): Inka. Könige der Anden. Darmstadt: Philipp von Zabern

2013, S. 196 ff.

Goede Montalván, Peggy (b): »Zeit des Umbruchs – die spanische Eroberung des Inka-Reiches«; in: Kurella, Doris / de Castro, Inés (Hrsg.): Inka. Könige der Anden. Darmstadt: Philipp von Zabern 2013, S. 205 ff.

Grimberg, Steffen: »Affäre um Konstantin Neven DuMont: Der beste Mann braucht Hilfe«; in: taz vom 31.10.2010; im Internet unter www.taz.de (Zugriff am 17.10.2016).

Grubb, Thomas M. / Lamb, Robert B.: Capitalize on Merger Chaos: Six Ways to Profit from Your Competitors' Consolidation and Your Own. New York: The Free Press 2001.

Grube, Nikolai: »Menschenopfer waren eine Notwendigkeit« (Interview), in: Inka – Maya – Azteken. Die geheimnisvollen Königreiche. Spiegel Geschichte Nr. 2/2014, S. 19 ff.

Hägler, Max: »Porsches übermütiger Plan«, in: Süddeutsche Zeitung vom 10.02.2014; im Internet unter www.sueddeutsche.de (Zugriff am 05.10.2016).

Hartmann, Michael: »Vor allem zählt der richtige Stallgeruch« (Interview); in: Zeit Campus vom 28.02.2013; im Internet unter www.zeit. de (Zugriff am 24.10.2016).

Hawranek, Dietmar / Kurbjuweit, Dirk: »Wolfsburger Weltreich«, in: Der Spiegel 34/2013, S. 58 ff.

Henkel, Hans-Olaf: »DaimlerChrysler und andere Katastrophen«, in: Süddeutsche Zeitung vom 21.05.2010; im Internet unter www.sueddeutsche.de (Zugriff am 31.08.2016).

Herzberg, Frederick et al.: The Motivation to Work. New York: Wiley, 2. Aufl. 1959.

Hesse, Jürgen / Schrader, Hans Christian: Die Neurosen der Chefs. Die seelischen Kosten der Karriere. Frankfurt a. M.: Eichborn 1994.

Hetzer, Wolfgang: »Ist die Deutsche Bank eine kriminelle Vereinigung?«; in: Die Kriminalpolizei März 2014; im Internet unter www.kriminalpolizei.de (Zugriff am 08.11.2016).

Hirt, Michael: »Die perfekte Post-Merger-Integration: Planungs- und Umsetzungsphase«, in: CFO aktuell Bd. 9, 2015, S. 105 ff.

Huntington, Samuel P.: Kampf der Kulturen. Die Neugestaltung der Weltpolitik im 21. Jahrhundert. Hamburg: Europa Verlag, 3. Aufl. 1997.

IfM (Institut für Mittelstandsforschung): »Unternehmensnachfolgen in Deutschland – Aktuelle Trends« (= IfM-Materialien Nr. 216). Bonn: IfM 2012 (Download im Internet unter www.ifm-bonn.org).

Kalbhenn, Patrick: »Compliance: Die größten Skandale in deutschen

Konzernen«; in: Handelsblatt vom 16.05.2012, im Internet unter www.handelsblatt.com (Zugriff am 08.11.2016).

Khurana, Rakesh / Nohria, Nitin, »Die Neuerfindung des Managers«, in: Harvard Business Manager Jan. 2009, S. 20 ff.

Krämer, Christopher: »Familienunternehmen: Die liebe Verwandtschaft«; Spiegel online vom 23.04.2012; im Internet unter www.spiegel.de (Zugriff am 22.11.2016).

Krohn, Philipp: »Unternehmerkinder: Nicht nur Tochter von Beruf«; in: Frankfurter Allgemeine Zeitung vom 17.10.2009; im Internet unter www.faz.net (Zugriff am 14.10.2016).

Kurella, Doris / de Castro, Inés (Hrsg.): Inka. Könige der Anden. Darmstadt: Philipp von Zabern 2013 (Katalog der gleichnamigen Ausstellung 2013).

Kurella, Doris: »Woher kamen die Inka?«; in: Kurella, Doris / de Castro, Inés (Hrsg.): Inka. Könige der Anden. Darmstadt: Philipp von Zabern 2013, S. 41 ff.

Lange, Kai / Schürmann, Lukas: »Valeants Rezept für ein Desaster«, in: Manager Magazin vom 07.06.2016; im Internet unter www.manager-magazin.de (Zugriff am 07.10.2016).

Langenscheidt, Florian / May, Peter (Hrsg.): Familienunternehmen hoch 10. Deutsche Standards 2014. Offenbach: GABAL Verlag 2014. (Darin S. 91 ff. Peter May, »Die Zukunft. Aktuelle Herausforderungen für Familienunternehmen und Unternehmerfamilien«).

Lehky, Maren: Die zehn größten Führungsfehler und wie Sie sie vermeiden. Frankfurt a. M.: Campus 2007.

Malik, Fredmund: Führen, leisten, leben. Wirksames Management für eine neue Zeit. Limitierte Sonderausgabe, Frankfurt a. M.: Campus 2013.

Maslow, Abraham: »A theory of human motivation«; in: Psychological Review 50, 1943, S. 370 ff.

May, Peter: Erfolgsmodell Familienunternehmen. Das Strategiebuch. Hamburg: Murmann 2012.

Mayer-Kuckuk, Finn: »Wie die ›Republik Samsung‹ funktioniert«; in: Augsburger Allgemeine vom 13.10.2016; im Internet unter www.augsburger-allgemeine.de (Zugriff am 31.10.2016).

McGregor, Douglas: The Human Side of Enterprise. Columbus, OH: McGraw-Hill Education, kommentierte Neuausgabe 2005 (1. Auflage 1960).

Noack, Karoline: »Die Staatsstruktur«; in: Kurella, Doris / de Castro, Inés (Hrsg.): Inka. Könige der Anden. Darmstadt: Philipp von Zabern 2013, S. 142 ff.

Neßhöver, Christoph: »Konstantin Neven DuMont – einst Medien-
mann, jetzt Immobilien-Investor«; in: Manager Magazin vom
19.04.2016; Download unter www.manager-magazin.de (Zugriff am
17.10.2016).

»Nokia: Etappen der 150-jährigen Geschichte«; in: Neue Zürcher
Zeitung vom 03.09.2013; im Internet unter www.nzz.ch (Zugriff am
02.04.2016).

»Nokia. Our Story«; im Internet unter http://company.nokia.com (Zugriff am 02.04.2016).

Neuberger, Oswald: Führen und führen lassen. Stuttgart: Lucius &
Lucius, 6., völlig neu bearb. und erw. Auflage 2002.

Patalong, Frank: »Der Gutsherr« (Zum Tode von Alfred Neven Du-
Mont); Spiegel online vom 31.05.2015; im Internet unter www.spie-
gel.de (Zugriff am 17.10.2016).

Pringle, Heather: »Die Inka auf dem Gipfel der Macht«; in: National
Geographic 4/2011; im Internet unter www.nationalgeographic.de.

Probst, Gilbert / Raisch, Sebastian: »Die Logik des Niedergangs«; in:
Harvard Business Manager März 2004, S. 37 ff.

Pundt, Alexander / Nerdinger, Friedemann W.: »Transformationale
Führung – Führung für den Wandel?«; in: Grote, Sven (Hrsg.):
Die Zukunft der Führung. Berlin / Heidelberg: Springer 2012, S. 27 ff.

Ramge, Thomas: »Der Kampf der Copycats«; in: Brand eins 01/2015,
S. 114 ff.

Rieck, Sophia: »Das Inkareich – Geschichte, Kultur, Religion und
Untergang«, Stuttgart: Klett Verlag 2007/2012; im Internet unter
www.klett.de.

Riese, Berthold: Machu Picchu. Die geheimnisvolle Stadt der Inka.
München: Beck, 2., überarbeitete Aufl. 2012.

Rochus Mummert: »Studie: Wertekultur in Unternehmen ist oft
nur Schall und Rauch« (2012), Download im Internet unter
www.rochusmummert.com (Zugriff am 14.11.2016).

Schulz, Matthias: »Land der angepflockten Sonne«; in: Inka – Maya –
Azteken. Die geheimnisvollen Königreiche. Spiegel Geschichte
Nr. 2/2014, S. 42 ff.

Schulz, Matthias: »Die Söhne der Sonne«; in: Spiegel 42/2013, S. 148 ff.

Schuster, Jochen: »Die Oetkers. Patriarch gesucht«; in: Focus 38/2016,
S. 56 ff.

Schwartz, Michael / Gerstenberger, Juliane: »Nachfolgeplanungen im
Mittelstand auf Hochtouren: Halbe Millionen Übergaben bis 2017;
Fokus Volkswirtschaft Nr. 91 vom 23.04.2015 (= KfW Economic
Research); Download im Internet unter www.kfw.de (Zugriff am

14.10.2016).

Schweikert, Christine: »Generische Compliance-Risiken in mittelständischen und Großunternehmen – Auswertung vorliegender Studien zu Compliance, Integrity und Wirtschaftskriminalität« (= KICG-Forschungspapier Nr. 8) 2014 (Download im Internet unter https:// opus.htwg-konstanz.de).

Sprenger, Reinhard K.: Mythos Motivation. Wege aus einer Sackgasse. Frankfurt: Campus, 20., aktualisierte Ausgabe 2014.

Stähli, Albert: Inka-Government. Eine Elite verwaltet ihre Welt. Frankfurt a. M.: Societäts-Medien GmbH 2013 (= Frankfurter Allgemeine Buch).

Thormann, Heike: »Dreißig Wahrnehmungsfehler« (Artikel vom 02.08.2016); im Internet unter www.kreativesdenken.com (Zugriff am 19.10.2016).

Tietz, Janko: »Delle im Universum«; in: Der Spiegel 35/2011, S. 87.

Uehlecke, Jens: »Bürokratie: Fallstricke für Mitarbeiter«; in: Die Zeit Nr. 2 vom 05.01.2006; im Internet unter www.zeit.de (Zugriff am 16.11.2016).

Wikipedia, Artikel »Inka« (eine ausführlich recherchierte und mit zahlreichen Quellen belegte Darstellung, die 2005 in die Liste »lesenswerter Artikel« aufgenommen wurde) (Zugriff am 29.08.2016).

Willmann, Urs: »Die Schule der Diktatoren«; in: Die Zeit vom 02.10.2013; im Internet www.zeit.de.

Zick, Michael: Die rätselhaften Vorfahren der Inka. Stuttgart: Theiss 2011.

Acknowledgments

We would like to thank a number people who, in various ways, have helped to make writing this book possible.

We'll start with Rosa Oliveira, who was the reason Paul was asked to travel to Peru in the first place. Thank you, Rosa, for the great work together and for your support later in helping to organize our research trip to Peru in 2016.

Special thanks to Nik Gowing and Peter May for contributing the Forewords. We feel honored to have two such successful and experienced personalities and authors prepared to write the opening pages of our book.

We would also like to express our gratitude to Dr. Doris Kurella, in charge of Latin American and North American History at the Linden Museum in Stuttgart, Germany, for the supportive discussion in spring 2016. We are also grateful to Cecilia Pardo, curator of "Colecciones—Arte Precolombino," Museo de Arte in Lima, and Dr Jeffrey Quilter at the Peabody Museum at Harvard University, Cambridge, Massachusetts, for their input and encouraging words in summer 2016.

Our thanks to all our interview partners, including those who chose to remain anonymous, for their faith in us and for being prepared to share with us some of their insights and experiences which have enriched the book a great deal.

A special word of thanks goes to our feedback-givers, who kindly gave of their time and expertise to provide critical and appreciative feedback on the first versions of the book prior to submitting to the publishers: Jörg Middendorf, Sandra Pfahler, Johannes Thönnessen, Freiherr Michael von Truchsess, and Dr. Timm Volmer for the German edition. For the English edition, Nick Boardman, Christine and Neil Darby, Dr. Doris Day, Manasi Ramanna, and, last but not least, Christian Velmer, who gave us his valuable input on both editions.

Our thanks to Martin Limbeck for his enthusiasm for the original idea, who told us quite clearly, "Guys, you have to do this!" and to Andreas Buhr for his encouragement and input during the concept phase, based on his experience as the author of more than ten books.

We would like to thank all of the people in Peru who were kind enough to receive us and for their motivating words that we should pursue our idea of connecting the story of the Incas to today's business world. A big *muchas gracias* to Marco Aveggio for opening a number of doors to contemporary academic and political life in Peru. A very special thank you to Dr. Max Hernandez, former Executive Director of Acuerdo National in Peru, physician, psychoanalyst, and author of one of the leading works on El Inca Garcilaso de la Vega, for his valuable input and support. We are particularly proud that such a prominent member of Peruvian society was prepared to write an Epilogue for our book.

Our thanks to Chris McGinty for the initial translation from German and for providing Paul with a great platform to fine-tune the English version of the book to his and Andreas's precise style of English.

We are grateful to the team at Mango Publishing Group in Florida for their faith in us and their terrific support in producing the international edition of the book.

The book was written in various places, but Senhalser Höfe on the river Mosel in Germany was particularly important and provided us with a wonderfully inspiring and creative atmosphere for putting the book together.

And last but not least, our thanks to Dr. Petra Begemann for her invaluable support as our writing coach and sparring partner for the German edition and in helping us to turn our crazy idea into a real book. Your two Incas will be grateful forever!

Andreas Krebs and Paul Williams

About Our Forewordists

 **Nik Gowing** coauthored (with Chris Langdon) *Thinking the Unthinkable* (published May 2018). It details the findings from hundreds of top-level confidential interviews and conversations with corporate and public service leaders, plus hundreds more conversations with the new generation of millennials. In the era of a new disruption, leaders reveal that they are "scared," "confused," and "overwhelmed," especially by the new short-termism.

Nik Gowing was a news presenter for the BBC's international twenty-four-hour news channel BBC World News from 1996 to 2014. He presented *The Hub with Nik Gowing, BBC World Debates, Dateline London,* and location coverage of major global stories.

For eighteen years, he worked at ITN where he was bureau chief in Rome and Warsaw, and diplomatic editor for Channel Four News (1988–1996). He has been a member of the councils of Chatham House (1998–2004), the Royal United Services Institute (2005–present), and the Overseas Development Institute (2007–2014), as well as on the board of the Westminster Foundation for Democracy (1996–2005) and the advisory council at Wilton Park (1998–2012). In 1994, he was a fellow at the Joan Shorenstein Barone Center in the J.F. Kennedy School of Government at Harvard University. He was a board member for the Hay Literature Festival (2004–2018) and is now a member of the Hay Festival Foundation.

His peer-reviewed study at Oxford University *Skyful of Lies and Black Swans* predicted and identified the new vulnerability, fragility, and brittleness of institutional power in the new, all-pervasive public information space. The work builds on his work initiated at Harvard.

In 2014, Nik was appointed a visiting professor at Kings College, London, in the School of Social Science and Public Policy. Since 2016, he has been a visiting professor at Nanyang University (NTU) in Singapore focusing on deepening and widening the "Thinking the Unthinkable" research. From 2014, he was a member of the World Economic Forum's Global Agenda Council on Geo-Economics. In September 2017, he was appointed as an adviser on leadership challenges to the president of the UN General Assembly.

He was awarded honorary doctorates by Exeter University in 2012 and Bristol University in 2015. They recognize his ongoing cutting-edge analyses and distinguished career in international journalism.

 **Prof. Dr. Peter May** is one of the leading experts on family businesses and a pioneer in providing strategic consulting to their owners. In a profile, a major German business newspaper described him as "the man who understands families." The lawyer and business administrator advises and supports well-known business families and is the founder of PETER MAY Family Business Consulting.

Back 1998, he founded INTES, the first company focused on consulting and qualification for business families in Germany, and developed it into the leading brand in its segment. In 2013, he sold INTES to PwC. Since then, he has worked as a strategic consultant and in numerous joint projects with PwC and INTES.

Peter May is an honorary professor at WHU–Otto Beisheim School of Management in Vallendar and has taught at various universities. From 2008 until 2009, he was Wild Group Chair of Family Business at IMD in Lausanne, Switzerland.

Early on, he called for an independent approach to business administration for family businesses. With the INTES Principle, the 3-Dimensional Model, the Owner Strategy, and the Family Constitution, he developed important concepts for advising family businesses and business families.

He has also launched numerous initiatives for family businesses. He initiated the world's first Governance Code for Family Businesses (2004 in Germany and 2005 in Austria) as well as the Family Business Owner of the Year Award (since 2004), the entrepreneurs association FBN Deutschland (since 2000), and the Institute for Family Business at WHU. Peter May is president of the Governance Commission, jury chairman of the Family Business Owner of the Year and managing director of FBN Deutschland. With the Business Owner Success Forum at Schloss Bensberg (since 1998), he has also created one of the most important conferences for family business owners.

Peter May is also an author and the publisher of numerous publications on the topic of family business. His standard works, *Erfolgsmodell Familienunternehmen* (*Family Businesses as Models of Success*) and *Die Inhaberstrategie im Familienunternehmen: Eine Anleitung* (*The Owner Strategy in Family Businesses: A Guide*), have been translated into various languages.

The areas of focus for Peter May's work are in in-depth personal support of business-owning families (including advisory and supervisory board activities) as well as taking on difficult and particularly exciting consulting mandates.

He says: *"Family businesses are my passion. I am happy to have been able to combine this passion with my penchant for sharing knowledge and experience and to turn my calling into a career. I love my work and everything connected with it."*

About Our Interview Partners

Dr. Rolando Arellano Cueva is president of "Arellano Consulting to grow" in Lima, Peru and an expert on marketing in developing countries. He is a psychologist, has an MBA, and gained his doctorate at the University of Grenoble. He has taught at a number of universities in Latin America, North America, and Europe, and is author of a broad range of books on sociopolitical, historical, and current topics within modern Peru. He is also a popular public speaker both in Peru and overseas.

Marco Aveggio was born in Lima in 1961. He is vice president of the Patronato Cultural del Peru, a Peruvian non-profit organization who run the Peruvian Pavilion for the Venice Biennale, a twenty-year project in partnership with the Peruvian government and the most relevant universities and museums of Peru in the fields of art and architecture. He is also responsible for the heritage recovery chapter of the Patronato, which manages the archaeological excavations at Chavin de Huantar. Marco has a degree in business from the University of Lima, has worked as an executive in the chemical and plastic industries and now works as a member of the board in various companies, foundations, and non-profit organizations.

Dr. Doris Day is a board-certified dermatologist who specializes in aesthetic dermatology in private practice in New York City and is a clinical associate professor of dermatology at New York University Langone Health. She has won awards for her work in laser research, teaching, and promoting the field of dermatology. Dr. Day is author of three books, the most recent titled *Beyond Beautiful: Using the Power of Your Mind and Aesthetic Breakthroughs to Look Naturally Young and Radiant.* She maintains her role as a freelance journalist, including as a host for her award-winning dermatology show on Doctor Radio on SiriusXM 110.

Dr. David Ebsworth is a senior manager with international experience in Europe, Canada, and the United States. His career in the pharmaceutical industry spans more than thirty-five years, including at Pfizer Germany, Bayer AG, and as CEO of various companies including Vifor Pharma and Galenica. He is currently an adviser to the CEOs of a number of well-known companies and chairman of the board at Verona Pharma.

Catherine von Fürstenberg-Dussman has chaired the Peter Dussmann Foundation since 2011. In this role, she oversees the Dussmann Group, which has 63,500 employees in eighteen countries. An American by birth, she studied psychology, English literature, and acting. After her husband fell ill, she joined the supervisory board of Dussmann Verwaltungs AG in 2008, taking over the chair one year later.

Dr. Max Hernandez is one of Peru's leading intellectuals. The psychoanalyst and historian played a leading role in the creation of the Peruvian Center for Development of Psychoanalysis. He is heavily involved in the development of a sustainable vision for the future of his country and, for ten years, he was executive director of the Acuerdo National (National Round Table). He has published a critically acclaimed book about Garcilaso de la Vega, one of the first chroniclers of the Incas and the Spanish conquest, and has been honored by his country as Grand Officer of the Order of the Sun of Peru and Commander of the Order of Isabella the Catholic of Spain.

Anke Hoffmann has been CEO of H/P Executive Consulting GmbH since 2016 and is an expert in the recruitment of management personalities. A business graduate, she held management positions in the banking sector before joining Kienbaum as partner and senior consultant and from 2006 continued her career there as managing director for Berlin and the new Federal States. From 2014 to 2016, she was managing shareholder of DEININGER Consulting GmbH.

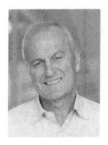

Rolf Hoffmann sits on numerous boards across Europe and the United States. He worked for three decades in two biopharmaceutical companies around the world, primarily running various geographies including Europe, Asia, Latin America, and the United States. Besides the board mandates, he teaches at UNC Chapel Hill and is involved with the World Anti-Doping Agency.

Rüdiger Lentz is the executive director of the Aspen Institute Germany. Between 2009 and September 2013, he served as the executive director of the German-American Heritage Foundation and Museum in Washington. From November 1998 until December 2009, he was the Washington bureau chief and senior diplomatic correspondent for *Deutsche Welle*. Prior to his assignment in Washington, he served as *Deutsche Welle*'s Brussels bureau chief. Before joining *Deutsche Welle*, Lentz worked as a correspondent for the German news magazine *Der Spiegel*, after having served in the German Armed Forces for eight years and as a TV commentator and reporter at ARD/WDR, Germany's largest public TV and radio station.

Dr. Iris Löw-Friedrich is a physician and senior executive. She has held leading management positions at different pharma companies (Hoechst AG, BASF Pharma, Schwarz Pharma AG). Since 2008, she has been a member of the Executive Committee of UCB S.A. in Brussels, chief medical officer and head of development. She holds several board mandates (Evotec since 2014, TransCelerate BioPharma Inc. since 2015, Fresenius SE since 2016). In addition, she is an adjunct professor for internal medicine at the University of Frankfurt.

Dr. Alexander von Preen has been CEO of Intersport (IDEA) since November 1, 2018. For many years, he was managing director of Kienbaum Consultants International GmbH and chairman of Kienbaum AG in Zurich. After training to be an officer, von Preen studied at the LMU in Munich before joining Kienbaum in

1997 as assistant to the managing director. He advised national and international companies in all aspects of corporate governance, executive search, strategy implementation, controlling, and remuneration. He sits on a number of supervisory boards.

Dr. Jeffrey Quilter is an associate of the Peabody Museum of Archaeology and Ethnology of Harvard University and former director (2012–2019) of and curator (2005–2012) in that institution. He is an archaeologist, an expert on Peru and Costa Rica, and co-directed various projects with national archaeologists in those countries. He taught at Ripon College, Wisconsin (1980–1995), and was director of pre-Columbian studies and curator of the Pre-Columbian Collection at Dumbarton Oaks, Washington, DC, (1995–2005) before moving to Harvard in 2005.

Joachim Rühle is a vice-admiral in the Bundeswehr (German Defense Forces) and, since summer 2017, vice chief of defense. Following a degree in engineering, he completed his training as a naval officer. After numerous national and international assignments with the Bundeswehr, between 2012 and 2017 he headed up several departments at the Federal Ministry of Defense, including the Planning, Armaments, and Human Resources departments.

Dr. Johannes von Schmettow has been a consultant at Egon Zehnder since 1998 and supports entrepreneurs and organizations in filling positions in their business leadership, executive boards, and supervisory boards. He was managing director (Germany) at Egon Zehnder as well as a member of the global executive committee. Before that, he was a consultant at the Boston Consulting Group for five years.

Werner Spinner was not only the ninth president of the football club 1. FC Cologne (2012–2019), but is also an internationally experienced manager. For many years, he worked for Bayer AG in the United States. In 1994, he became head of consumer care, and between 1998 and 2003 he was a member of the executive board at Bayer. For fifteen years he has been a member of several supervisory boards in Germany, the UK, and Netherlands, as well as at significant businesses in Asia.

Dr. med. Christoph Straub has been the CEO of BARMER since 2011. Before that, the trained physician was on the board of Rhön-Klinikum AG and deputy CEO and head of business development at the health insurer Techniker Krankenkasse. Upon completion of his PhD, Christoph Straub started his career at the Verband der Angestellten Krankenkassen e.V (VdAK)—Federal Association of Substitute Sickness Funds—where he led the department dealing with questions about basic health care and medical science.

Gerd W. Stürz is managing partner at Ernst & Young and Vice President of the British Chamber of Commerce in Germany. He can look back on more than thirty years working as auditor or adviser to international companies, as well as several international leadership roles at EY and before at Arthur Andersen. Today, he leads the "Life Sciences, Health & Chemicals" market segment at EY for Germany, Switzerland, and Austria.

Johannes Thönnessen is a graduate psychologist, author of numerous books, managing partner of MWonline GmbH and an independent consultant specializing in communication, organizational development, and HR management tools. For many years, he worked in personnel development at Bayer AG and since 1998 has run the website "Managementwissen online" (Management Know-how online) where, together with other authors, he comments on current trends in management.

Dr. Timm Volmer is a senior manager and management consultant. A veterinary surgeon, economist, and master of public health (Harvard University), he has held management positions at GlaxoSmithKline and was managing director of Wyeth Pharma GmbH in Germany. In 2010 he founded SmartStep, a consultancy for the pharmaceutical and medical technology industries, which helps its customers gain effective market access for their products in Germany and across Europe.

Christine Wolff is a management consultant, a member of several supervisory boards, and a business mediator. She has a degree in geology and an MBA. She worked for more than twenty years in international engineering businesses, most recently as director for Europe and the Middle East at URS Corporation (now AECOM), a listed US engineering company with more than fifty-six thousand employees worldwide. As senior vice president, she was in charge of operations in fifteen countries.

About the Authors

 **Andreas Krebs** is an entrepreneur, an internationally experienced manager, and an expert on leadership, globalization, and entrepreneurship. He is one of the few Germans to have made it to the executive board of a "Big Pharma" company in corporate America. Andreas currently runs his own venture capital business, Longfield Invest, which invests in young start-ups and growth businesses covering many sectors and operating in the New Economy. Up until 2010, Andreas held international leadership positions with Bayer AG and the Wyeth Corporation, latterly serving on the main board in the United States, where he was responsible for more than eight thousand employees in ninety-six countries. He worked in seven countries, in the UK, Austria, nine years in Latin America, in Asia, Canada and, finally, in the United States. From 2010 until 2019, he was chairman of the board at Merz KGaA, Frankfurt, and holds other board positions across various sectors. In addition, he dedicates time as chairman of the private NGO Girassol e.V., supporting children and young people living in poverty in São Paulo, Brazil.

For more information: www.inca-inc.com

 **Paul Williams** is an internationally experienced manager, executive coach, and entrepreneur. Since 2003, he has been managing partner at the consulting firm Paul Williams & Associates in Langenfeld, Germany, which specializes in leadership coaching, self-management, management diagnostics, and organizational development. Early in his career, the natural scientist and native Englishman held positions in international sales, marketing, and general management in Europe, Australasia, the United States, the Middle East, and Africa at the pharmaceutical division of Bayer AG. From 1995, Paul assumed responsibility for human resources in international business operations and later for global research and product development. He is married and lives with his wife Steffi in Leverkusen.

For more information: www.inca-inc.com or www.paul-williams.net

Mango Publishing, established in 2014, publishes an eclectic list of books by diverse authors—both new and established voices—on topics ranging from business, personal growth, women's empowerment, LGBTQ studies, health, and spirituality to history, popular culture, time management, decluttering, lifestyle, mental wellness, aging, and sustainable living. We were recently named 2019's #1 fastest growing independent publisher by Publishers Weekly. Our success is driven by our main goal, which is to publish high quality books that will entertain readers as well as make a positive difference in their lives.

Our readers are our most important resource; we value your input, suggestions, and ideas. We'd love to hear from you—after all, we are publishing books for you!

Please stay in touch with us and follow us at:
Facebook: Mango Publishing
Twitter: @MangoPublishing
Instagram: @MangoPublishing
LinkedIn: Mango Publishing
Pinterest: Mango Publishing

Sign up for our newsletter at www.mango.bz and receive a free book!

Join us on Mango's journey to reinvent publishing, one book at a time.